NEW TACTICS IN HUMAN RIGHTS

A RESOURCE FOR PRACTITIONERS

NEWTactics
in Human Rights

**THE CENTER
FOR VICTIMS OF
TORTURE**

NEW TACTICS IN HUMAN RIGHTS

A RESOURCE FOR PRACTITIONERS

A workbook created by
The New Tactics in Human Rights Project

A project of
The Center for Victims of Torture

The New Tactics in Human Rights Project
A project of the Center for Victims of Torture
717 East River Road
Minneapolis, MN 55455
+1 612 436 4800
www.cvt.org
www.newtactics.org

Writing and Editing: Tricia Cornell, Kate Kelsch, Nicole Palasz

Design: Matthew Rezac, MCAD DesignWorks, Minneapolis College of Art and Design, www.mcad.edu
Type Design: Locator and Bryant, Eric Olson, Process Type Foundry
Photography: Dick Bancroft (except pages 26 and 153 by Ann Bancroft)

Printing: Friesens

CONTENTS

Prevention Tactics

Intervention Tactics

Restorative Tactics

Building Human Rights
Cultures and Institutions

Resources

Index

INTRODUCTION

In the past two decades the world has seen the beginning of a new era for human rights, one in which the weight of international law and international public opinion has come increasingly to bear. In the arena of international law, new mechanisms have transformed the way we think about and achieve justice. And at the same time, the creative thinking and innovative spirit of individuals and organizations have changed the way we think about what is possible in human rights — and therefore what we can achieve.

All around the world and at all levels, in small villages and in national governments as well as at the highest levels of international justice, people are creating and using innovative tactics to make their work more effective. The New Tactics in Human Rights Project captures these tactical innovations and shares them with others striving to advance human rights. I invite you to join me in celebrating this work and in making use of the valuable resource you now hold in your hands.

In reflecting on my own area of work, I have seen new opportunities for obtaining justice arise for victims of the gravest human rights abuses. The establishment of the International Criminal Tribunals for the former Yugoslavia and Rwanda, which were the first war crimes courts to be created with the full weight of international opinion behind them, opened new doors for justice. The international teams working on the tribunals, people from dozens of countries, were doing something that had never been attempted before — making new law, setting new precedents, handing down indictments that did not look like indictments that had ever been handed down before in any country. Together a new tactic was created, one that paved the way for another, even more powerful tactic, the International Criminal Court. This court could now provide a tool to achieve justice no matter where or by whom crimes against humanity are perpetrated.

Within the context of the International Criminal Tribunal for the former Yugoslavia, we used another new tactic: We made rape a war crime that could be prosecuted on its own, rather than as a secondary offense that was only appended to other offenses. When the tribunal indicted eight Bosnian Serb military officers on charges of systematic rape of Muslim women, it represented a sea change in the way the world thought about gender-related crimes and human rights. This tactic has made it possible to achieve justice in many more cases since.

Ten years ago legal experts would have laughed at the prospect of indicting and extraditing a powerful former dictator like Augusto Pinochet. This was not a tactic that seemed available to us. Perpetrators at that level, no matter how barbarous their crimes, moved about the world with impunity. Pinochet's arrest and extradition changed the way we think about what is possible in international justice. It added a tactic to the human rights arsenal, one that is sure to be used again and again in the future.

I applaud efforts by human rights advocates to use national and international courts and other public forums to call attention to crimes against humanity, wherever they occur, and to call loudly and boldly for justice. But these are just a few among the many new and innovative tactics being used by people around the world, in spheres and regions as diverse as human experience itself, to promote and protect basic human dignity.

I am proud to join the New Tactics in Human Rights Project in presenting this resource. While it could never claim to be an exhaustive catalogue, it is a rich compendium of this fresh and innovative thinking, one which we hope will be valuable to you in your work.

— Justice Richard J. Goldstone

Justice of the Constitutional Court of South Africa, retired

Chief Prosecutor of the UN International Criminal Tribunals for the former Yugoslavia and Rwanda

Chairperson of the International Independent Inquiry on Kosovo

Chairperson of the International Task Force on Terrorism established by the International Bar Association

ACKNOWLEDGEMENTS

This workbook would not have been possible without the assistance, advice and support of countless individuals and organizations around the world. We are grateful to the people and organizations mentioned in this workbook for their initiatives and for the time they gave responding to our inquiries, informing us of their work and, in several cases, writing or editing pieces. We would also like to thank those who recommended organizations to interview for consideration in the workbook.

Kate Kelsch, project manager of the New Tactics in Human Rights Project, wrote and coordinated earlier editions of the workbook, edited and oversaw the creation of this one and infected us all with her avid dedication to quality and accuracy. Tricia Cornell wrote and edited portions of the text. Nicole Palasz wrote tactical summaries, researched tactics, coordinated research on tactics and was responsible for their selection and organization. Nancy Pearson developed the training resources. Rachel Tschida provided guidance and expertise. Susan Everson edited the text. Pam Arnold, Matthew Rezac and the staff at the Minneapolis College of Art and Design's DesignWorks program patiently, skillfully and enthusiastically shepherded the book from raw text to finish product. Douglas A. Johnson created the original vision and framework for the New Tactics project, without which this book would never have been possible.

A number of generous donors provided financial support for creating the vision and content of the workbook, including the John D. and Catherine T. MacArthur Foundation, the Paul & Phyllis Fireman Charitable Foundation, The Sigrid Rausing Trust (formerly known as the Ruben and Elisabeth Rausing Trust), the United States Institute of Peace and donors who wish to remain anonymous. Other donors have created a strong foundation for this book by supporting CVT's involvement in other elements of the New Tactics project; these include the International Center on Nonviolent Conflict, the National Philanthropic Trust, the Organization for Security and Cooperation in Europe, the Rockefeller Foundation and the foundation's Bellagio Conference Center in Italy, and the United States Department of State. CVT's partners in the project have also received financial support from a number of organizations, making their participation possible.

We extend our appreciation to the New Tactics Advisory Committee and Working Group members (a full list of members is included on page 24) as well as other supporters who reviewed and commented on the workbook. Their experience with the realities of the struggle to advance human rights, and their understanding of what will be truly helpful to colleagues around the world, guided the development of the workbook and continue to guide the New Tactics project.

Justice Richard A. Goldstone, Murat Belge, Morten Kjaerum, Sofia Macher, Kailash Satyarthi all contributed pieces that have enriched the content of the workbook.

Others contributed their fine editorial and analytical skills in reviewing chapters, including Susan Atwood, Tanya Cromey, Phil Deering, Basil Fernando, Barbara Frey, Deanna Gallagher, Paul Haupt, Carine Kaneza, Salma Khan, Mark Ritchie, Liz Sevcenko and Bruce van Voorhis and his colleagues at the Asian Human Rights Commission. Paul Dalton, Clarence Dias, Liam Mahony, Paul Milne, Suzanne Miric, Boris Pustintsev, Sir Nigel Rodley, Edson Spencer and Rajesh Tandon helped us shape the thinking behind the current format.

The current edition was built on the strong foundation of two previous editions. Among the more than 50 volunteers who helped research, write, edit and review those volumes we wish especially to thank Aron Cramer, Bennett Freeman, Barbara Frey, Edward Halpin, Eileen Kaufman, Morten Kjaerum, John Salzberg, Robert Shoemake and David Weissbrodt. Phil Deering edited the second edition and Deanna Gallagher, Kenei Sato, Kathryn Weber and Wendy Weber wrote chapters.

While we are grateful to all of these people and countless others for their talent, time, insight and generosity, we willingly acknowledge any oversights or errors that remain in the book as our own. Additionally, the opinions, findings and conclusions or recommendations expressed in this book are those of the New Tactics project and do not necessarily reflect the views of our funders.

THE NEED FOR NEW TACTICS

BY DOUGLAS A. JOHNSON

The modern human rights movement has made enormous strides in the past few decades in the advancement of the human rights ideal and the establishment of specific protections. The movement created new international conventions condemning torture and protecting the rights of women and children and developed an international consensus regarding the definition of legitimate political activities that deserve protection and support. Political prisoners have been protected from harm and many have been freed. And in many nations, sophisticated institutions have been developed to promote adherence — on both domestic and foreign policy levels — to international human rights standards. We cannot overstate how important these accomplishments are or how difficult they were to achieve.

Three tactics, predominantly, led to these advancements: 1) setting international norms that created a body of conventions, treaties and standards; 2) monitoring compliance to these standards; and 3) denouncing or shaming government actions and inaction when the standards were violated. Over the years, the infrastructure and skills these approaches demand have grown dramatically.

It is clear that these tactics have brought about tremendous advances and thus should continue to be supported and pursued. It is equally clear that there are great limits to what we can accomplish in this way and that these approaches are not, in and of themselves, enough to solve seemingly intractable human rights problems.

Consider the problem of torture. There are, for example, more international conventions and standards, more constitutional protections and national legislation against torture than against any other single human rights abuse. There is more monitoring of torture, not only by the infrastructures of treaty bodies, but by national and international nongovernmental organizations. Add to this capacity the creation of over 250 treatment centers for torture survivors around the world, each of which brings medical resources to bear on documenting torture in thousands of victims and elevates the forensic capacity to document torture. Torture is the most documented and denounced of all abuses.

Yet when Amnesty International launched its third international campaign against torture in 2000, it concluded that torture was as widespread then as it was when the organization launched its first global campaign in 1974.

In the past decade alone, we have witnessed human rights violations shocking in their scope — in Bosnia, Rwanda, Sierra Leone and the more than 150 countries that still perpetrate or allow torture. I must state the obvious: *something is not working.*

It is the contention of this workbook that advancing human rights requires the creation of a broader human rights field, one that incorporates many more people and sectors of society than are currently engaged. It also requires the development of more comprehensive strategic approaches that can only be accomplished by using a far broader array of tactics than are currently in use.

All over the world dedicated human rights practitioners have begun this work: developing innovative approaches, building unexpected strategic alliances and learning from unexpected sectors. The New Tactics in Human Rights Project aims to bring these innovators together and inspire others with their work. This workbook includes more than 75 stories of tactical innovation — by students, villagers, government commissioners and others who use sophisticated technology or the tools already at hand, and who work to achieve goals as seemingly diverse as fair elections, clean water and freedom for political prisoners.

Individually these stories are inspiring. Together, in the workbook that follows, they represent a vision of what can be accomplished in human rights.

The Limits of Curent Strategy

The persistence of torture represents a significant challenge to the global community. When the three most common tactics of the human rights movement have not significantly reduced the incidence of torture, it is time to take a good look at the limits of current strategy. Some sense of those limits emerges from a process I call "tactical mapping."

Beginning with the relationship between the torturer and the victim, a group of ten experts on torture diagrammed other relationships in which that fundamental perversion is embedded and which enable the torture to occur. For example, torturers are usually members of a team with strong hierarchical leadership; they may also be part of a particular police station or military unit. We followed these relationships vertically to understand the chain of command that plans, organizes and funds the use of torture. But we also looked at each level horizontally, in order to understand other possible influences and relationships. Police stations, for instance, also have civilians and physicians in attendance; they, in turn, have relationships to the outside world that have some degree of control or influence over them. The initial map developed using this process diagrammed over 400 relationships, from the highly local to those in the international community.

We posited that every relationship on the diagram was a possible place to begin an intervention to interrupt or control the torturer/victim dyad. With the help of the diagram, we mapped the relationships targeted by various tactics and then the logical chain of relationships that they must influence in order to interrupt the dyad (hence the name, the "tactical map").[1] In doing so, we reached several important conclusions:

1   Most tactics were initiated on the far edges of the diagram, such as on the international level, meaning they had to work their way through many layers of other relationships before they indirectly affected the torturer/victim dyad. We speculated that this weakened or dissipated the force of the action.

2   Rather than brittle and easily disrupted, systems that use torture are often highly complex, allowing the different institutions which benefit from torture's use to support each other. As one part of the system is attacked, other parts (such as the police structure, the system of prosecutors, the indifference of the judiciary) help protect the target and allow it to self-repair. We understood this to mean that the system will not yield to individual tactics. Rather, the system needs to be affected in multiple areas at the same time to create disequilibrium and prevent self-repair. This requires the use of multiple tactics working in conjunction as part of a more comprehensive strategy.

3   Most organizations in the field incorporate a limited number of tactics within their repertoire. Organizations tend to focus on a narrow set of tactics, and rarely cooperate or collaborate on them. Not only does this limit influence to very narrow sectors in a complex, mutually reinforcing system, but each organization is shaping its strategy based on this isolated capacity rather than on what is needed to affect the situation. We do what we can do, not what we need to do. We speculated that more coordination between tactics would make them more effective.

4   So many relationships on the diagram were unaffected or uninvolved in any form of current action. Their strengths and concerns were not called forth to action. We speculated that a much wider array of tactics would be needed to engage these potential actors.

[1] Tactical mapping was developed with support from the Organization for Security and Cooperation in Europe's (OSCE) Advisory Panel for the Prevention of Torture and an in-kind donation from the Rockefeller Brothers Fund.

"I am not arguing, then, that tactical thinking or training supersedes strategic thinking, but rather that tactical development enriches strategic thought."

I believe these same conclusions hold true in other social and human rights issues. We need to find new ways of working together — and new ways of working — in order to create effective strategies of change. Some current strategies require a macro-framework, in which the limited resources of many are more effectively combined in a unified campaign. This might require what I call a "strategic convenor," an institution or person with the moral credibility to pull us together in a new working relationship. But others can be initiated by organizations that begin to test new ways of pressuring complex systems and stimulating action by new actors in the social web. This book is part of an overarching project, the New Tactics in Human Rights Project, to develop a dialogue within the human rights community about how that could come about and to broadly illustrate some of the tools at our disposal for more effective action.

An Emerging Idea

The Center for Victims of Torture (CVT) was founded in 1985 as the first comprehensive treatment facility for torture survivors in the United States. From the outset, CVT's leadership conceived of its work as developing a new tactic of use to the human rights community. As we began to understand what tactics could emerge from our work, we also encouraged the development of other treatment programs for torture survivors. These new institutions created new strategic opportunities for the human rights movement: restoring, for example, leadership stolen by repression, helping communities come to terms with the legacy of fear, and organizing the health care community as a new human rights constituency. In the course of our work we also began to collect stories of other groups and people who were innovating outside the mainstream's focus.

The New Tactics project was conceived in 1995. Shortly thereafter, CVT convened advisory groups in Turkey to explore the idea of a "best practices" symposium examining tactics used around the world to resolve — or more effectively struggle with — widespread human rights abuses. We wanted to focus on solutions rather than problems and to proceed from the idea that, at least in part, abuses continue because both civil society and government are stymied by a lack of specific examples of what to do. Although we believed that a problem orientation was useful, it was already being done quite well by the mainstream movement; we believed that not enough attention was focused on effective solutions. There was already a lot of attention to the "what" but too little attention on the "how."

The idea found resonance and respect with a broad sector of leaders in Turkey. In 1997, CVT formed a partnership with two Turkish organizations — Helsinki Citizens Assembly and the Human Rights Centre of the Turkish and Middle Eastern Institute for Public Administration — to develop the New Tactics in Human Rights Project. Systematic research on innovative tactics began in earnest in 1999 with support from the John D. and Catherine T. MacArthur Foundation. We also established an International Advisory Committee of nine world leaders to provide visibility and political support and a Human Rights Working Group, composed of 21 human rights leaders in nearly every region of the world to help identify promising tactics and contribute to the project's overall direction.

The Working Group met with members of the Turkish advisory group in 2000 in Istanbul. The former prime minister of Canada, the Right Honourable Kim Campbell, represented the International Advisory Committee and chaired the gathering. The group engaged in discussions on innovative approaches to advancing human rights, modeled cross-training approaches and formulated action plans for the future work of the project.

Individuals who have worked in the human rights field for much of their lives commented on how the ideas and information shared at the meeting helped them think differently about opportunities to engage new people and approach matters from fresh perspectives. We have continued to build on this initial vision by providing tools — including this book and a web page, www.newtactics.org — and by training human rights advocates in tactical innovation and strategic thinking through a series of regional cross-training workshops.

Framework of Our Thinking

Working at CVT over the past sixteen years has taught me that there are important social and political implications in providing treatment to torture survivors. It has reshaped my thinking about the assumed distinctions between preventing torture and caring for survivors. CVT staff have discovered that the care of survivors is about recovering leadership and helping communities overcome the legacy of fear. We've found that the metaphor of healing creates safer political space that allows communities to gather, to work and to learn to take risks. Treatment centers like CVT bring new groups, such as educators, health care professionals and policy makers, into human rights work. And from our position as a treatment center we advocate for an end to torture and for policies and laws that will improve the lives of torture victims. Though we didn't frame it as such, in the early years at least, we were broadening the definition of human rights work and implementing new tactics.

Also framing my thoughts on New Tactics was my role in the international baby food campaign in the 1970s and 1980s. In late 1976 I headed a grassroots activist group working on hunger issues; we had a program budget of $500 a year, plus my own subsistence salary. A small group of us began working together across the country and created the Infant Formula Action Coalition (INFACT). With those meager resources we launched a boycott against the world's largest food corporation, Nestlé, to force changes in its marketing of breast milk substitutes. We built a network of 300 American chapters; created a coalition of over 120 national endorsing organizations with over 40 million members; created the first grassroots international boycott, operating in ten countries; formed the first transnational issue network, IBFAN, operating in 67 nations; became one of the first NGOs invited as an equal participant with nations and corporations into a UN meeting and eventually negotiated the first and only corporate marketing code to emerge from the UN; and, after damaging Nestlé's revenue by about $5 billion, signed a joint agreement with the company to change its marketing practices in alignment with the international code — an agreement that was hailed as "the most important victory in the history of the international consumer movement."

I am proud of that campaign and of nearly a decade of work. But, like all beginners, we made a few mistakes. I can trace many of those mistakes to my limited knowledge of tactics. For example, I initially confused tactics with strategy. Strategic thinking is really about how you make the best of what's available to you and since, in my mind, I had only one tactic available to me, this was, perhaps, inevitable. As with so many leaders who emerge at the grassroots level trying to right a wrong, I began at the level of an activity, graduated to thinking about tactics and struggled to understand how to shape strategy, with only limited notions of the tools that were available to me.

As I have had more experience in shaping the strategy of an organization, it has become clearer to me that the more we understand about tactics, the more flexibility we have to set new strategic directions. I am not arguing, then, that tactical thinking or training supersedes strategic thinking, but rather that tactical development enriches strategic thought.

Goals, Strategy and Tactics

While a focus on tactics is essential, it is not an organization's first priority. An organization must first set broad goals that reflect the values and beliefs of its founders, leaders or members and that incorporate its mission and purposes. These goals must be clear in order to focus planning. An organization will also need to establish intermediate goals that more closely state what it will accomplish over time and that embed a strategic vision of what is feasible to accomplish.

There is nothing mysterious about strategy, though it is often difficult to think strategically. Strategy is not a single decision, but rather a confluence of decisions: the selection of key objectives and appropriate targets, an understanding of needed constituencies and resources and decisions on which tactics to use and when. More than two thousand years ago, Sun Tzu taught that strategy emerges from understanding the adversary (its goals, strategy, strengths and weaknesses), understanding ourselves (our allies, what are our strengths and limits) and understanding the terrain (where a battle will be fought). The adversary's tactics are a key component to its strategy and knowledge of such tactics aids us in counteracting them. What we can accomplish, including which tactics we know and which we can successfully implement, will affect the formation of our strategy. Tactical thinking is therefore a critical component of strategic thinking.

A tactic is a specific action that one takes within a strategy and a way to organize our resources to effect change in the world. A tactic may be an activity, a system or even an institution in one situation and a technique in another. Tactics will manifest themselves differently depending on the size, capability and resources of the organization. Tactics embody how one goes about making change, while a strategy involves decisions on which tactics to use, which targets deserve focus and which resources can be employed. Our knowledge of tactics also shapes the strategy we choose.

Tactical thinking is essential to an effective struggle for human rights. Let me describe this reasoning in greater detail.

1   **What we know how to do influences what we think is possible to do; tactics help determine strategy**.

    I don't want to be overly deterministic here. Innovations happen all through human history whenever someone creates a new response to a problem. Nonetheless, human history is full of examples where the same solution is tried over and over again without success, or where a new tactic replaces an old one. Two good examples come from military history: 1) the development of the Greek phalanx, which created a system of fighting that overcame the traditional reliance on disorganized but overwhelming horse warriors, and 2) the incorporation of the long bow into the English armies of Henry V, which overcame the heavily armored knights. Tactical innovation paved the way to new strategic opportunities.

    Similarly, when our thinking about how we can act is narrowly defined, we restrict our views of what is possible to accomplish. I rejected a lot of good advice during the baby food campaign because I did not know how to carry out the activities suggested — and couldn't afford to pay those who did!

2   **Different tactics are effective against different targets.**

    Not all tactics affect all targets equally. Letter-writing campaigns aimed at democratic governments will get a different reaction than the same number of letters to autocratic governments. An economic boycott requires a target concerned with its economic condition and vulnerable in a way that can be touched by the participants.

We must learn to tailor our tactics to our targets, finding those that will have the fullest possible impact. When tactics fail to affect our targets, we must innovate new and more effective tactics.

3   Different tactics appeal to different constituencies.

Each of us has our own learning style. Good teachers recognize this and help us learn by changing their teaching tactics. To engage the broadest range of people in human rights work, we need the same attitude toward social change tactics.

Some people find picketing in front of a torturer's home a very frightening tactic; others find letter writing too removed from where the change is needed. We can debate who is right or we can recognize that people respond differently to a tactic based on their notions of causation, their tolerance for risk, the time they have available or their way of processing information.

If the human rights community responds by offering only one or two tactics to engage the public, we will appeal only to the narrow constituency to whom those tactics make sense. Legal tactics, for example, are notoriously difficult to use with wide sectors of the population: they tend to be long-term and esoteric efforts in which there is little for anyone beyond a small group of professionals to do. We need to employ other tactics that give more people the chance to be participants rather than observers.

In cultures that have experienced repression, people have learned to withdraw from public life. To engage constituencies in cultures such as these we need to offer tactics that appeal to different risk tolerances and different views of social change.

4   Tactical flexibility is the source of surprise.

As we repeat the same tactics, our adversaries learn to counter them and contain their impact.

When we initiated the boycott against Nestlé, the company overreacted and made many mistakes that ended up strengthening the boycott. But as the campaign wore on, Nestlé developed the expertise to smooth over the criticism and implemented effective counteroffensives. We were constantly changing our tactics to throw the company off balance so its counteroffensives would be ineffective.

The fact that human rights continue to be violated underscores the existence of smart, powerful adversaries with substantial resources. One can imagine the power of the first letter-writing campaign from Amnesty International because the tactic was so surprising. But we can also imagine how, after 30 years, most states have learned to bureaucratize a response and protect themselves from the tactic.

Creating surprise keeps the adversary off balance. This can lead to mistakes that undermine its position. It can also lead to learning, as the tactic's target may gain new insight or come to understand the need for positive change. Inflexibility leads to repetition in our thinking, as well as the adversary's. Flexibility promotes learning by both parties.

5   Tactics teach participants and observers how to engage in the world.

The first baby food campaign (1975–1985) created a new way of conducting global politics. It was a challenge because each stage of the campaign created new precedents; there was no one to coach us on what to do next. Since then other international campaigns have formed and operated within the same framework and have been able to move much more quickly. Think of the international campaign to ban landmines, which accomplished its goals in 18 months, when INFACT took us nearly ten years.

I think of this phenomenon as something similar to a musician learning a new piece of music. As we practice, the muscles learn how to move, giving the brain the opportunity to plan subtle variations and improvements. As we practice, it gets easier.

Another example comes from Uruguay. For 70 years, a provision of the Uruguayan constitution that allowed a public referendum to overturn parliamentary legislation had never been used. The Uruguayan human rights community dusted off this provision and collected petitions from 25 percent of eligible voters to try to overturn the impunity of those who tortured and killed citizens during the dictatorship. Although the referendum failed by a narrow margin, the Uruguayan population learned a new way of doing politics; the referendum was used eight more times in the next 12 years.

6   **Tactics are the training systems for engaging participants and allies in the organization's work.**
Some tactics may be short-term (such as a march), some longer-term (such as a boycott). But as systems of acting, all of them require planning, coordination and direction. They create opportunities for many citizens to be involved, to learn and to become more committed to the work of the organization or campaign. Involvement on a tactical level is an excellent training ground for younger or newer staff and volunteers.

When CVT first proposed introducing the Torture Victims Relief Act[2] in the U.S. Congress (a legislative tactic), we used the opportunity to engage other human rights organizations, the religious community and other potential allies. Through their engagement, they became more knowledgeable about the work of torture treatment programs and the experiences of survivors and began to incorporate our understanding of torture into their language.

Tactical innovation is critical to the successful implementation of human rights around the globe. By expanding our thinking both tactically and strategically, the human rights community has the opportunity to be more effective. In summary:

1   A narrow range of tactics leads to narrow constituencies; a broader range of tactics appeals to, and involves, broader constituencies.

2   An over-reliance on any single tactic leads to its application in the wrong circumstances and to missed opportunities to expand strategic targets; flexible tactical thinking creates the opportunity for refined strategic targeting.

3   An overused tactic encourages the adversary to systematize a response and makes it easier for adversaries to defend their position; tactical flexibility creates surprise and learning.

We do not intend this workbook to be a "cookbook" for creating strategies or to promote any particular set of tactics. Tactical choices must be influenced by a group's capacities, its tolerance for risk, its analysis of the adversary or adversarial conditions and the context in which the tactics will be used.

We instead hope to inspire human rights practitioners to think strategically and to increase their own vocabulary of tactics, presenting a small glimpse of the scope of innovative work being done around the world. And we challenge ourselves, within governments and human rights instiutions, to invest in the development of new strategic tools that will enable us to work together more effectively.

Douglas A. Johnson
[2] The Torture Victims Relief Act is U.S. legislation designed to develop a comprehensive American strategy against torture and provide support for the rehabilitation of torture victims around the world. The bill originally authorized $31 million dollars for the treatment of victims of torture. It was reauthorized and expanded in 2003.

NEW TACTICS IN HUMAN RIGHTS: A RESOURCE FOR PRACTITIONERS

Tactics and Tactical Thinking

In the past twenty-five years, strategic planning has become the norm in nongovernmental organizations. Curiously, the notion of tactics has not accompanied the development of strategic planning and still remains, for many, a pejorative term. We commonly say something or someone is "tactical" rather than "strategic," meaning subject to limited, short-term thinking rather than long-term, core thinking. "Tactics" implies maneuvering for short-term gain or position, perhaps in an unethical manner and because it is not often used in the human rights field the word has raised a number of questions. "Isn't this a military term?" "The word is confusing!" "What do you mean by tactics?" "People in my region don't use this word." So, you may ask, why are we using the word "tactic" rather than another word such as approach, methodology or technique?

In the New Tactics in Human Rights Project, we use "tactic" because of its integral relationship to the concept of "strategy." Strategy defines what is important to do, tactics embody how to do it. The relationship between "the what" and "the how" is an important one in understanding — and demystifying — the concepts of strategy and tactics. Tactics — which may be activities, systems, techniques or even institutions — are one of the key building blocks of strategy.

Another source of confusion is that a strategy for one group may be a tactic for another. A government, for example, could develop a strategy of creating new institutions for protecting human rights. One of the tactics in this strategy may be creating a national commission on human rights. But as an entity, the commission must define its own strategy and the tactics it will use to implement it more precisely.

Building successful strategies also relies on tactical flexibility and access to a broad range of tactics. As I explain in "The Need for New Tactics" (p. 12), people, organizations and movements that rely too much on a narrow range of tactics may end up using them in the wrong circumstances or may miss opportunities to use other, more appropriate tactics. They may not be able to attract as broad a range of supporters as they would using more diverse tactics. Also, repeatedly using the same tactics allows the targeted adversaries or systems to adapt and change, rendering the tactics themselves less effective.

This book, while by no means exhaustive, is an illustration of the breadth of tactics being used by the international human rights community. It is a testament both to the creativity — often born of necessity — of human rights practitioners and to the power of tactical and strategic thinking.

Douglas A. Johnson
Executive Director
The Center for Victims of Torture

USING THE WORKBOOK
AS A RESOURCE

Whatever your role in the struggle to promote the basic dignity of the human being, whether you are a community organizer, a government official or the head of a multinational corporation, we hope that this book changes the way you think about what's possible in your work. In the stories that follow we want you to see new opportunities, new partnerships and new tactical approaches to help you advance human rights.

We also want to challenge you to examine your own work in terms of tactics and strategies. With so much important work and so few resources, human rights advocates may see this kind of examination as a luxury. But when we think tactically and strategically we can often do better work faster. The worksheets in the back of the book (pp. 155–156) may help you outline your goal, choose a target, develop your strategy and choose tactics to implement that strategy. The article "The Need for New Tactics" (p. 12) explains the place for tactical thinking in the human rights movement as a whole.

We hope these worksheets and this book as a whole can be a starting point for your own thinking, or for discussions in your organization or within any group working to improve human rights. Get together to find inspiration in the stories that follow and brainstorm ideas of your own. Use the questions throughout the book to help you look more closely at individual tactics and the aspects of them you might use in your own work.

As you browse through the book, the tactics that might catch your eye at first may be the ones that have been used in your region or in fields of work similar to yours. But these tactics may not necessarily the most useful to you. Instead of organizing this book geographically or by human rights area, we have grouped the tactics into four categories:

1   Those that aim to prevent imminent abuse (in the Prevention Tactics chapter, pp. 28–47).

2   Those that intervene to stop ongoing abuse (in the Intervention Tactics chapter, pp. 50–81).

3   Those that help restore and rebuild people and communities after abuse has ended (in the Restorative Tactics Chapter, pp. 84–113).

4   Those that promote human rights by building communities and cultures where those rights are understood and respected (in the Building Human Rights Cultures and Institutions chapter, pp. 116–151).

You might want to think about the primary challenge you face — intervention or prevention, for example — and start browsing in that chapter. At the same time, you will quickly find that tactics can often be used for several purposes and may address more than one of these goals. However you approach it, we urge you to read with an open mind, ready to consider what you might learn or adapt from each tactic. Some of the tactics you read about will be readily useable in your situation, others will require greater analysis and adjustment. The worksheets in the back of the book include a list of questions to consider when adapting tactics (pp. 161). If you want to browse an expanded and continually growing list of tactics, see our searchable online database at www.newtactics.org.

Neither this book nor the New Tactics project seeks to promote any particular tactic or to tell you what would be appropriate in your situation. It is up to you to consider tactics in the context of your :

overall strategy

financial resources

human resources

political openings

cultural considerations

We hope you will find this workbook a valuable resource, one that inspires you to reexamine your own work and see new possibilities for advancing human rights. Given the nature of its content, this book will always be a work in progress, never an exhaustive catalogue of tactics. The New Tactics project will continue to research innovative tactics being used around the globe and promote them through the other tools we create — including the searchable online database (available at www.newtactics.org), training workshops, tactical notebooks and others. Your comments, additions and suggestions will always be welcome. Please use the form at the back of this book or contact us at newtactics@cvt.org.

Key Terms
These are some of the important terms we use throughout the book. These words are used to mean many different things in other contexts. This is the way we define them for our purposes.

Goal The aim or purpose toward which an effort is directed.

Strategy An outline of key steps and approaches in accomplishing the goal.

Tactic(s) A specific action taken to implement a strategy. Tactics are the levers or mechanisms to carry out a strategy. They are the means through which a change is made, while a strategy defines what is important to do. Tactics are about "the how," while strategies are about "the what."

Target(s) The person, place or thing the tactic is intended to affect.

Active allies People or organizations who actively and openly support and are involved in your work.

Passive allies People or organizations who support your goals but have not yet become involved in advancing your work.

The Research Process

The tactics included in this workbook, in the database on the New Tactics web site (www.newtactics.org) and in New Tactics workshops are drawn from a broad range of work. Some have been used by people who identify themselves and their work as part of the human rights struggle and others by individuals working in business, government, law enforcement, conflict resolution, environment, labor, women's rights and other movements for social change and justice. All of these people work to promote the basic dignity of the human being, as defined in the foundation documents for human rights law.

These documents are collectively known as the International Bill of Human Rights: the Universal Declaration of Human Rights (1948), the International Covenant on Civil and Political Rights (1966), its Optional Protocol and the International Covenant on Economic, Social and Cultural Rights (1966). These documents were followed by more than twenty human rights conventions — treaties that become binding law in those countries that ratify them.

We have included only nonviolent tactics in this workbook because we believe that they are the most appropriate to protect and advance human rights. When people who are frustrated by social injustice have used violence, it has often prompted repressive social measures that, in turn, have violated human rights. We recognize that the pursuit of human rights will involve struggle. It is our hope that by learning about tactics from around the world, people will find effective ways of working for human rights without using violence.

In November 1999, CVT staff and volunteers began researching tactics being used to advance human rights. In particular, we sought tactical approaches that would inspire others to think creatively and to take effective action. We cast the net widely, surveying work done by civil society organizations, international agencies, government bodies, businesses and other organizations to discover what people were doing to build constituencies, pressure for change and promote human rights. Volunteers, including students, professors, health professionals, public relations professionals, business consultants, journalists, computer specialists and others, contributed countless hours to this effort. The New Tactics Working Group and Advisory Committee also offered invaluable assistance.

Researchers contacted funders of human rights work, attended conferences, searched written materials and the Internet and conducted countless interviews over the phone and in person. We have made every reasonable effort to contact the organizations involved and to verify the information we have included. When this was not possible, the New Tactics team decided whether the information was sufficient to be useful and whether it was already public. If an organization was not comfortable with having a tactic summary or contact information included, that information was removed.

The first draft of the New Tactics in Human Rights Workbook was printed in September 2000, followed by a second draft in 2001. The third edition builds on the substantial work done in those two drafts.

As with all work, this workbook reflects its authors' biases, including the places we looked for ideas and what was available to us within the limits of research and technology. Due to the constraints of time, available information and resources, some sections and examples are more complete than others. Readers can help us improve later editions by sending in information, indicating biases that distort the facts and suggesting additional tactics and materials to include. We welcome your contributions in these areas as well as in any part of the workbook.

About the New Tactics in Human Rights Project

Led by a diverse group of international organizations and practitioners and coordinated by the Center for Victims of Torture (CVT), the New Tactics in Human Rights Project promotes tactical innovation and strategic thinking within the international human rights community. It works to enhance the effectiveness of practitioners and organizations worldwide by developing tools and networks for sharing creative ideas and fostering tactical innovation.

This workbook is one of several tools developed by the New Tactics project to illustrate the wide range of tactical possibilities in human rights work.

The New Tactics web site, www.newtactics.org, includes a searchable database of tactics and forums where people can build networks and exchange ideas.

The Tactical Notebooks are a series of first-person, in-depth case studies that provide a detailed look at how a tactic was implemented and the challenges that were faced along the way.

The Regional Training Workshops, held in each region of the world, bring together people who have used innovative tactics to train each other on those tactics. Participants work hard and leave with a new range of tactics available to them, new confidence in their training ability and a new network of colleagues across a range of human rights fields.

About the Center for Victims of Torture

The Center for Victims of Torture works to heal the wounds of torture on individuals, their families and their communities and to stop torture worldwide.

At its founding in 1985, CVT was the first torture treatment center of its kind in the United States and the third in the world. Today CVT provides torture survivors with counseling, medical care and social services in a holistic treatment model; trains educators and medical professionals who may work with survivors of torture or war trauma; conducts research on the effects of torture and effective treatment; and lobbies locally, nationally and internationally to put an end to torture.

The New Tactics project emerged from CVT's own experience as a creator of new tactics and as a treatment center that also advocates for the protection of human rights from a unique position — one of healing and of reclaiming civic leadership.

For more information, see our web site: www.cvt.org.

The Center for Victims of Torture

717 East River Road
Minneapolis, MN 55455
612 436 4800
cvt@cvt.org
www.cvt.org

Partner Organizations

Access to Justice, Nigeria

The Center for Victims of Torture, United States

The Danish Institute for Human Rights, Denmark

The Helsinki Citizens' Assembly, Turkey

The ICAR Foundation, Romania

National Coordinator for Human Rights, Peru

Turkish and Middle Eastern Institute for Public Administration, Turkey

International Advisory Committee

The Hon. Morton I. Abramowitz, former President of the Carnegie Endowment for International Peace and former United States Ambassador to Turkey and Thailand

J. Brian Atwood, former Administrator of the U. S. Agency for International Development; Dean, Hubert Humphrey Institute for Public Affairs, University of Minnesota

The Rt. Hon. Kim Campbell, former Prime Minister of Canada and former Consul General of Canada in Los Angeles

The Hon. Justice Richard J. Goldstone, former Justice of the Constitutional Court of South Africa and former Prosecutor for the International Criminal Tribunal for the former Yugoslavia and Rwanda

Ioanna Kucuradi, Chair of the National Committee of Supreme Coordination Council of Human Rights in Turkey

The Hon. Walter F. Mondale, former Vice President of the United States and former United States Ambassador to Japan

Orhan Pamuk, Turkish novelist

The Hon. Michel Rocard, President of the Commission of Employment and Social Affairs of the European Parliament and former Prime Minister of France

Edson W. Spencer, former Chief Executive Officer of Honeywell Inc. and former Chair of the Board of the Ford Foundation

Mario Vargas Llosa, Peruvian novelist

Elie Wiesel, Nobel Peace Laureate

Human Rights Working Group

Mariclaire Acosta, Mexico, Former Under-Secretary in the area of Human Rights and Democracy, Mexican Government

Miguel Darcy de Oliveira, Brazil, Director, Institute for Cultural Action

Clarence Dias, United States, Director, International Center for Law in Development; Chair of the Board, Human Rights Internet

Camelia Doru, Romania, Director, ICAR Foundation

Basil Fernando, China, Executive Director, Asian Human Rights Commission

Claudine Haenni, Switzerland, Research Fellow, University of Bristol

Bahey El Din Hassan, Egypt, Director, Cairo Institute for Human Rights Studies

Salma Khan, Bangladesh, former Chair and current Member, United Nations Committee on the Elimination of Discrimination Against Women; board member, Women for Women, Bangladesh

Morten Kjaerum, Denmark, Director, The Danish Institute for Human Rights

Norine MacDonald, Canada, Executive Director, The Gabriel Foundation

Sofia Macher, Peru, former member, Truth & Reconciliation Commission; former Executive Director, National Coordinator of Human Rights

Liam Mahony, United States, Board Member, Peace Brigades International and Lecturer in Human Rights, Princeton University

Pat Naidoo, Kenya, Associate Director, Rockefeller Foundation, Africa Regional Office

Joseph Otteh, Nigeria, Director, Access to Justice

Boris Pustintsev, Russia, Chairman, Citizens' Watch

Mark Ritchie, United States, President, Institute for Agriculture and Trade Policy

Sir Nigel Rodley, United Kingdom, former Special Rapporteur on Torture for the United Nations and Member, United Nations Human Rights Committee

Kailash Satyarthi, India, Chairman, South Asian Coalition on Child Servitude

Rajesh Tandon, India, Executive Director, Society for Participatory Research in Asia

Patricia Valdez, Argentina, Executive Director, Memoria Abierta

Glenda Wildschut, South Africa, former Member, Truth and Reconciliation Commission

Michael Windfuhr, Germany, Executive Director, FoodFirst Information and Action Network International

PREVENTION TACTICS

Just a little more than a decade ago, human rights organizations focused primarily on denouncing past or ongoing violations. The main tool in the human rights tool box was a hammer, and the major players in human rights work relied on "naming and shaming" countries for documented abuses. While in its own way this is valuable work, the tool box has been dramatically expanded by the many new actors involved in human rights work.

We have seen a striking change in the human rights environment in the last decade. The agenda moved from creating an international legal framework to serious discussions about on-the-ground implementation. At the same time, there has been a shift from international efforts to local work, and local groups often include both intervention and prevention in their goals. A local NGO, for example, might approach the police about a specific case of torture and discuss how to keep it from happening in the future. These groups are using new tactics that weren't available to traditional human rights organizations. They are not only criticizing: they are forming partnerships with government institutions to help reform legislation; they are offering training to police forces and creating curricula; they are making their presence known in crucial ways.

The work of protecting human rights and preventing abuse continues to change, advance and improve. The tactics you will read about in this chapter perhaps will be part of making the next decade even better.

— Morten Kjaerum
Director
Danish Institute for Human Rights
Copenhagen, Denmark

In order to prevent human rights abuses we must recognize when people are in physical danger; when freedom of movement, the right to work or to adequate housing will be curtailed; when a group is in danger of losing its voice in society or a community is in danger of falling into poverty; or when an indigenous way of life is disappearing.

The tactics in this chapter aim to prevent imminent abuse. Sometimes the most effective way to do that is just to be there. The physical presence of others — whether that means one volunteer from a country with a powerful government or a crowd of bystanders who will serve as witnesses — can deter potential abusers.

Sometimes abuse occurs because people don't have the information they need to prevent it. Getting information into the right hands — of those who will be directly affected by the abuse or of others who can mobilize against it — can stop abuse from happening.

And sometimes the best way to preserve human rights is to remove the possibility for abuse. Recognizing the pattern of abuse makes it possible to change the situation, so that abuse is far less likely to occur.

The tactics in this section are divided into three sections:

1   Physical protection tactics that prevent harm through physical presence.
2   Tactics that get critical information into the hands of people who can prevent abuse.
3   Tactics that anticipate abuse and create obstacles to stop it.

PHYSICAL PROTECTION

We can show no greater solidarity than physically to stand up for — or next to — fellow human beings who are in danger. The tactics in this section go beyond symbolism, using the physical presence of volunteers to protect the safety of others. This is a relatively simple and powerful idea: safety in numbers. People or groups who are willing to hurt someone may be unwilling to do so in front of others, fearing witnesses or bad press or the consequences of harming someone who has the backing of an influential group or government. This leads to another powerful idea: show that you have friends in high places.

Bodyguards for Human Rights: Protecting and encouraging endangered human rights activists through the presence of international volunteers.

Peace Brigades International (PBI) sends international observers to accompany human rights activists who are threatened by the government or paramilitary organizations. If they witness abuse, observers alert authorities in the country, their own native government and activists around the world. Knowing they can expect an international response, abusers are deterred from their planned attacks. At the same time, the accompanied activists are empowered to continue and expand their work for human rights. PBI was one of the first to 'institutionalize' the idea of accompaniment, beginning in Guatemala in the early 1980s. PBI currently sustains over 80 volunteers on the ground in Colombia, Indonesia, Mexico and Guatemala.

Although the volunteers themselves are the most visible aspect of this tactic, the tactic's success depends on the actions of many others around the world. The volunteer must be able to attract international attention immediately in the event of an attack or threat. To this end, PBI has networks of activists in the home countries of the volunteers. Additionally, volunteers bring networks of family and friends to their work, and often draw on extensive activist experience and past contacts.

International accompaniment can be difficult for both human rights activists and volunteers, who face constant danger, stress and constraints on their personal lives. PBI places the highest value on the empowerment and encouragement of local grassroots activists, offering accompaniment only upon request and never imposing itself in the internal affairs of those it accompanies.

Read more about this in a tactical notebook available at www.newtactics.org, under Tools for Action, and see *Unarmed Bodyguards: International Accompaniment for the Protection of Human Rights*, by Liam Mahony and Luis Enrique Eguren, Kumarian Press, 1997.

ONLINE

This tactic builds on the universal reality that we are all subject to moral and political pressure. National leaders don't want bad press. Low-level killers don't want a witness watching their dirty work. Everyone prefers anonymity in their crimes, and no one wants witnesses. By putting an international witness right in the face of the perpetrators, and simultaneously placing external pressure on the leaders, the attacks are deterred. Meanwhile, by showing threatened activists that international solidarity extends to the point of taking risks right at their side, they are emboldened and strengthened in their courageous work.

Accompaniment has since been used as a tactic in other situations where people are in physical danger and perpetrators of abuse are likely to be swayed by international opinion. Other groups using this tactic include the Nonviolent Peaceforce in Sri Lanka, Christian Peacemaker Teams in the West Bank, the National Organization in Solidarity with the People of Guatemala, the Ecumenical Accompaniment Program in Palestine and Israel, the Fellowship of Reconciliation in Colombia, the Centro Fray Bartolome de Las Casas in Mexico, and others.

These dynamics can be used in other settings as well. The symbolic power of church workers or journalists, for instance, often has a protective or calming influence in situations of tension and violence, because perpetrators don't want to be seen misbehaving in such a presence. In Haiti, Partners in Health employs community health workers called *accompagnateurs* who make daily visits to HIV/AIDS and tuberculosis patients, which, in addition to providing medical and emotional support, shows members of the community that they need not fear casual contact with people who have the illness. Here again, the symbol and physical presence of a committed third party carries a moral and social weight that can change behavior.

How can you focus international attention on your struggle?

Region	Initiating Sector	Target Sector	Focus	Human Rights Issue	**PREVENTION**	**New Tactics in Human Rights**
Americas	Civil Society	Civil Society	National	Civil and political rights	Physical Protection	
Asia			International	HIV/AIDS		
Multiple						

Plan B: Protecting arrested demonstrators by protesting outside the police stations where they are being detained.

In Serbia, under the Milosevic regime, a group of young activists built on the idea of safety in numbers, using secondary demonstrations to protect members arrested during demonstrations and to render the threat of arrest ineffective. They also used humor and theater to lessen the population's fear of government power.

Otpor! ("Resistance!" in Serbo-Croatian) prepared secondary demonstrations — their "Plan B" — outside police stations to respond immediately to arrests during protest events. The police were less likely to beat or detain the activists, knowing that large crowds and a number of journalists were waiting outside for them, while the activists felt less afraid, thanks to the support they knew they were receiving.

Once arrests occurred, Otpor! put Plan B into action by mobilizing its extensive network of contacts:

1   A nearby observer with a mobile phone observed the arrest and determined which police station received the arrested activists.
2   Lawyers went immediately to the police station to negotiate for the activists' release.
3   Other Otpor! activists gathered, within an hour, in front of the police station and at the organization's office. They played games and sang songs to keep the crowds upbeat, calm and involved. Activists remained outside the police stations until the detainees were released.
4   Media contacts went to the police station to report on the protests and take statements from the activists' after they were released.
5   Opposition parties condemned the arrest and sent their members to the police station.
6   Local NGOs informed international organizations and asked them to condemn the arrests.

Otpor! put substantial time and effort into building a strong, extensive and loyal network that could be mobilized quickly. Extensive planning outlined who would call whom and exactly what each person was to do after the arrests, so that the second demonstration would follow the arrests almost instantaneously. Most contact information for the network was stored on individual members' mobile phones, so that the police could not seize or destroy the information.

ONLINE | Read more about this in a tactical notebook available at www.newtactics.org, under Tools for Action.

Otpor!'s "Plan B" is a fascinating example of a tactic that met the aims described in each section of this workbook. People using this tactic prevented the imminent torture of activists inside the police station. They intervened to stop the ongoing abuses of the Milosevic regime by weakening police power. They helped heal and restore the confidence of protesters who had been arrested, and helped volunteers overcome the fear of being arrested. And the visibility of the demonstrations built awareness of the regime's abuses and the growing democratic resistance movement.

Otpor!'s success depended on a number of critical factors. While the country was suffering under an autocratic regime, Otpor!'s lawyers were still able to meet with the activists and have some influence with the police. Similarly, the police and the regime still feared a large public gathering and international public opinion. In a totally closed society, neither of these things would be true.

What is your plan B?

" " | *All our arrested activists became heroes. Because they had the support of hundreds of people waiting for them at the station, they were not afraid any more. Competitions started for who was the "most wanted" activist and who got arrested more. We were laughing in the face of the regime and the entire world learned about what was happening to us.*

— Zorana Smiljanic, Otpor!, Serbia

	PREVENTION	Region	Initiating Sector	Target Sector	Focus	Human Rights Issue
	Physical Protection	Europe	Civil Society	Government Society	National	Torture

A Protective Presence: Maintaining a physical presence at the site of potential abuse to monitor and prevent human rights violations. | TACTIC

Throughout the West Bank, Machsom Watch uses the presence of Israeli women to protect Palestinians passing through Israeli checkpoints and ensure that their rights are respected.

Machsom Watch monitors several Israeli checkpoints every morning and afternoon during the periods of highest traffic to protest the checkpoints and to protect the rights of individual Palestinians who must pass through them. All of the volunteers for Machsom Watch (*machsom* means checkpoint in Hebrew) are Israeli women. The organization began in January 2001 with three women and has since grown to 300 volunteers.

Monitors view the checkpoints as a violations of human rights, restricting the Palentinians' right to free movement and hence the right to education, medical treatment and work.

The monitors perform three primary functions at the checkpoints: they prevent abuses, they document abuses that they witness and they show solidarity with the Palestinian people.

The very presence of the Israeli women discourages some soldiers from abusing the people passing through the checkpoints, according to both monitors and Palestinians. When soldiers try to keep people from crossing or to confiscate ID cards, monitors quietly but assertively intervene if they think it could make a difference. When they witness serious violations, monitors often complain to higher-ranking army officials and encourage Palestinians to do the same.

Monitors who witness abuses make detailed reports and publish them on their website. They invite journalists, politicians and others to join them at the checkpoints. And they wear tags that read in Arabic "No to the checkpoints!" This show of support is heartening to many Palestinians, who may not have a positive image of Israelis.

Machsom Watch has faced several challenges in its work. There are many checkpoints and not enough monitors to cover them all. Volunteers admit that the army does not feel committed to report to the monitors, or necessarily acknowledge them. This is exacerbated by the fact that Israeli soldiers are rotated into and out of their positions fairly frequently, so the monitors are not able to develop a relationship with them, and some of the work begins anew with each new rotation of soldiers. So far, Machsom Watch has not succeeded in its broader goal of ending the occupation and the removal of checkpoints. However, it has helped to make the Israeli public and people all over the world more aware of the abuses occurring at the checkpoints.

The physical presence of an individual is often more effective when it is backed by an influential network that can move information quickly to a large number of people or to the right people in key positions of influence. Machsom Watch uses the Internet to share its monitoring experiences more widely and to raise awareness among Israelis and the international community.

How can you use respected people in your community to assist potential victims of abuse?

When we arrived at the checkpoint, there were men, women, children, taxis, lorries loaded with produce, an ambulance and also a long line of cars from the other side. As soon as people saw us they rushed towards us as if we were their last hope, each with his own story... We tried all sorts of phone numbers, and finally a jeep arrived with a high-ranking officer. At first he refused to talk to us, saying that we only come to the checkpoints to make trouble for the soldiers and to make an impression... A doctor and his wife who were there had taken their daughter to hospital in Ramallah, and though the border policemen were prepared to let him return home to Hebron, they would not let his wife, as they maintained that she had passed illegally and her midwife documents were out of date. We kept pleading for some people. We don't know why or at what point the officer softened, but suddenly he gave orders, and everyone started going through. Within five minutes the checkpoint was empty, and there was no checking on the way, but the doctor's wife was left standing and sobbing. The soldiers had taken her ID. Next thing we knew, she had her ID back, and was on her way to join her husband on the other side. As we left, we heard shouting from the other side of the checkpoint, and saw our doctor and other people jumping up and down and waving their arms at us, shouting "Shukran! Shukran!" (Thank you! Thank you!).

" "

— volunteer, Machsom Watch,
Abu-Dis checkpoint, Israel

Region	Initiating Sector	Target Sector	Focus	Human Rights Issue	**PREVENTION**	New Tactics in Human Rights
Asia	Civil Society	Government	Local	Freedom of Movement	Physical Protection	

SHARING CRITICAL INFORMATION

The right information in the right hands can go a long way toward preventing abuse and advancing human rights. However, even in today's globalized and technology-saturated society, this can be a real challenge. The tactics included in this section demonstrate innovative ways to share critical information with people who can help prevent abuse, with those who may be in danger of suffering abuse and with large groups of people who can speak out to prevent it. Some of these tactics make sophisticated use of new technologies while others rely on person-to-person contact. All of them demonstrate the old maxim: knowledge is power.

New Tactics
in Human Rights

PREVENTION

Sharing Critical
Information

34   www.newtactics.org

Anti-Violence Phone Network: Using mobile phones to create a network of communication that can stop violence before it escalates.

In the seemingly intractable conflict in Northern Ireland, finding common ground between politicized Catholic and Protestant factions has often proven nearly impossible. And yet there are people on both sides who want to prevent outbreaks of violence. This tactic involves identifying leaders in each community who want to prevent violence and arming them with needed information.

Interaction Belfast (formerly known as Springfield Inter-Community Development Project) created a mobile phone network to prevent outbreaks of violence between volatile neighborhoods in Belfast. Volunteers in both Catholic and Protestant communities are given mobile phones to communicate with their counterparts across the interface when potentially violent crowds gather or when rumors of violence start to spread.

An "interface" is an area where Catholic (Nationalist/Republican) and Protestant (Unionist/Loyalist) neighborhoods abut one another. Typically divided by physical walls, neighborhoods along the interfaces tend to be among the most economically deprived communities in Northern Ireland. Suspicion about what is happening on the other side of the wall can cause or escalate violent incidents.

Volunteers from both sides meet weekly and their phones are always on. During events that are likely to cause violence, such as sporting events or Protestant parades through Catholic neighborhoods, the network plans ahead to monitor key areas. Volunteers recognize that they are able to intervene most effectively in cases of "recreational violence" — youth seeking excitement or responding to rumors — but are able to do little in cases of organized or paramilitary violence.

When volunteers see or hear of crowds gathering along the interface, or hear rumors of violence about to occur on the other side, they call their counterparts across the interface. Volunteers calm crowds on their own sides before the incidents become violent.

Since the program began, the phone network has both prevented violence and provided communities on both sides of the interface with more accurate information when violence does occur. The weekly meetings of volunteers have also created a core group of people engaged in regular cross-community dialogue. As these relationships have matured, the network has also begun to address other common problems facing both communities, including long-term revitalization of the area.

The widespread use of mobile telephone technology has made rapid responses to imminent and ongoing abuse more possible now than ever. In Northern Ireland the telephones made communication possible even when the two sides did not at first have a particularly strong relationship, but were committed to ending the violence.

When kids gather at the interface rumors often spread as to what they're up to, and that in itself can attract others to gather at the other side of that interface.... But when you can phone people on the other side and check whether anything is actually going on or not, it means you can go back to your own crowd and quell those rumors.

Before we had the network established, we had kids on our side of the interface coming up and claiming, "They're doing this over there" or "They're doing that," and we didn't know any differently. But now we have a means of counteracting all that.

" "

— **Member of the Springfield Inter-Community Development Project Phone Network,**
now Interaction Belfast, Northern Ireland

Region	Initiating Sector	Target Sector	Focus	Human Rights Issue	**PREVENTION**	New Tactics in Human Rights
Europe	Civil Society	Society	Local	Peace	Sharing Critical Information	

Mobile Phones Help Keep Elections Honest: Transmitting vote tallies by mobile phone to prevent tampering.

Mobile phone networks can also be useful in other situations when time is of the essence. For example, during and immediately following elections, control of ballot boxes and vote tallies is critical. In Kenya, mobile phone networks have been used to keep elections fair and honest — thereby preserving people's right to take part in the government of their country — by reporting vote tallies before they could be tampered with.

During Kenya's 2002 presidential elections, independent monitoring groups used mobile phones to keep the election process honest by immediately reporting vote tallies from each polling place.

In previous elections, votes had to be physically transported to key counting points before any results could be released. Although observers monitored this process, the delay did leave open the possibility of fraud, or at least the suspicion of fraud. The instant communication provided by mobile phones (in many Kenyan polling stations there are no fixed land lines) made it difficult to change results.

Two groups given credentials by the election commission to observe the vote count monitored the election: the Institute for Education in Democracy (IED) and the Kenya Domestic Observer Programme (K-DOP). IED volunteers were stationed in 178 of Kenya's 210 constituencies. Volunteers used their own phones and were given an allowance of 2000 Kenyan shillings (about US$26). They called a central IED office to report as soon as votes were counted; the numbers were posted immediately on the Internet. Volunteers also called in to report violence and malpractice. The IED results were available even before the official results of the Kenya's electoral commission, largely because the commission had a more complicated protocol for releasing results.

K-DOP also used a network of volunteers, but did not have standard provisions for reimbursement. Kenyan election commission officers also reported results by phone, using government-supplied satellite phones or their own mobile phones where no land lines existed.

The transparency created by the quick and independent reporting of these several networks helped prevent the violence that may have occurred had people on the losing side of the election suspected fraud. The fast reporting forced both the major candidates and their supporters to accept the results as legitimate.

Mobile phones are increasingly used to ensure that elections are fair and to preserve the basic human right of expressing one's will in a free and genuine election. Even fast communication, however, cannot always speed up bureaucracy. One observer in Kenya noted that, while officials used mobile phones to report problems such as voters not included in the rolls, some voters were still turned away because of the complicated protocols involved in fixing the problem.

Mobile phones have been used in other recent elections around the world. During the 2000 elections in Peru, nonpartisan monitors from the Peruvian organization Transparencia telephoned turnout numbers, evaluations of the quality of the voting and counting processes, and precinct election results to a central data analysis center from a randomly selected sample of polling stations across the country. Some reports came from remote regions of the Andes and Amazon regions. Transparencia's data analysis prompted national and international pressure for Alberto Fujimori to accept a run-off election.

How might you be able to use mobile phones or other forms of technology to improve your work and help strengthen human rights?

	PREVENTION	Region	Initiating Sector	Target Sector	Focus	Human Rights Issue
	Sharing Critical Information	Africa	Civil Society	Government	National	Democracy

Survivors Know What Questions to Ask: Involving survivors of human rights abuse in the identification and rescue of potential victims.

Survivors of human rights abuse have a unique knowledge of the form abuse can take and a unique ability to recognize it. Such information can be used to prevent others from suffering the same fate. The organization Maiti Nepal enlists women who have been trafficked to help save other women and girls.

Maiti Nepal works to stop trafficking of women and girls across the Nepal-India border by interviewing those who appear vulnerable. The Maiti interviewers are more likely to recognize others in dangerous situations because many of them, too, are survivors of trafficking.

Increasing demand for sex workers in Indian brothels and other markets is increasing trafficking in Nepal. One way to combat the problem is to prevent traffickers from crossing the border, but border police often fail to identify potential victims or simply look the other way.

Maiti Nepal works closely with the border guards at 11 transit points along Nepal's borders to confront suspicious travelers. They stop every car and rickshaw. If there are women or girls traveling with men, the border guards question the men while Maiti Nepal's staff question the women. They ask questions such as "Why are you going to India?" and "How long have you known this man?" and observe the women's body language, dress and make-up. During the interview, they also tell the women about the sex trade in India.

If the travelers' stories are inconsistent, the suspected traffickers are apprehended by the police and the women and girls are taken to safe transit homes Maiti Nepal has constructed near the border. Here they receive food, counseling, and, if they wish, medical exams and transportation back to their home villages. In the event that relatives are unwilling to take someone back, or are found to have participated in the trafficking, Maiti Nepal provides counseling and job training.

Hundreds of potential victims have been rescued as a result of this tactic and cases have been brought against alleged traffickers, putting pressure on local administrations to take action against the criminals.

In situations that involve trafficking, domestic violence, child molestation or forced prostitution, outsiders may not always recognize abuse as easily as survivors do. Potential victims may also be more likely to respond to someone with personal knowledge of what they are going through. The participation of abuse survivors is thus central to the implementation of this tactic. When victims are willing to prevent future abuses, their unique knowledge of how human rights violations are carried out can be invaluable to those working to end such violations. Also crucial in the tactic is Maiti Nepal's successful collaboration with the border guards and its care not to return girls to families complicit in their trafficking.

Region	Initiating Sector	Target Sector	Focus	Human Rights Issue	**PREVENTION**	New Tactics in Human Rights
Asia	Civil Society	Government Society	National	Trafficking	Sharing Critical Information	

www.newtactics.org   37

Protecting Rights on a Time Limit: Informing potential victims of their rights when there is a time limit on protecting those rights.

Sometimes laws themselves impose arbitrary and brief windows of opportunity for individuals to act to protect their rights. The Centre for Equality Rights in Accommodation (CERA) in Ontario, Canada, uses a rapid-response tactic to inform people of their rights and their deadline for action.

The Centre for Equality Rights in Accommodation (CERA) in Ontario, Canada, contacts tenants at risk of eviction and gives them the information they need to avoid eviction. Canadian law limits to five days the time tenants have to dispute evictions, and many people do not have the information or resources to react quickly enough to prevent eviction.

In 1998, a new law was passed in Ontario that allowed landlords to raise the rent to market rates when a rental unit is vacant, giving them an incentive to evict tenants, particularly in communities with low vacancy rates. Every year approximately 60,000 people in Ontario face eviction.

CERA petitioned the Ontario Rental Housing Tribunal for lists of tenants facing eviction. It receives the lists on the condition that it maintain the privacy of the tenants. CERA mails an information package to each tenant whose landlord has applied for an eviction order. Volunteers then follow up with a call to inform tenants of their rights before the five-day period has lapsed. During these conversations, the volunteers inform tenants that their landlords applied to evict them, discuss possible options and refer them to relevant agencies. They also ask tenants about the situation that lead to the eviction, which provides important information about the causes of housing insecurity that CERA and other organizations can use to prevent the problem in the first place.

CERA reaches about 25,000 people each year. After the program started, eviction rates for those reached by telephone declined more than 20%. Since March 2003, however, CERA has been unable to continue the Eviction Prevention project due to a Privacy Commission ruling prohibiting the release of eviction data. CERA is currently in the process of appealing the decision.

While Ontario housing laws do give people the right to dispute their evictions, not all tenants have the information they need to protect those rights in the limited time allowed. CERA's tactic helps get that information to them in time to use it. CERA did need to obtain a list of people facing eviction, and the challenge in other cases may a lack of such information. In addition, not all tenants are reachable by telephone, and not everyone is willing or able to put in the effort to fight for their rights.

Is a rapid response network needed for your struggle? If so, what type of network would be useful?

New Tactics in Human Rights

	PREVENTION	Region	Initiating Sector	Target Sector	Focus	Human Rights Issue
	Sharing Critical Information	Americas	Civil Society	Society	Local	Right to housing

38   www.newtactics.org

Skills for a Population At Risk: Using nonformal education techniques to give an at-risk population the skills needed to thrive in a changing economy.

In Mongolia in the 1990s, as in many other societies in transition, the shift from a state-run to a market economy threatened to leave women (and therefore children) behind, in danger of poverty, hunger and abuse. The Gobi Women's Project sought to bring the women of Mongolia's isolated rural areas the information they needed to succeed in the emerging economic system.

The Mongolian government used nonformal education tools such as the radio, printed materials and visiting teachers to reach out to marginalized and vulnerable Gobi women and teach them the new skills they needed to survive in a market economy.

After the collapse of the Soviet Union in 1991, Mongolia's centralized, state-run economy also came to an end. People who had lived their whole lives on collective farms became responsible for obtaining their own herds and producing and marketing their own goods and services. Many did not have the skills or resources to do this. Nomadic women in the Gobi Desert, an area with an extremely harsh climate and poor communication and transportation systems, were particularly vulnerable. Without trade and commercial skills the women and their children were at risk of poverty, malnutrition and, potentially, violence and abuse.

The government formed the Gobi Women's Project and invited all women in the Gobi Desert to a community planning forum to look for ways to address the problem. The group decided that single mothers with at least three children were the highest priority group, and that radio programs, combined with other nonformal education techniques, were the best way to reach them. (Nonformal education refers to learning programs that are not obligatory and take place outside of a school.)

The radio programs provided information on trade skills (such as producing wool, refining camel fleece and making felt, saddles and traditional clothes), commercial skills (such as negotiating prices and planning) and health issues (such as family planning, hygiene, nutrition and first aid). The programs were broadcast twice a week at times when most women would be likely to listen, usually in the evening. Cassettes were available in local learning centers for anyone who was not able to hear the program. Companion materials were produced for use with the radio programs, and visiting teachers checked the women's progress and offered supplementary materials.

The nonformal education approach succeeded in mobilizing the women to take control of their economic future. They organized local markets, initiated collaborative projects across communities, and encouraged broadening the project to include their husbands and children.

In this case, this skills-building tactic was used to ensure economic rights, but similar nonformal education programs are used to reach distant populations on other issues as well. It is vital to note that the staff of the Gobi Women's Project took into account the lifestyle and the culture of the women they were trying to reach when designing their programs and choosing their media.

How could nonformal education programs be used to strengthen human rights in your community?

Region	Initiating Sector	Target Sector	Focus	Human Rights Issue	**PREVENTION**	**New Tactics in Human Rights**
Asia	Government	Society	National	Development	Sharing Critical Information	

Providing Information and Skills Needed to Claim Rights: Empowering people to use the legal system to exert their rights.

Constitutional guarantees of certain rights are often not protected by law or implemented in reality. Soldiers' Mothers of St. Petersburg gives people the information and skills they need to claim their constitutional right not to serve in the military or to return to units in which they have suffered ill-treatment.

Soldiers' Mothers of Saint Petersburg educates conscripts, army recruits and family members of Russian soldiers about their legal rights so that they can effectively exercise them.

In Russia all young men are required to serve in the military. While a 1993 law exempts men for reasons of poor health or hardship (e.g. their parents are retired or ill, or they are still in school), inscription commissions regularly violate this law. Soldiers' Mothers has documented cases in which young men with physical or psychological problems that should have exempted them from military service have been forced to serve. Inscription commissions have even been known to conduct round-ups with the cooperation of police, on the street, in schools and in dormitories, even going house to house. Once in the military, the young men are subject to terrible conditions, including degrading and substandard living conditions, nightly beatings and torture.

At the school for human rights run by Soldiers' Mothers, known as "Let Us Protect Our Sons," students are taught how to make use of the laws that protect their rights. They are also encouraged to trust that the law can protect them and to support each other and help each other deal with their fears.

Training sessions are held once a week and last three hours. They include specific instruction on how to write statements to the authorities, as well as role-playing and discussions about the law and human rights. A guidebook is also published annually.

Most people are able to obtain documentation from civilian physicians to present to the military physicians. Soldiers' Mothers, with a staff of ten as well as many Russian and foreign volunteers, follows up with participants through questionnaires and keeps a file for each person and district. Participants who succeed in their petitions for exemption are asked to speak to later groups. About 120,000 people have participated in the training sessions over 12 years, and 90,000 have protected their legal right not to serve in the army. Approximately 5,000 people who were tortured in the army have successfully petitioned not to return to their units.

While, in theory, constitutional protections do exist in Russia for young men who fear abuse or who have been abused in the military, lack of information and fear of using the legal system (a system that has not been commonly used by individuals) keeps them from taking advantage of those rights. Soldiers' Mothers provides information about those rights, skills such as letter-writing, and guidance through the legal system.

New Tactics in Human Rights

PREVENTION	Region	Initiating Sector	Target Sector	Focus	Human Rights Issue
Sharing Critical Information	Europe	Civil Society	Society	National	Police and military abuses

40   www.newtactics.org

Fighting Corruption through Transparency: Tracking the work of government officials online to fight corruption.

In South Korea the government of Seoul is encouraging its own officials to act more honestly by sharing critical information with anyone who has an Internet connection.

The city government in Seoul, South Korea, has created an online database to increase government transparency. Online Procedures Enhancement for Civil Applications (OPEN) allows city residents to monitor details of civil applications related to 70 municipal government tasks that have been identified as the most prone to corruption, including housing and construction projects, environmental regulation and urban planning.

Before OPEN's development, applicants for government permits were not able to see how their applications were being processed. The process was opaque, rather than transparent, allowing corrupt government officials to demand a bribe to move the application forward.

Now, when officials receive or update applications, they fill out standardized data entry forms. The forms are used by each department to update the online database. Through the database, applicants can find out who has their applications, when they can expect the application process to be complete, reasons for delay and, if an application has been declined, reasons for its rejection.

OPEN was instituted in conjunction with other initiatives to fight corruption. These include stricter penalties for officials who solicit or accept bribes, a Corruption Report Card to the mayor, a phone line citizens can use to alert the mayor's offices to cases of corruption and rotating officials among departments to prevent cronyism.

The OPEN website receives about 2,500 hits per day. An Internet survey by the Seoul City Government reported that 78.7 percent of citizens surveyed believed OPEN was effectively decreasing government corruption. Recently, the government also started disclosing information about 35 city government committees. This means that citizens can also monitor the management of committees through the OPEN System.

While OPEN serves to prevent corruption in individual applications for government services, it is also an intervention on a broader level, seeking to end ongoing abuses. One factor in the system's success has been the active involvement and ongoing support of the mayor's office. Without such support of high-ranking people with public legitimacy, a system like OPEN would be difficult to implement. The success of this anti-corruption tactic is also strengthened by widespread Internet use in the country.

Region	Initiating Sector	Target Sector	Focus	Human Rights Issue	PREVENTION	New Tactics in Human Rights
Asia	Government	Society	Local	Corruption	Sharing Critical Information	

REMOVING OPPORTUNITIES FOR ABUSE

There is often a pattern to human rights abuses — they occur in predictable places under predictable circumstances. Recognizing those patterns and disrupting them can be key to protecting human rights. If torture is known to be a problem in prisons, then keeping people out of prisons may prevent torture. If a government can erode intellectual freedom by seizing personal information, then making sure that few records exist in the first place may prevent that loss of freedom. The tactics in this section have all been used to prevent human rights abuses and problems by making them impossible — by simply removing any opportunities for abuse.

**New Tactics
in Human Rights**

PREVENTION

Removing
Opportunities
for Abuse
42   **www.newtactics.org**

Workers Saving their Factories and Saving their Jobs: Using an expropriation law to ensure economic rights are protected.

When businesses close and jobs disappear, individuals, families and communities risk falling into poverty. In Argentina's recent economic downturn, many businesses have closed or gone bankrupt.

Workers in Argentina have tried to prevent job losses by refusing to stop working when their employers' businesses go bankrupt. Jobs at nearly 200 *fabricas recuperadas*, or recuperated factories, have been saved by workers who use a little-known expropriation law to prevent removal of equipment by creditors and to seek receivership of the factories. The businesses range from ice cream factories and metal works to four-star hotels and shipyards.

Once hailed as an "economic miracle," Argentina slipped into recession in the late 1990s, pushing many Argentineans into poverty. The factory occupation movement arose spontaneously in response to economic decline. The approach has followed a general pattern.

First, the business falls into bankruptcy or is abandoned. The workers take over the business and run it cooperatively, preventing creditors from removing machinery while seeking a court order granting them the right to continue the business in compensation for unpaid back wages. This order is granted under a law originally intended to allow local governments to seize property for public works projects. The workers must agree to pay the owners the fair value of the assets over an established period of time and can pay themselves only if they turn a profit.

More than 10,000 jobs have been saved as a result of this tactic and workers in several recuperated factories are on their way to owning the assets of the businesses they occupied.

The use of the expropriation law to justify this occupation arose in desperation and yet has the potential to do more than simply keep the businesses open. It is a step toward preventing the poverty that could spread through vulnerable communities and toward raising the standard of living. It is an expression of the right to work and protect one's livelihood, as set forth in the Universal Declaration of Human Rights.

| **Community Mediation:** Creating alternative mechanisms of dispute resolution to prevent the involvement of the police, who are potential abusers.

This tactic arises from the idea that we can keep people out of police stations — and thus out of danger of being tortured — by mediating conflicts outside of the court system.

As an alternative to the criminal justice system, the Centre for Victims of Torture (CVICT) in Nepal has created a process of community mediation. This process keeps some people from being needlessly arrested and brought to police stations, where 60 percent of prisoners are tortured into giving confessions.

CVICT conducted research on what types of disputes were occurring, then developed a training course for community leaders, including women and Dalits (of the untouchable caste), on settling disputes with a rights-based community mediation method. Community mediation would be available for disputes other than violent crimes and to everyone, regardless of age, sex, class or social caste. To recruit trainers, CVICT held mass meetings in each community and asked for nominations. The trainers were then trained in human rights, local laws and methods of handling disputes. Many who were already involved in mediating disputes could build on their existing skills. These trainers then trained others at the local level.

These people make up committees that mediate disputes at the local level. Each committee is made up of at least 30 percent women and has at least one representative from the community's ethnic minorities. The steps and rules in the mediation process are very clear, beginning with a request for mediation and involving self-representation for both parties.

During the mediation session, five to nine trained mediators are placed between the parties of the dispute, who can also bring others to support them. The mediation committee explains the structure of the mediation process and the parties and their supporters each state their case. The mediators then involve the parties in a discussion of possible options for agreement. In general, the solutions emerge this way, from the parties in conflict and the community. However, the mediators are also empowered to decide that further investigation or legal action is necessary. The mediator can decide to file a case on behalf of one of the parties, which has resulted in the wealthy being willing to engage in the process.

In the three districts that have implemented it, the mediation system is improving access to justice and the dynamics of power. It is also greatly reducing the number of arrests; in the first year, two-thirds of cases were resolved through mediation while one-third went to the police and the courts. CVICT's community mediation project has been able to resolve a large number of local disputes, create awareness about human rights and reduce conflict within families and between neighbors. CVICT is expanding the project to twelve districts, where one-third of the country's population will have access to it.

Because torture in Nepal is often used in police stations as an interrogation tool, mediation is an effective way of preventing torture by keeping people out of the stations. This tactic has other significant benefits as well: it expands access to justice for people who may have no other ways to resolve their disputes or bring complaints against the wealthy and it trains local people to take on or expand their leadership roles in their communities.

" " | *I come from a village. Many of my colleagues work at the village level. People are always complaining about the time it takes to resolve disputes. When people can resolve their disputes in this way, it helps to prevent torture as well as giving people more time for development activities.*

— **Bhogendra Sharma, Centre for Victims of Torture, Nepal**

New Tactics
in Human Rights

44

	PREVENTION	Region	Initiating Sector	Target Sector	Focus	Human Rights Issue
	Removing Opportunities for Abuse www.newtactics.org	Asia	Civil Society	Society	Local	Torture

Disposing of Records: Protecting freedom of thought and the right to privacy by destroying records that could be demanded by the government.

In the United States, a national professional organization is increasing its efforts to prevent potential infringements of privacy rights and intellectual freedom by making sure that as few records as possible are kept.

Traditionally, librarians throughout the United States have prevented restrictions on intellectual freedom by destroying unnecessary library records as soon as possible. The American Library Association (ALA) — the largest library association in the world, with over 64,000 members — has used its influence with members to oppose changes to federal law that reduce protection of library records.

Forty-eight states have laws on the books that make library patron records confidential. The ALA code of ethics and its confidentiality policy also protect patron privacy. The 2001 USA Patriot Act, however, specifically authorizes federal law enforcement agents to search library records and public computer terminals to see what books patrons are reading and what websites they are accessing as a way of preventing terrorism.

In response to the Patriot Act, libraries are reviewing their record retention policies to ensure that unnecessary records are purged as soon as possible. The ALA has developed guidelines that include recommendations for reducing unnecessary library patron records and eliminating all records as soon as they are no longer useful. Librarians across the country have the support of a powerful national organization behind them when they choose to eliminate patron records, which is fully within the bounds of the law.

The ALA, a powerful national organization, is using a fairly simple act of resistance and, when done across the country, one that is relatively safe for individual librarians. In more repressive contexts, such resistance, even though perfectly legal, may lead to reprisals.

Region	Initiating Sector	Target Sector	Focus	Human Rights Issue	PREVENTION	New Tactics in Human Rights
Americas	Civil Society	Government	National	Freedom of thought	Removing Opportunities for Abuse	

Publishing Indigenous Knowledge Online: Protecting cultural and economic rights of indigenous people by recording traditional ecological knowledge.

Many indigenous groups have found their ways of life greatly diminished when private corporations patent their traditional knowledge. A national science organization is working to stop this from happening.

The Science and Human Rights Program of the American Association for the Advancement of Science (AAAS) has created an online searchable database of traditional ecological knowledge to prevent private companies from patenting that knowledge. The Traditional Ecological Knowledge Prior Art Database (T.E.K.*P.A.D.) is located at ip.aaas.org/tekpad.

Indigenous people all over the world have systematically cultivated plants and developed methods of using them for the benefit of their communities. Companies from the developed world have in some cases patented this knowledge without the permission of the communities themselves. The patents allow the holders to control the use and sale of the subject of the patent for a period of time, without any obligation to share profits with the communities. In some cases, the patent holder may be able to prevent those communities from using or benefiting from their own knowledge.

The database helps end this by making indigenous knowledge available in the public domain, thus defining it as "prior art." An invention can be patented only if it is new, useful and not obvious. If the invention or knowledge has been published somewhere — one form of what is called prior art — it is demonstrably not new. Traditional knowledge has been vulnerable to patenting by outside corporations because it has rarely been published anywhere or, if it has, is often overlooked.

Once the information is added to the database it is more easily located by U.S. Patent and Trademark Office (USPTO) and other patenting authorities during prior art searches. AAAS actively researches traditional knowledge that is unprotected and in the public domain, then adds the information to the database to further protect it.

T.E.K.*P.A.D also allows people to submit entries. Individuals who submit entries must prove that they have prior consent from their communities. AAAS encourages communities to explore the issues associated with various options, including applying for patents themselves, before adding their knowledge to the database. A handbook developed to help communities evaluate their options is available at shr.aaas.org/tek/.

T.E.K.*P.A.D.'s database currently protects 30,000 plants cultivated and managed by indigenous communities from patent exploitation.

When private corporations are allowed to hold patents on traditional knowledge that may form the basis of some communities' livelihoods, those communities may lose their cultural and economic rights. When they are no longer allowed to use that knowledge, or are forced to pay royalties, their livelihoods and traditions may be irreparably destroyed. The use of a recording and publishing tactic helps prevent that from happening.

It is intriguing that technology is being used to protect indigenous peoples' right to benefit from knowledge that is, in some cases, hundreds or thousands of years old. Online databases have also been used to build awareness of abuse, such as high levels of pollution in impoverished areas or widespread corruption, or to pressure for policy changes.

PREVENTION
Removing
Opportunities
for Abuse
www.newtactics.org

**New Tactics
in Human Rights**

47

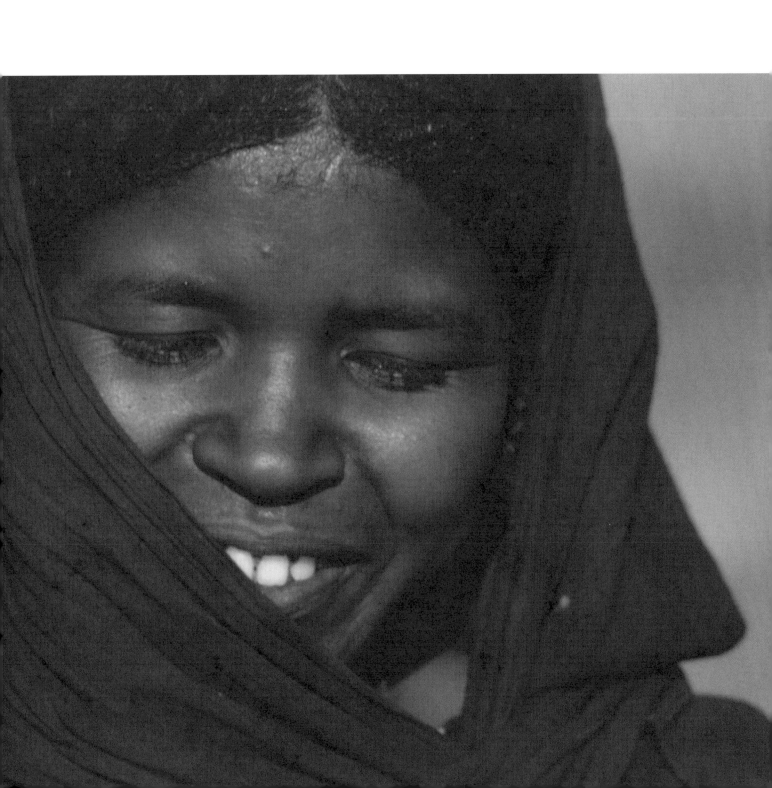

INTERVENTION TACTICS

I have been fortunate to be involved in several campaigns to intervene on behalf of victims of human rights abuses. I have observed many other successful campaigns around the world. In the late 1980s, I helped launch Rugmark, the first effort to discourage the use of child labor in rug manufacturing through voluntary labeling. My organization, Bachpan Bachao Andolan (BBA)/South Asian Coalition on Child Servitude (SACCS), has rescued and rehabilitated more than 65,000 children from bondage and brought the problem to worldwide attention through the 1998 Global March Against Child Labour.

Around the world, other consumer campaigns, including the Carpet Consumers, Clean Clothes and Foul Ball campaigns, have also tapped into the power of consumers to help end abuses. At the same time, mass mobilization campaigns — for labor rights and a clean environment in Latin America, for example, and for women's rights in Africa — have demonstrated opposition to ongoing abuse and disrupted the perpetrators' ability to continue it.

What these campaigns have in common is that they were initiated at the grassroots level. While the numbers and extent of laws and regulations are increasing, people are living in the same or worse conditions than ever with regard to human rights. The truth is that we cannot realize human rights through laws alone. People on the ground need to intervene when rights are under attack or when abuses are being perpetrated.

In this chapter you will read about individuals and organizations who have worked to stop ongoing human rights abuses through campaigns like these and through other innovative tactics. I hope that you, like me, will be inspired to continue standing up to human rights abuse.

— Kailash Satyarthi

Chair

Global March Against Child Labour

South Asian Coalition on Child Servitude (SACCS)

Global Campaign for Education (GCE)

New Delhi, India

The tactics here have been used to intervene in situations involving ongoing abuses and the denial of human rights. For this reason they are among the most challenging — and the most inspiring. People here are operating in crisis situations. They are fighting entrenched power, trying to overturn the status quo. They are challenging long-held expectations and beliefs, and questioning local traditions. And they are standing up to corruption and abuse that have become accepted as cultural norms.

Very often they are operating from the bottom of the power structure — and drawing on remarkable resources to do so. Sex workers have banded together to save young girls from being forced into their profession. Child workers have formed unions to protect their own rights. Landless peasants have started to farm unused land. Local governments have spoken out against laws and policies put forth on the federal level.

You will also find here, however, a few noteworthy and laudable examples of businesses — perched atop the power structure — using their own power and influence to intervene in situations of ongoing abuse.

In many of these tactics people take the tools of those in power and turn them around to fight abuses of power. They study budgets and laws and publicly hold governments to their promises. They draw on the strengths of traditional cultures and respected leaders to hold their communities to higher standards for the protection of human rights.

The tactics in this chapter are divided into four sections:
1   Resistance tactics demonstrate opposition to abuse.
2   Disruption tactics use direct action to influence a perpetrator to end the abuse.
3   Persuasion tactics use respected leaders or nonconfrontational institutional mechanisms to negotiate an end to violations.
4   Incentive tactics provide alternatives to human rights abuse.

RESISTANCE TACTICS

Resistance tactics demonstrate opposition to ongoing abuse or the denial of rights. These tactics serve two important functions: They make abuse visible — whether locally, nationally or internationally — to those who are affected by it, to those who have the possibility to change it and even to those who are perpetrating it. They also set the stage for further tactics that can effect changes.

These tactics can be deceptively simple. A tactic in Turkey required just the flicking of a switch — well, in the end, millions of switches! — while another in Estonia began as a choral gathering. They can also involve the sophisticated use of complex mechanisms such as budgets and laws, mechanisms that have not been thoroughly exploited in the past.

With the Flick of a Switch: Creating a single mass expression of protest based on a simple activity that citizens can safely carry out in their own homes.

TACTIC

In Turkey, the participation of large numbers of people in a campaign not only provided a measure of safety, but encouraged more and more people — millions, ultimately — to become involved.

The Campaign of Darkness for Light mobilized 30 million people in Turkey to flick their lights on and off as a public demonstration against government corruption. Corruption had been an open secret and yet the public felt apathetic and powerless to end it. With many citizens afraid to participate in political action, organizations needed a tactic of low personal risk that would help overcome the sense of isolation that comes with fear. The Campaign gave people an easy and no-risk action everyone could take — simply turning off their lights at the same time each evening — to show their displeasure with the lack of concerted action against corruption.

The campaign was originally conceived in response to a scandal that revealed extensive connections between government officials and organized crime. In the month prior to the event, organizers launched a massive publicity campaign. They formed alliances with grassroots organizations and unions, asking them to fax petitions and information on the protest campaign to their members, who in turn would send the fax on to their friends and contacts. They also enlisted columnists, radio personalities and TV broadcasters to post public reminders.

Organizers initially proposed that citizens turn off their lights for one minute each night. People then began to blink their lights on and off. By the second week, communities began to improvise, initiating different street actions, including banging pots and pans. By the time organizers halted the action, the campaign had gone on for more than a month.

Although some of the officials implicated in the scandal remain in parliament, there has been a great deal of political and legal change since the campaign, including the trial of several businessmen, police, military personnel and mafia leaders, campaigns within parliament against corruption, and the replacement of many politicians who failed to deal with state corruption.

Read more about this in a tactical notebook available at www.newtactics.org, under Tools for Action.

ONLINE

The action people were asked to take was extraordinarily simple. It required no preparation and very little commitment, encouraging wide participation. The tactic is thus conceptually easy to adapt to other situations. In fact, similar tactics have been used in many situations around the world. People in Zambia honked their car horns at a given time every Friday to protest the president's decision to change the constitution in order to remain in power. People in Chile protested the Pinochet regime by blaring their car horns, banging pots and pans in their apartment windows and marching in the streets. Common to each campaign is the attempt to make the widespread nature of public concern evident to a population which has been ruled by fear and feels isolated, alone and defeated.

Tactics of this nature have the virtue of making the invisible visible. They should be measured by their ability to stimulate a sense of solidarity in a population and to help redefine new political space in which more citizens are willing to act together.

But, while these tactics may be conceptually simple, their success is not easy to replicate. Organizers were not able to revive their tactic on the same scale just months later, despite the existence of many of the same issues and mechanisms. Once achieved, the momentum of such a tactic needs to be harnessed to drive the movement forward.

When might you use such a tactic? Is there an abuse in your country that people know of, but, through fear or apathy, do not speak out against?

Region	Initiating Sector	Target Sector	Focus	Human Rights Issue	**INTERVENTION**	**New Tactics in Human Rights**
Asia	Civil Society	Government Society	National	Corruption	Resistance	

| **Singing Revolution:** Asserting cultural identity en masse to express opposition to an oppressive regime.

In Estonia, in the 1980s, those who opposed the Soviet regime invited people to come out and sing publicly the songs sung in their homes and among friends all their lives.

In June of 1988 hundreds of thousands of Estonians (by some estimates, as many as 300,000, or one-third of the Estonian population) gathered for five consecutive nights in the capital city of Tallinn to sing forbidden or politically risky folk songs. Similar festivals were held that summer in Latvia and Lithuania. This "Singing Revolution," as it became known, was an important step toward the independence of all three Baltic states from the Soviet Union in August 1991.

The Soviet system actively sought to destroy people's connection to their own national identities. Some elements of this identity had been preserved openly in ways that the regime deemed innocuous (such as certain folk songs); others had been hidden (such as references to "Estonia" rather than "the Estonian Soviet Socialist Republic" and the observance of pre-Soviet national holidays) but still remembered by some. Those who had preserved these traditions used them to remind their fellow Estonians of their identity, motivate them to protect it and, in the context of glasnost, give them a safe way to express it.

The song festivals galvanized and popularized the nascent resistance movement by using powerful folk cultural symbols. Many participants came to the stadium wearing traditional dress and sang songs that emphasized their Estonian identity. Under a regime that had used the homogenization of culture as a tool of repression, the festivals gave Estonians a chance to stand up publicly as Estonians rather than Soviet citizens. The presence of 300,000 compatriots took some of the risk out of such a stance.

The festivals were organized by the Estonian Heritage Society (Eesti Muinsuskaitse Selts), an unofficial organization that took advantage of the relative openness of the glasnost era to push for public celebration of important national anniversaries and to revive key pre-Soviet national symbols, such as the blue-black-and-white Estonian flag and the national anthem. In the nearly bloodless battle for independence in the Baltics, these symbols were among the most powerful weapons.

The Singing Revolution drew on cultural traditions that were particularly deep in the Baltic countries, including public song festivals with a history that went back formally more than 100 years and informally for many centuries. Other cultures may have similarly strong traditions of song, dance, theater or other forms of art or symbolic expression. Families of the disappeared, for example, have used a traditional folk dance learned by all Chileans and danced in pairs. When a spouse danced with a missing partner in a traditional paired dance, others could visualize the missing person and his place in the family and community.

When you want to mobilize large numbers of people, the challenge is often making them feel safe enough to speak out and providing assurances that they will not be alone. The organizers of the song festivals were counting on safety in numbers: The presence of hundreds of thousands of fellow singers offered some measure of safety for participants, though by no means was that safety assured.

In a case of repression, what cultural traditions might draw people in your community together?

New Tactics in Human Rights	INTERVENTION	Region	Initiating Sector	Target Sector	Focus	Human Rights Issue
	Resistance	Europe	Society	Government	National	Cultural Rights

54   www.newtactics.org

Comparing Paper with Reality: Creating people's platforms (public hearings) where citizens can publicly challenge officials on the difference between promises and reality.

In India, a group is holding the government accountable by organizing public hearings on public expenditures. Organizers prove that even funding allocations, usually a technical topic, can draw a crowd.

Mazdoor Kisan Shakti Sangathan (MKSS) organizes public hearings in India to expose acts of corruption, such as the embezzlement of funds dedicated to development projects, through a comparison of official records to actual events and to reports by villagers in attendance.

In India, as in many countries, corrupt officials and rural elites can manipulate development schemes to their own advantage. This prevents projects from benefiting the poor and perpetuates poverty and social inequality.

MKSS activists and area residents investigate allegations of corruption in villages or districts, often at the initiative of local residents who feel they have been cheated or abused. At the village council or at higher levels of government they request copies of relevant official records. Most often, despite a legal entitlement, the process of obtaining the required information is a struggle with many hurdles. Once obtained, the accounts are cross-checked through site visits and interviews with villagers.

MKSS then holds public hearings that are attended by hundreds of villagers. Organizers invite the press, government officials and those suspected of corruption. MKSS activists, most of whom are from the area, read and explain the official documents claiming, for instance, that a certain health clinic was built in the village, or that laborers in a construction project were paid a certain amount. These documents are then contrasted with actual events. Activists present the results of their research and attending villagers provide their own testimony. The hearings last several hours, as organizers review one development project or instance of corruption after another. More recently, public hearings have also been organized around the operations of a local hospital and the public health system and around the functioning of food security schemes and the public distribution system.

While the impact on transparency and accountability issues has been dramatic, the effects on follow-up official action have been mixed — a few officials have been arrested and government investigations have started to move forward. In some villages the corrupt local officials attending the hearings have voluntarily agreed, when faced with the evidence, to cooperate with the investigations and even return the funds. Usually, however, MKSS activists must follow the public hearings with continued agitation and pressure in order to ensure official action.

Essential to MKSS's work is access to government records, including records of public expenditures. MKSS used a series of tactics to convince the state of Rajasthan to pass a right-to-information law. The organization mobilized villagers from several districts, staged sit-ins and generated publicity around the issue. As a result a law was passed that compels officials to provide, upon request and at a nominal price, copies of documents on any sphere of government activity, including development programs, public resources and expenditures. This also sparked a national right-to-information movement that has led to the passage of similar laws in several other states, and to a Freedom of Information Bill in the national parliament.

What tactics can be used to ensure your local government spending is helping uphold the rights of the local people?

"We have used the demand for information as a means to assert the people's democratic right to ask questions and demand answers. The demand for specific information is being used in different ways by people in different parts of India to control corruption and the arbitrary use of power. It is eventually a demand not just for information, but a share of governance."

— activist, Mazdoor Kisan Shakti Sangathan, India

Region	Initiating Sector	Target Sector	Focus	Human Rights Issue	INTERVENTION	New Tactics in Human Rights
Asia	Civil Society	Government	Local	Corruption	Resistance	

All Politics are Local: Encouraging local governments, organizations and individuals to oppose, through the use of education and resources, federal legislation that endangers human rights.

As demonstrated here, local organizations and local government can work together to resist legislation made on the federal level.

In the United States, the Bill of Rights Defense Committee (BORDC) creates tools and resources to help local advocates of the Bill of Rights educate members of local governments and communities about how federal anti-terrorism legislation and policies violate their rights. Many of the local groups work with their city, town or county governments to formally register opposition to violations of civil liberties, passing resolutions or ordinances upholding the Bill of Rights. These ordinances instruct local law enforcement and other government employees not to cooperate with requests to violate residents' constitutional rights.

The USA Patriot Act was signed into law in late 2001. It created a new crime, "domestic terrorism," and gave the federal government greater rights to wiretap phones; monitor emails; survey medical, financial, library and student records; and enter homes and offices without prior notification. Under this Act and other legislation, non-citizens can be deported and detained without judicial appeal. BORDC believes these provisions violate key civil and political rights provisions of the U.S. Constitution.

Recognizing that much of the work authorized by the Act and other antiterrorism policies and legislation is ultimately carried out by local law enforcement, a group of advocates (who would eventually create BORDC) held a community-wide forum in Northampton, Massachusetts. They circulated a petition to gain support for a city council resolution opposing key components of the legislation and requesting that local law enforcement refrain from carrying out any order that violates the civil liberties of community members. They received additional support by inviting businesses, individuals and organizations to participate in public forums. Many joined the activists, providing funding and helping distribute the petition, rallying support for the resolution at city council meetings, and lending it credibility by demonstrating its broad support and appeal.

The coalition convinced the city council president to sponsor a resolution. BORDC then began encouraging similar efforts in neighboring towns and across the nation. Their web site has been central to their organizing efforts. It explains in detail the steps taken to educate citizens and gain public support for passing municipal resolutions. It contains sample resolutions, petitions, press releases, fliers, FAQs and news articles. It also describes how their public forums were organized and provides alternative campaign approaches.

Resolutions have been passed in 267 cities, towns and counties and in three states (as this book goes to press), demonstrating growing momentum to revoke provisions of the legislation that could have an impact on human rights. The combined population of these "civil liberties safe zones" has topped 47 million. BORDC's web site also offers information to help students and faculty, religious groups, unions and professional groups organize.

BORDC members began by mobilizing for change in their own community and then decided to make their efforts national, sharing their experience with other communities. They helped cities and communities recognize that people can take a stand against deteriorating human rights, sending a strong signal to the national government. Although a particularly potent form of resistance in a political system with delineated and separated authority, this can be adapted to systems with even vertical political structures, though the risks to local authorities may be much higher.

How would something like this work in your country?

" " It is the municipality's responsibility to ensure that its residents feel safe and protected by just laws from unfair treatment, invasion of privacy without probable cause and detentions without charges and in secrecy. When most local elected officials take office, they swear to uphold both the state and federal constitutions, including the Bill of Rights in their municipality.

— From www.bordc.org.

New Tactics in Human Rights	INTERVENTION	Region	Initiating Sector	Target Sector	Focus	Human Rights Issue
	Resistance	Americas	Civil Society	Government	National	Civil and political rights

Petition Power: Organizing a large-scale petition drive to pressure the government to change.

A group in Argentina uses a little-known and under-utilized provision in the constitution to educate the public and mobilize for change, while at the same time convincing the parliament to pass legislative reforms.

In 2002, Poder Ciudadano (Citizen Power) collected signatures on a petition that, under a constitutional provision, the Argentine congress was then obligated to consider. The constitutional provision requires the congress to deliberate any proposed legislation brought before it by community members or organizations, as long as that legislation bears the signatures of 1.5 percent of Argentine citizens in at least six of 24 districts.

Poder Ciudadano was created in 1989 by a group of citizens concerned about the defense of civil rights in Argentina. Its petitions, initiated in the several years since the country's economic collapse, have focused on key problems of hunger and excessive retirement benefits for government officials. The petition related to hunger proposed to feed all impoverished pregnant women and Argentine children under the age of five. Over half of the Argentine population have been living below the poverty line since the economic collapse. Children represent the largest population in poverty and few social programs address hunger among children. The goal of the petition was not only to obligate the congress to address this problem, but also to propose solutions.

Poder Ciudadano wrote the petition, recruited 250 volunteers around the country and trained them with crucial instruction sheets that explained who was eligible to sign, where to send the completed petitions and what information was needed from signatories. Most volunteers were recruited through the organization's web site and the project coordinator. The volunteers met at public locations in their communities to collect the signatures: markets, bookstores, pharmacies, newsstands and phonebooths. Poder Ciudadano partnered with several organizations and the media, including a prominent radio personality who gave the locations of signature collection tables on air and a major newspaper updating readers on the number of signatures collected.

The initiative was very well received by Argentine citizens and Poder Ciudadano presented it to the congress, which, by late 2002, passed the proposal with some modifications. The right-to-food initiative collected over one million signatures and was accepted by the congress as a state obligation. The program to combat hunger is currently in the early stages of implementation and the first food centers have recently opened.

Poder Ciudadano transformed widespread apathy into real change. People with no faith in government or its responsiveness to citizens were able to see their own voices have a direct effect on legislation. Poder Ciudadano built a strong network of volunteers, allied organizations and the media to spread word about the petition and gather the enormous number of necessary signatures.

Region	Initiating Sector	Target Sector	Focus	Human Rights Issue	INTERVENTION	New Tactics in Human Rights
Americas	Civil Society	Government	National	Right to food	Resistance	

Bucket Brigades: Independently collecting air-quality data on the community level in order to pressure for change.

Communities can demonstrate opposition to abuse — in this case, environmental violations — by acting on their own to collect information.

Many communities across the United States have begun or joined "bucket brigades," programs that teach people living near industrial polluters to build and use simple air monitoring devices, or "buckets," which have been approved by the U.S. Environmental Protection Agency. In the absence of strong environmental laws, standards or enforcement bodies, buckets give communities the means to independently monitor the air quality of their neighborhoods and provide them with evidence to pressure for change.

The bucket itself is a relatively simple and inexpensive air sampling device composed of a Tedlar sampling bag inside a five-gallon plastic bucket and a vacuum or tire pump used to suck air into the bag. The bucket brigade includes volunteer members in three jobs: sniffers, samplers and community bucket coordinators (CBCs). Sniffers are responsible for alerting the samplers to pollution incidents. Samplers keep the air sampling devices in their homes and take a sample when a pollution incident is suspected. They record where, when and why the samples are taken and call a CBC to retrieve the sampling bag and arrange for delivery to the analytical laboratory. Results are recorded in a database and provided to the community through local media, community meetings and other methods. Community members use the data at their own discretion to request further investigations on pollution from community groups, government agencies and health facilities. The brigade also provides residents with fact sheets on health effects associated with pollution levels.

Low-income, minority communities in the United States have been particularly receptive to the idea of bucket brigades and the tactic is gaining widespread acceptance. Media attention has helped to create change in many communities. Contra Costa County, California, adopted an "environmental justice policy," reinforcing industrial pollution regulations, expanding occupational medical facilities and including residents in decisions regarding nearby industries. In Louisiana, air samples proved that the Diamond neighborhood, which was slowly being engulfed by the Shell Chemical plant, was no longer safe; the company eventually agreed to relocate the entire neighborhood.

This approach is useful when governments or businesses do not provide information about pollution or when communities are concerned that official information is false. Setting up a bucket brigade is a powerful public statement that chemical plants and government agencies do not have the right to control data on pollution and that communities can gather this evidence on their own, make it public and place pressure on a company to respond. The method is so simple that it has spread quickly from community to community, and beyond the U.S. as well, making possible something rather unusual: victims of abuse (rather than outsiders) documenting abuse as it is happening. This tactic has been adapted in South Africa, India and the Philippines.

New Tactics in Human Rights	INTERVENTION	Region	Initiating Sector	Target Sector	Focus	Human Rights Issue
	Resistance	Americas	Civil Society	Business	Local	Environment

58   www.newtactics.org

Training Victims as Human Rights Monitors: Training victims of human rights abuses to monitor and defend their rights.

A group in Mexico trains indigenous communities to monitor abuses. Armed with new skills in documentation and legal defense, members of these communities are able to take their complaints to the highest levels.

The Chiapas Community Defenders Network (Red de Defensores Comunitarios por los Derechos Humanos or Red) trains young indigenous community members to monitor and defend their human rights.

The extensive military presence in Chiapas, as well as the increasingly paramilitary nature of the conflict between the Zapatistas and the Mexican government, has resulted in widespread human rights abuses, including illegal detention, military harassment of civilians (particularly at checkpoints), illegal killings and detention and sexual abuse of women by military and paramilitary groups.

In 1999, Red trained 14 people representing seven Chiapas regions and communities. In 2001, a second class of defenders began training. The defenders were appointed by their communities and actively involve community members in their work.

Defenders are trained through monthly seminars covering the theories and concepts of human rights work as well as the practical skills needed to ensure human rights violations are documented, reported and prevented. Through this process, they learn what constitutes a rights violation and how to document it through the use of video, photography and computers. They also learn various ways to respond.

Defenders present complaints to the government, give information to the press and human rights monitoring groups and seek the release or legal defense of people unjustly detained. They are able to locate detainees and present requests of habeas corpus (the right to be brought before a judge to determine if an individual was lawfully detained) when rights are in jeopardy. They know how to file a request for precautionary measures when human rights violations are imminent and who to approach to denounce violations when they occur. For cases that go before the courts or require long-term legal strategies, attorney advisors work collaboratively with the defenders.

At home, defenders engage in a range of work depending on community need. They collect testimony from victims and witnesses of human rights violations, gather video and photo evidence of abuse and determine appropriate ways to intervene when a violation has occurred. They also train other community members in this work.

This approach has led to numerous successes and has also increased the autonomy of indigenous communities by eliminating dependence on external actors such as NGOs.

The model of Red places communities and local leaders at the center of the struggle for human rights, with outsiders serving only as advisors. Training a network of local people to independently defend human rights in their communities can be done by organizations seeking to strengthen human rights advocacy in any region. The tactic of training victims of human rights abuses to monitor and defend human rights can serve to both increase human rights awareness and defense in indigenous communities as well as build those communities' capacity to function autonomously.

The defensores [defenders] do legal "first aid." That is, they are trained to be the communities' first line of defense. They know what a rights violation is, what is needed to document it and how to go about doing so. As a result of this tactic, a stable group of indigenous community representatives have been prepared to carry out their communities' legal defense and they are, in turn, training others.

" "

— Miguel Angel de los Santos,
   Red de Defensores Comunitarios
   por los Derechos Humanos, Mexico

Region	Initiating Sector	Target Sector	Focus	Human Rights Issue	**INTERVENTION**	**New Tactics in Human Rights**
Americas	Civil Society	Society	Local	Indigenous rights	Resistance	

Search and Seizure

Operation SalAMI used what it called a "Citizen Search and Seizure Operation" to pressure the Canadian government to release a secret draft treaty that members believed could undermine human rights. The group was able to generate public condemnation of the secrecy used to shield the government and the treaty from public scrutiny. **Philippe Duhamel**, an organizer and trainer, describes the operation:

" "

For months, the government had adamantly refused to make public the draft papers for the Free Trade Agreement of the Americas (FTAA), a trade liberalization treaty being negotiated among 34 countries of the Americas. We announced our intention to pick up the hard copies of the FTAA texts at the Department of Foreign Affairs and International Trade on April 1, 2001. First, we would hold a legal demonstration in Ottawa, where one of two things would happen: either we would joyfully pick up the boxes of documents given to us, or the offensive secrecy of the process would be made public. If the texts were not released, we would use a nonviolent blockade to shut down the building and attempt a "search and seizure" operation, a citizens' raid to obtain the documents through a strictly nonviolent intervention.

When the government did not comply, a group of citizens declared, "We ask you, police officers, to do your duty and help us retrieve the documents to which we have a right. Do not become accomplices of the secrecy and manipulation of this government. If you refuse to seek and retrieve the texts on our behalf, we will have no option but to attempt to retrieve those ourselves." One by one, they then gave their names and said, "I am here to exercise my rights as a citizen. Please let me through." Groups of two then proceeded to climb over the barricade. Close to 100 people were arrested and held overnight. No charges were filed. Across the country, people asked, "Why is the government refusing to give us these documents and choosing to arrest its own citizens instead?"

The action, and the vast campaign around it, were covered by virtually every media outlet in the country. The government was forced to act. One week after the Citizen Search and Seizure Operation, the Canadian government, after consulting the other negotiating partners, finally agreed to make the documents public.

ONLINE

Read more about this in a tactical notebook available at www.newtactics.org, under Tools for Action.

New Tactics in Human Rights	INTERVENTION	Region	Initiating Sector	Target Sector	Focus	Human Rights Issue
	Resistance	Americas	Civil Society	Government	National	Right to information

60   www.newtactics.org

DISRUPTION TACTICS

Some human rights abuses call for advocates to step in physically to end the abuse, to simply make it impossible for the abuse to continue. You can lobby and you can campaign and you can protest, but sometimes you need to change the situation yourself: give people the land they need to thrive or the medicine they need to survive, take the young girls out of the brothels, rescue enslaved children from the factories. The brave people who use such tactics all risk physical danger. Some, like sex workers organized in Bangladesh, would seem to be unlikely participants, yet they turn out to be vital to the effort.

Resisting Unfair Property Law: Settling landless people on unfarmed land to pressure the government to carry out land reforms.

The Brazilian Landless Workers Movement puts pressure on the government to enact reforms while at the same time providing support — in the form of peacefully occupied farming land — to victims of abuse.

Since its creation in 1984, the Brazilian Landless Workers Movement (Movimento Dos Trabalhadores Rurais Sem Terra, or MST) has addressed the issue of land reform by organizing large groups of landless farmers to settle and farm unused land belonging to wealthy landowners. After occupying an area MST attempts to gain the land legally through petitioning and legislation, using an article in the Brazilian constitution stating that unproductive land is available for agrarian reform.

Although the Brazilian government has promised land reforms for the last 20 years, little land has actually been redistributed through government programs. Half of Brazilian land is currently owned by one percent of the population, while nearly five million agrarian workers are landless.

MST sends organizers into a new area to contact landless families and recruit them for an occupation. The organizers consult with the local community to choose a site that is not being farmed and is known to be fertile, and whose legal ownership is disputed. Often, organizers will remain in the community for six months or more to prepare local people for the occupation. The local community divides the work of preparing for the occupation, which allows them to take ownership over the process. On the day of the action, landless families go to the site, peacefully cross any barriers to the land and occupy it. If they are evicted, they leave peacefully but return to the same place when the eviction order has ended.

The occupations are brought to the attention of the national agency that deals with land reform, where activists pressure for legalization of the occupation, often through the expropriation of land. As part of this pressure, MST organizes marches and occupations of government buildings and publicly denounces the government for failing to abide by its own constitution. The legalization process can last as long as five years. Once a new settlement is established, schools and health clinics are built and the land is used for sustainable farming, allowing settlers to access their right to food. This tactic has been extremely successful, although it has been met with occasional violence. MST has gained land for about 250,000 families living on over 1,600 settlements.

MST's story is a remarkable one: peaceful occupations leading to real change for thousands of people who can now support themselves agriculturally. While the occupations alone would have been divisive and dangerous, when combined with pressure on the government to enact promised land reforms they became part of a successful campaign. MST is able to safely use this tactic by ensuring that a sufficient number of people participate. If landowners or local authorities use violence against the peaceful occupiers, MST activists generate pressure through the media attention.

There are numerous examples of land occupations in other parts of the world that have not been peacefully carried out or that have resulted in high incidents of violence. The use of this approach carries great risk in some contexts and must be very carefully planned and carried out to ensure nonviolence.

When do you use an unlawful tactic to ensure access to human rights and strongly pressure the government for change?

The Agrarian Reform Law states that all property should either have a social function, or should be used productively to produce jobs and food. Our struggle has law as an ally, but if we leave the government to do the agrarian reform, it will not happen because the main landowners have a lot of power in the National Congress and Senate.

— Wanusa Santos, Movimento Dos
Trabalhadores Rurais Sem Terra, Brazil

" "

Region	Initiating Sector	Target Sector	Focus	Human Rights Issue	**INTERVENTION**	**New Tactics** in Human Rights
	Civil Society	Government Society	National	Economic rights	Disruption	

| **Defying International Patent Law:** Defying laws in order to pressure for their change.

In South Africa the Treatment Action Campaign engaged in civil disobedience by circumventing national laws, then pressured the government to change these laws in order to ensure treatment for people with HIV/AIDS.

In June 2000, the Treatment Action Campaign (TAC) began importing generic HIV/AIDS drugs in defiance of patent laws, trying to pressure drug companies to reduce drug costs and to compel the South African government to allow the importation of generic versions of patented drugs. The goal of the tactic was to increase access to affordable HIV/AIDS prescription drugs for all South Africans. Over four million people are infected with HIV in South Africa and high prices for patented drugs have made treatment inaccessible to most people.

Fluconazole is an essential drug used to treat illnesses related to HIV. Like many other HIV/AIDS medications, Fluconazole is produced by multinational companies under patent and imported into South Africa at a very high price. Generic versions of the drug are significantly less expensive. Pfizer's patent of the drug, however, prevented the South African government from importing these generic versions. Although the South African Patent Act gives the government power to import or produce cheap copies of patented drugs, the government did not attempt to use this power.

Before importing medications, TAC worked with the World Health Organization and Medecins Sans Frontieres to confirm that they were safe and effective, and arranged systems for their purchase and import. For example, TAC organized a trip to Thailand, where a generic form of Fluconazole called Biozole was available to the public for less than US$0.28 per tablet.

When the Biozole tablets reached the border, the South African Medicine Control Council confiscated them while members of that Council debated the issue of granting them an exemption. In November 2000, under pressure from TAC and its international and local supporters, the Council permitted the generic drug to be distributed to patients by one of TAC's partners. The pharmaceutical company Pfizer had promised to deliver its own medication to patients in March 2000; the exemption — an exercise of the government's discretionary power — would be reviewed once this delivery actually occurred.

By drawing attention to low-cost alternatives, this act of civil disobedience demonstrated the urgency need for access to HIV/AIDS medications. The activists were prepared to suffer the consequences of breaking the law in order to save lives, thereby applying sufficient pressure to affect national policy.

Even as it defied South African law and international patent agreements by importing generic drugs, TAC also supported the South African government in a case brought by a group of 39 pharmaceuticals, called the Pharmaceutical Manufacturers' Association (PMA). The PMA alleged that the Medicines Act, which includes provisions allowing the government to import patented drugs from other countries if they are available at a lower prince, violated patent laws. The PMA ultimately withdrew its case.

South Africa continues to live under the specter of a grave human rights crisis: millions of people have HIV/AIDS and have no access to effective medicine. In August 2003, however, under pressure from TAC, the South African government agreed to make anti-retroviral drugs available without charge to all South Africans and confirmed this promise in a new plan unveiled in November of the same year.

New Tactics in Human Rights

INTERVENTION	Region	Initiating Sector	Target Sector	Focus	Human Rights Issue
Disruption	Africa	Civil Society	Government Business	National International	HIV/AIDS

64   www.newtactics.org

Taking Young Women Out of Brothels: Using people with direct experience and knowledge to rescue victims of abuse.

In Bangladesh, a local association intervenes in private sector activities that violate human rights.

The Ekota Sex Workers Association in Bangladesh uses surveillance teams made up of older prostitutes to rescue girls who are being kept against their will in brothels.

Senior sex workers play an important role in the sex trade. Most are madams or rent rooms to prostitutes who stay in the brothel. They have more spare time than younger workers and they also have a deeper knowledge of the industry. Their position of economic power within the brothels offers these senior sex workers a unique ability to influence who can be in the brothels and when they rent quarters to younger prostitutes they clarify that no under-age girls are allowed.

Despite this policy, however, younger prostitutes sometimes bring girls into a brothel. When this happens, the senior sex workers keep track of where the girl is being held and communicate with her through small windows and openings. They try to find out whether she came there willingly, what village she is from, how old she is and who her relatives are. They then notify the sex workers association, which sends a trusted person to the girl's home to inform parents or relatives of her whereabouts. In many cases the family is able to come to the brothel to rescue the girl. In some, however, the family itself has sold the girl into prostitution and is unwilling or unable to help her.

When it began rescuing girls from the brothels, the sex workers association contacted a range of local nongovernmental organizations (NGOs) to support their work and help the girls. The NGOs play a critical role in rehabilitating those girls who are unable to return to their families.

Despite their efforts to remove underage girls from brothels, the sex workers receive little support from the local community, which views prostitution as a social threat. In addition, the rescue of children by the sex workers threatens those who benefit from the sex trade. This places the senior sex workers and the association in danger. The women rely on the local NGOs for support in influencing local government officials to increase protection for the sex workers and to remove underage prostitutes from the brothels.

This tactic is effective largely because the older sex workers who are involved are in a unique position both to monitor and to recognize the problem. They have also built a solid network, through their association, that can safely gather and transmit information. This tactic intervenes at the very last stage of abuse, when the girls are already in the brothels, and facilitates their physical removal from the situation. Other exploited groups — perhaps survivors of domestic abuse, forced labor or forced migration — would also be in a position to use their experience to keep others from suffering the same fate. But it is important to note that they, like these women in Bangladesh, would be placing themselves in physical danger.

Region	Initiating Sector	Target Sector	Focus	Human Rights Issue	INTERVENTION	New Tactics in Human Rights
Asia	Society	Society	Local	Trafficking	Disruption	

| **Throwing Open the Factory Doors:** Rescuing child laborers through factory raids.

In India, the South Asian Coalition on Child Servitude intervenes physically to rescue child laborers.

The South Asian Coalition on Child Servitude (SACCS) organizes raids and rescue operations to liberate child laborers. A conglomeration of more than 400 human rights groups throughout South Asia, SACCS aims to eradicate bonded and child labor.

The International Labour Organisation says that there are more than 60 million bonded child workers in India. These children are denied their fundamental rights to childhood, to education, to fair remuneration and to adequate health care and living conditions because they are forced to work more than 12 hours every day. Most of them are held as slaves in factories where they are subjected to beatings and widespread disease.

Since its inception in 1989, SACCS has addressed this problem using a two-pronged strategy that involves both direct and indirect action. SACCS Direct Action Rescue Operations are planned raids against industries known to use child labor. After receiving tips that identify an industry using child laborers or being approached by parents whose children have been taken into bondage, SACCS organizes its own teams, families of stolen children, local supporters and a few policemen armed only with sticks to forcefully free the children. They open the factory doors that lock the children in at night and remove the children before the owner is alerted. In order to secure police protection the local administration is informed about the impending raid beforehand, but exact details are never revealed so as to avoid collusion between the administration and the industries.

After the children are liberated, their official release certificates must be secured from the local administration. Because the administration is sympathetic toward the industries this can take a long time. The children are then introduced to SACCS rehabilitation programs that provide free education before being returned to their families, when that is possible. Through its direct action raids SACCS has released more than 65,000 laborers from servitude in the last two decades.

SACCS intervenes directly at the site of the abuse: the factories where children are being held as slaves. Their actions not only rescue thousands of children, but build community awareness of the problem when word gets out about the freed children and the conditions in which they were held. Their actions also make it impossible for the government to continue to be complicit in child labor. Once made aware of the problem and SACCS's intended action, the government can no longer protect the factories without being publicly exposed.

This is also a dangerous tactic that could have repercussions for the children and the community, forcing the factories to hide the problem even more deeply or to move to another area. The SACCS team members may themselves be in physical danger and must plan for a number of contingencies. But when a problem is this extreme — whether it is child slavery, human trafficking or unlawful detention — there are sometimes people brave enough to take that danger upon themselves.

INTERVENTION	Region	Initiating Sector	Target Sector	Focus	Human Rights Issue
Disruption	Asia	Civil Society	Business Society	National	Child labor

Shifting Tactics

Knowing when it's time to switch tactics can be just as important as knowing which tactics to use in the first place. The Free Burma Coalition recently decided to end its ten-year-old campaign of boycotts against PepsiCo, Apple Computer, Heineken, Texaco and other companies doing business in Burma — not because the campaign had been ineffective or because the coalition had achieved all of its goals, but because it was time for a shift in tactics. **Zar Ni**, one of the coalition's founders, explains.

Boycotts have a lot of potential to do good. They can be like the heavy artillery in a military campaign: They wear down the enemy, but the real job is done by the people on the ground, in the country itself. And, once you've crippled your enemy, you have to be ready to strike the next blow.

The boycotts raised awareness of the situation in Burma and convinced several international companies to pull out of the country, but this alone was not enough.

We officially ended the boycott in 2003 because we realized that we needed to use a new set of tactics to start to reframe the issue and bring our campaign to another level. We realized that unless we changed the way people tell the Burma story, we would not win. With the boycott the centerpiece of the campaign, the focus would always be on the regime and not on the Burmese people. We need to focus attention on the people and our own road to the future.

Now we are exploring strategic partnerships with others involved in international human rights campaigns. Reframing the issue and incorporating new tactics into our campaign will open up new strategic avenues and new options for us.

Region	Initiating Sector	Target Sector	Focus	Human Rights Issue	INTERVENTION	New Tactics in Human Rights
Asia	Civil Society	Government	International	Gross violations of human rights	Disruption	

PERSUASION TACTICS

Persuasion tactics are used to end human rights abuses without confrontation, without demonizing the abusers or those facilitating abuse. Often abusers simply need support and encouragement to end their participation in human rights violations.

While intervention tactics are often associated with protest and resistance, some of the most dramatic successes in ending human rights abuses have resulted from negotiation and persuasion. Through pressure that is at times quiet and at times more visual, advocates are able to make significant improvements in human rights, often very quickly. These tactics use nonadversarial relationships with governments and businesses, even offering assistance to help end the abuse. They put respected community leaders in the forefront of negotiations or education efforts. They operate within an atmosphere of collaboration.

People and relationships are an essential resource to consider when evaluating the range of tactics available to you. Who is close to your target? Who has their respect? Who can influence your target?

The Power of the Airwaves: Using the power of the media to send targeted messages to people in a position to end abuses.

Journalists can use their position in society to raise awareness of human rights abuses and to influence those in power to make changes. Through the use of radio, journalists in Burundi were able to persuade key leaders to end human rights abuses occurring in hospitals.

African Public Radio (APR) used its power as a media entity to influence individuals and groups who could help fix the situation in Burundi's hospitals, where poor people were being held against their will because they could not pay their bills. Eventually, in partnership with local NGOs, APR successfully pressured the government to order the people's release.

In war-stricken Burundi, many cannot afford needed medical care. Adding to the problem, a general system breakdown in the 1990s reduced the state's capacity to support the health system. Facing a budget crisis and growing debt, hospitals began to detain people who could not pay their bills. Because the hospitals felt they were being wronged by those who would not pay, they did not see this as a human rights issue.

After gaining access to detainees and winning their trust, APR secretly interviewed them and broadcast their testimonies. The broadcasts included messages targeted to specific groups and individuals who had power to fix the situation. After the first broadcast, APR joined forces with national and international NGOs, hosting a *café presse* — an elaborate press conference — on health care with government officials and other influential people. The final discussion addressed the detentions themselves and put moral pressure on the government to respond.

In April 2002, the Council of Ministers forbade hospital detentions and ordered the hospitals to free all detainees. The government also created a commission to examine the larger issues of access to health care and reforms of national health policy.

A key element of this tactic was identifying the target of the broadcasts: What group or groups would have the power to change the situation in the hospitals and at the same time be receptive to the message? In this case it was government officials, who were morally bound to act after the stories became public. This tactic also demonstrates the power of stories. The victims' stories, once in the hands of individuals with access to a podium, changed national policies.

The tactic could have backfired, however, as some had feared, if the hospitals had decided to deny future care to patients who had appeared on the radio program. It might also have resulted in embarrassment for those patients if there were any stigma surrounding their illnesses. To be successful, this tactic requires that journalists be engaged in and willing to work for the advancement of human rights issues.

How might radio be used to inform people about your human rights issue and to pressure for change?

Region	Initiating Sector	Target Sector	Focus	Human Rights Issue	INTERVENTION	New Tactics in Human Rights
Africa	Civil Society	Government	National	Civil and political rights	Persuasion	

Enlisting Local Leaders to End Harmful Customs: Engaging local leaders to use their influence to help end abuse.

When looking for allies in a campaign to end abuse, community leaders are a natural choice. They might be tribal leaders, elders, religious leaders, local politicians or just individuals with charisma and influence.

The Commission on Human Rights and Administrative Justice in Ghana solicits the support of respected community leaders — chiefs and queen mothers — to address the problem of *trokosi*, a system in which women and young girls are kept in fetish shrines without their consent. Families give their girls to the shrines to atone for the sins or crimes committed by a family member, and to thereby end or reverse a family's bad luck.

The Commission has the power to enforce laws against trokosi, but it took this tactical approach because it recognized that the tradition is based on deeply held beliefs and, if not transformed voluntarily, might simply go underground. To prepare for the campaign, the Commission researched the beliefs behind trokosi and built an alliance with International Needs Ghana, an NGO that counsels and rehabilitates former victims of trokosi. Together they host meetings with the victims and the fetish priests at which everyone is encouraged to share their views.

Local leaders then help the Commission emphasize the need to abandon the practice and use their position in the community to convince the fetish priests to free the women and girls. Liberation ceremonies bring the community together to publicly recognize the priests' decision and help fulfill the community's spiritual needs. These ceremonies are covered by the media, demonstrating to the broader public that the local leaders support ending the practice. This tactic has freed about 3,000 women and girls.

ONLINE | Read more about this in a tactical notebook available at www.newtactics.org, under Tools for Action.

Calling for an end to a traditional practice without addressing the underlying beliefs and structures that keep it in place, or without proposing an alternative that allows those beliefs and structures to be transformed, can drive communities to hide the practice rather than end it. This tactic depends upon the respect of a community for its leaders, and the willingness of those leaders to set an example for the community to follow. To end the trokosi practice, it is essential that communities be convinced that they do not need to relinquish their family members to the priests in order to atone for their sins. The liberation rituals and the reassurances from community leaders are essential in alleviating fears of reprisals from the gods and in building trust within the community.

This tactic could be useful in helping to transform or eradicate other traditional or entrenched social practices that violate human rights, such as female genital cutting or domestic violence.

New Tactics in Human Rights	INTERVENTION	Region	Initiating Sector	Target Sector	Focus	Human Rights Issue
	Persuasion	Africa	Government	Society	Local	Slavery

Follow the Money: Examining budgets to reveal social and economic inequities and persuade the government to rectify them.

Sometimes individual leaders hold moral and political sway over governments, and sometimes numbers and data speak for themselves. Budget analysis can uncover inequities in the fulfilment of social and economic rights, can be a tool to help persuade governments to rectify these inequities and can help hold governments accountable to their commitments.

The Children's Budget Unit (CBU) at the Institute for Democracy in South Africa (IDASA) uses national and provincial budgets to reveal whether the government is meeting its commitments in protecting the rights of children and to provide evidence and recommendations for rectifying the failure. South Africa's constitution states that every child has the right to basic nutrition, shelter, health care and social services. However, millions of children go hungry, do not have the material means to attend school or receive health care and find it impossible to live healthy and secure lives.

The CBU first determines the government's obligations based on the constitution and international commitments. It then measures the extent of child poverty. This is followed by a comprehensive analysis of budget allocations and expenditures and of the delivery of key services to children, revealing the government's fiscal priorities. This analysis and compilation of the budgetary facts allows CBU to clearly illustrate where the national, provincial or local government is not meeting its obligations. It also provides solid facts and data from which to make recommendations and strongly pressure for change. In some cases, local governments do not even collect this data and welcome the information that IDASA provides as a way to improve their own work.

This tactic has resulted in new legislation and better relationships with key government institutions, some of which now request information from the CBU. The tactic has spread globally, with similar monitoring units being opened in parts of Asia, South America and across the continent of Africa.

Read more about this in a tactical notebook available at www.newtactics.org, under Tools for Action.

ONLINE

To monitor government programs the CBU gathers information that the government itself is either unable or unwilling to obtain. This tactic merges two historically separate discourses — of budget analysis and of human rights — to improve budget transparency, accountability and good governance practices. Rather than becoming an adversary, the CBU persuades the government to accept, use and even request this data in order to improve the lives of the children in the community. The CBU also maintains its monitoring role to ensure that the information gathered is credible and can be used by the country's human rights lobbyists. To do its work, the CBU needs access to budgets, which may not be available in less open societies. The first step in using such a tactic, then, is to ensure that local laws allow public access to budget information and to pressure for this access if it does not exist.

This tactic can be used to monitor national and local government commitments, donor commitments, foreign aid and Poverty Reduction Strategy Policies, as well as conditions governments must adhere to in order to access certain types of donor funding from institutions like the World Bank and the International Monetary Fund. The budgeting approach can also show what progress is being made on a wide range of human rights issues, including disability rights and the rights to education, housing and health.

> *The budget is government's operational plan to deliver a better life for our people. It sets out what you will pay in taxes, how we will spend that money and what we will deliver. It is a synthesis of all our government policies. The budget is our contract with the nation.*

> — Trevor Manual, Minister of Finance, South Africa

Region	Initiating Sector	Target Sector	Focus	Human Rights Issue	INTERVENTION	New Tactics in Human Rights
Africa	Civil Society	Government	National	Children's rights	Persuasion	

Civilizing the Bureaucrat: Building collaborative relationships with government officials to promote change from within the system.

A Russian organization has shown that persuasion tactics can promote change from within. In other words, you can catch more flies with honey than with vinegar.

Citizens' Watch identifies democratic Russian officials who are supportive of human rights and reform and provides them with opportunities to strengthen democratic processes in Russia. The legacy of Soviet rule and totalitarianism left extremely challenging conditions for the development of democracy in Russia. Government officials had no experience in being responsive to the public, an essential practice in a democracy.

Citizens' Watch carefully monitors the actions of leading government officials, including individuals in the Interior Ministry, police and judiciary. They then identify officials who demonstrate an interest in a more democratic government and support for human rights — people they also believe will be open to change — and tailor their approaches to suit each individual, always being respectful and supportive. In some cases, this involves translation of international documents that support democracy and respect for human rights or are otherwise useful to the bureaucrat's job. In others, Citizens' Watch invites officials from abroad for seminars or supports the travel of Russian officials to meet with colleagues in other countries. During Soviet rule, few officials had opportunities to travel and learn of the democratic work of colleagues abroad. Citizens' Watch therefore uses travel and exchange opportunities both to train government officials and to entice them to actively seek change.

The group's hope is that access to these international documents and exposure to international colleagues will help illustrate the possibilities, and even prestige, in government collaboration with citizens and in work to uphold human rights. It also provides government officials with concrete information and examples of ways to improve government and human rights in their own country.

As a result of these efforts, Citizens' Watch has formed numerous collaborative relationships with government officials and institutions. Approaching officials in a variety of fields, and supporting them in their efforts to reform their departments, helps strengthen civil society and creates a more democratic relationship between the government agencies and the community.

ONLINE Read more about this in a tactical notebook available at www.newtactics.org, under Tools for Action.

Citizens' Watch is trying to remind officials that they are citizens first, with constitutional rights that must be respected, and only next are they governmental servants. What we can learn from Citizens' Watch is that, even in government systems with no tradition of engaging with the public or working in a democracy, there are openings for change. Other organizations hoping to take advantage of such openings in their countries will need to keep in mind that this approach requires a high level of individual diplomatic talent, along with a fairly deep pool of resources. These diplomatic skills and resources are also essential to another key aspect of the tactic: providing continued support to those who do want your assistance to advance human rights.

What tactical approaches can you use to turn adversaries (or potential adversaries) into allies?

" " *Heavy authoritarian traditions don't die easily and sometimes get the upper hand for a time, throwing us a few steps back down the ladder. For example, in March 2004, Citizens' Watch, along with justices of the peace from several Russian regions, organized a two-day conference to discuss problems in developing courts in the Russian northwest and other regions. We invited a couple of Supreme Court judges who, to our knowledge, had been most active in this process, as well as administrators from St. Petersburg and other population centers in the region.*

Two weeks before the conference, we were informed that the Supreme Court superiors had forbidden the judges to participate in our confer-ence or in any events organized by NGOs. But the local judges showed themselves to be worthy of the independent status they were given in 1992: They showed up in force to the conference, which took place in the St. Petersburg City Court — also a supporter of the initiative. The judges who came were brave enough to publicly denounce their higher-ups — proving that we had not been working in vain.

— Boris Pustintsev, Citizens' Watch, Russia

New Tactics in Human Rights	INTERVENTION	Region	Initiating Sector	Target Sector	Focus	Human Rights Issue
	Persuasion	Europe	Civil Society	Government	National	Corruption

Shareholder Power: Presenting shareholder resolutions to press companies to adopt more socially responsible business practices, including comprehensive human rights policies and practices.

Shareholders and investors are often overlooked as potential actors who can improve human rights protections in businesses.

The Interfaith Center on Corporate Responsibility (ICCR), a coalition of 275 faith-based institutional investors in North America, promotes shareholder resolutions to change unjust or harmful corporate policies and practices. As of 2003, the current combined portfolio of ICCR member organizations was estimated at about $110 billion.

ICCR members examine the social and environmental performance of the companies in which they invest. Rather than selling the stock of companies whose practices are harmful, the ICCR uses their financial holdings as a tool to pressure the companies to change their practices.

As shareholders, ICCR members place resolutions on social issues onto company ballots to be voted on at the annual meetings. In one example, nine ICCR-affiliated institutions co-filed a shareholder resolution with Amalgamated Bank and several other institutions. The resolution urged Unocal to adopt new company-wide policies based on the International Labor Organization's (ILO) Declaration on Fundamental Principles and Rights at Work, and was submitted to Unocal shareholders in 2002. The shareholders argued that Unocal's image was suffering because of questionable business practices in its Burmese pipeline project and that this was discouraging investment in Unocal. The proposed resolution received the highest vote on record in support of a human and labor rights shareholder proposal and caught the attention of the board and top management. In 2003, Unocal adopted policies based on the ILO declaration. In 2004, after ICCR members filed a resolution, Occidental Petroleum agreed to adopt a comprehensive human rights policy. ICCR publishes an annual *Proxy Resolutions Book* containing shareholder resolutions filed that year so that managers can make informed decisions about proxy voting and investors can see trends in corporate responsibility.

Each year ICCR-member institutions submit more than 100 shareholder resolutions on social and environmental issues. In many cases, these resolutions open the door for negotiations between religious investors and company executives.

While shareholder resolutions are not binding on companies, they do prompt company action when they receive support of a substantial number of shareholders. ICCR has been able to make its voice heard on important issues since 1971. Just as importantly, its tactic gives more people opportunities to participate in the advancement of human rights by changing the way they invest.

Region	Initiating Sector	Target Sector	Focus	Human Rights Issue	INTERVENTION	New Tactics in Human Rights
Multiple	Civil Society	Business	International	General human rights	Persuasion	

Mock Tribunals: Organizing mock tribunals to raise awareness of human rights abuses and influence public policy.

We don't have to wait until a particular form of human rights violation has ended to begin using stories for healing and reconciliation and to mobilize public opinion. In Nigeria, a group convened a mock tribunal focused on women's rights.

BAOBAB for Women's Human Rights, along with the Civil Resource Development and Documentation Centre, organized the first National Tribunal on Violence against Women. Held in March 2002 in Abuja, Nigeria's capital, the tribunal was unofficial and not legally binding, but the testimony was real. Thirty-three women testified, sharing their experiences in order to help the public learn about the abuses suffered by women in their homes, in their communities and at the hands of the government, including sexual harassment, domestic violence, rape and female genital mutilation.

The judges on the tribunal, all Nigerians, were selected based on their prominence and their concern for women's rights. They included two judges, one a Supreme Court justice, a former ambassador, a member of the National Human Rights Commission and a former attorney general. The tribunal was open to the public and the organizers took special care to invite journalists, police, commissioners, legislators and international observers. Different types of human rights abuses were grouped into different sessions. The panel of judges heard the testimony and asked questions, then convened in private. Afterwards, rather than handing down a sentence, the judges made public policy recommendations.

The tribunal and the media coverage around it created greater public awareness that abuses against women do exist and that they are serious. It helped facilitate the passing of state legislation on different issues affecting women and advanced a national bill on violence against women.

ONLINE | Read more about this in a tactical notebook available at www.newtactics.org, under Tools for Action.

Since the tribunals can raise awareness only when word spreads to the general public, BAOBAB's success required a good media strategy, along with strong leadership and a shrewd assessment of their political needs. BAOBAB chose, for example, not to invite any international experts to serve as judges, so the Nigerian government would have no opportunity to disregard its findings as "outside meddling." Others who wish to implement this tactic will also need to carefully tailor the make-up and scope of their tribunals in order to have the most impact on their intended audience. Tribunals such as these have been used in communities in many parts of the world for a number of purposes, such as recognizing abuses and raising public awareness.

" " | *Finding people to testify was a very big challenge — both the search and the process of counseling and encouragement. Some people had religious and cultural beliefs that inhibited them from telling their stories. Some expressed fears that they would not want their identity disclosed. The most common fear was of what their communities would think of them after giving their testimonies in the public. They were afraid of being rejected by their community. We responded to this by disguising them during their testimonies.*

— Mufuliat Fijabi, BAOBAB, Nigeria

New Tactics in Human Rights	INTERVENTION	Region	Initiating Sector	Target Sector	Focus	Human Rights Issue
	Persuasion	Africa	Civil Society	Government Society	National	Women's rights

INCENTIVE TACTICS   The tactics in this section make it easier for

people — parents, business owners and consumers, for example — to choose to do

the right thing by providing them with an incentive.

When parents feel like they need to send their children to work in order to survive,

financial support can give them an incentive to send the children to school instead.

When businesses are tempted by lower labor costs to hire children, they may be

convinced not to do so when their loans are tied to labor practices or when lucrative

markets for humanely produced goods open up. And when businesses are look-

ing to build their brands, they may find a powerful incentive for supporting human

rights in a generation of consumers who are vocal about their values.

The tactics we include here all involve financial incentives, but other things can be

powerful motivators as well — recognition, prestige and standing in the internation-

al community, for example, can motivate both people and governments.

From the Streets to School: Providing parents with funds that allow them to send their children to school rather than to work.

Poverty is one of the root causes of child labor. Many families would like to send their children to school but cannot afford to do so because they need the income those children can earn. A program has been created in Brazil to provide economic support to families, thus allowing their children an education.

The Bolsa Escola program in Brazil provides families with a monthly stipend so that children can attend school rather than working in the streets. The program, which began in the city of Brasilia, was created with the realization that the working children of today are the poor adults of tomorrow. Bolsa Escola was expanded to a federal program in 2001.

The Bolsa Escola program is managed by the Department of Education. Qualifying families receive monthly payments and ATM cards (electronic bank cards) that allow them to access the stipends directly. Families must meet the following criteria: the children must be between the ages of six and 15 and cannot miss more than two days of school per month; each unemployed adult in the family must be registered with the National Employment System (SINE) and actively seeking employment; and the family must have lived in Brazil for at least five years. The family receives the stipend for a minimum of two years to a maximum of eight. If a child does not meet the mandatory attendance rate, the stipend for that month is withheld.

In addition to combating poverty and encouraging children to complete their education, this tactic has significantly decreased the numbers of child laborers and reduced the numbers of school dropouts. To date the Bolsa Escola has helped the families of 8,289,930 children. When the federal program was created, Bolsa Escola became the broadest social program in the world.

Families are often complicit in the use of child labor — because of need, rather than choice — and this tactic gives them an alternative. Providing ATM cards that look like and can be used like other ATM cards also helps recipients avoid the stigma associated with poverty and public assistance. This approach clearly requires significant financial resources and also demands a great deal of administration and coordination among the various agencies and institutions.

What incentives, in addition to money, will motivate your adversaries or your potential allies?

Region	Initiating Sector	Target Sector	Focus	Human Rights Issue	**INTERVENTION**	New Tactics in Human Rights
Americas	Government	Society	National	Child labor	Incentive	

Linking Loans to Human Rights: Offering loans with favorable terms to small-business owners with the condition that they not use child labor.

A group in Bangladesh gives communities an alternative to using child labor, providing loans with favorable terms to businesses that agree not to hire children.

The Bangladesh Rural Advancement Committee (BRAC) administers the Micro Enterprise Lending and Assistance (MELA) program, which offers loans with favorable terms to small businesses that would not normally be able to secure funds, on the condition that they agree not to use child labor.

The lending program provides credit to new or existing small businesses that show entrepreneurial promise, including enterprises in the textile, food processing, service and transport sectors. Borrowers are often eager for the loans, which range from US$300 to US$3500 with a 15 percent service charge. The average loan size is approximately $1,000. Borrowers agree to their terms because regular banks are unwilling to lend to rural people and require repayment in lump sums, rather than in equal monthly installments. Borrowers repay their loans over a period of one to two years.

BRAC also monitors the activities of its borrowers to ensure that they comply with the terms of their loans and field staff are prepared to take immediate action upon finding any human rights violations, regardless of whether they involve BRAC borrowers.

Since its inception in 1996, the program has lent to over 45,000 borrowers in Bangladesh, all in enterprises that do not use child labor. The program simultaneously generates employment by injecting new capital into local businesses, creates awareness of the problem of child labor and reduces the use of the practice.

The incentive here is clear: BRAC has identified a need and fills it, while spelling out its requirements for respecting human rights. This tactic could also be used in other situations where there is a connection between financial activity and human rights, such as in guarding against discrimination, in guaranteeing fair wages or in providing safe working conditions. The loans themselves have to be attractive enough to provide an incentive, perhaps by having lower interest rates or better repayment terms than those provided by ordinary banks.

New Tactics in Human Rights	INTERVENTION	Region	Initiating Sector	Target Sector	Focus	Human Rights Issue
	Incentive	Asia	Civil Society	Society	National	Child labor

78   www.newtactics.org

Sometimes consumers, lenders, shareholders and others who are far removed from the abuse itself — from the use of child labor, from unfair labor practices, from the environmental degradation in another country — have incentive to change their behavior. They may also feel that they have no alternatives or they lack the information needed to make humane and just choices. One foundation provides people who are far away from the sources of their purchased products with the information and alternatives they need to make choices that support human rights.

The Rugmark label, which shows a smiling face on a carpet, has become the trademark for a promising initiative to identify and promote hand-knotted carpets made without child labor. The Rugmark Foundation awards licenses to carpet exporters who agree not to use child labor and who voluntarily submit to a monitoring system that includes surprise inspections and cross-checking of export records and looms. Children who are found to be illegally working during inspections are rehabilitated and schooled by Rugmark.

Rugmark implements a three-step process of investigation:

1   License approval after a series of inspections. Inspectors are hired and trained by the Rugmark Foundation, and measures are taken to ensure the investigations are carried out properly. The inspectors either approve the manufacturers or, upon finding evidence of child labor, give them a limited time to stop the practice.

2   Random surprise inspections, only after which carpets made in that period will be certified.

3   Carpet tracking, whereby each Rugmark carpet can be tracked by maker, location and exporter.

Rugmark has faced some challenges in its efforts. Due to the widely scattered location of looms in India, regular inspections are difficult. The structure of the industry is not uniform. While some exporters are closely connected to the looms, many employ intermediaries, making it difficult to enforce the tracking component of the certification process. Nevertheless, upwards of 4,000 children in India, Pakistan and Nepal have been rehabilitated through Rugmark programs and, from the publicity generated by Rugmark, thousands of other children have been prevented from working at the carpet looms altogether.

Essential to Rugmark's success is the understanding that there is an increasing demand for products made without child labor. Because Rugmark deals with carpet importers, not directly with consumers, it must convince importers that there is a market for these carpets. Importers of Rugmark carpets pay, in addition to the cost of the carpets, a 1.75 percent royalty on the total yearly cost of the imports, a portion of which goes to rehabilitation and education programs for the children. In return, Rugmark promotes the retailers carrying their carpets. These retailers are mentioned in Rugmark's outreach materials and at events in which Rugmark plays a role, such as the World Day against Child Labor. Retailers are also provided with promotional materials explaining the importance of purchasing Rugmark carpets. Rugmark tells importers and retailers that carrying certified carpets not only helps them reach the consumers who wish only to purchase child labor-free carpets, but enhances the public image of their stores.

The Rugmark label, like many other labeling systems created in the last decade or so, provides consumers with the information they need in order to avoid contributing to human rights abuses. At the same time, it raises awareness of the problems associated with a particular product, and creates demand for products that are produced and moved to market humanely. Because producers want access to that market, they have an incentive to participate.

Such programs risk dilution of the meaning of their "brand" if they are not associated with a suitable stringent monitoring process — which can be complicated and resource-intensive. They may also need to be used in conjunction with other awareness-raising tactics in order to inform consumers and producers and convince them that they have a reason to care about changes in the production process.

Region	Initiating Sector	Target Sector	Focus	Human Rights Issue	INTERVENTION	New Tactics in Human Rights
Asia	Civil Society	Business	International	Child labor	Incentive	

| **When Businesses Lead the Way:** Concentrating all steps in the production process in facilities to make it easier to monitor and eliminate the use of child labor.

Reebok is one of the best-known brands in the business, a brand that has been protected in part by the company's efforts to protect human rights though monitoring.

In 1996 Reebok International initiated factory monitoring, product labeling and education programs to prevent the use of child labor in the manufacture of their Pakistani-made soccer balls.

An estimated twenty percent of laborers in soccer ball production facilities in Sialkot, Pakistan, were children. Reebok human rights standards require that workers in its factories be 15 years old at a minimum, or older, depending on applicable local laws.

When it entered the soccer ball market, Reebok acted to prevent the use of child labor by containing all production, including stitching, in a single state-of-the-art manufacturing facility in Sialkot. All work is performed on-site and is free of child labor. Monitors inspect the production facilities periodically, interviewing workers and supervising inspectors who oversee the shipments of panels in and out of the factories. They also maintain ties with the local community and visit surrounding villages to confirm that no Reebok balls are stitched outside the factories. The soccer balls are then labeled "Guaranteed: Manufactured Without Child Labor." This provides consumers a choice regarding how their soccer balls are produced and builds awareness about child labor in the soccer ball industry.

As a result of concentrating production in child labor-free facilities, Reebok has been able to produce tens of thousands of soccer balls without the use of child labor.

In 1997, Reebok created the Reebok Educational Assistance to Pakistan program (R.E.A.P.) and allocated US$1 million from the sales of these balls to support local education in the region where the balls are manufactured. In 1997 Reebok joined with the Society for Advancement of Education in Sialkot to establish the Chaanan Institute, which works with local families to place children in schools and keep them out of the labor pool.

Reebok saw a market for products made without child labor and decided to fill it. For several years public awareness had been building around this issue. As a multinational corporation with a strong market share, Reebok was in a unique position to influence the entire chain of production and distribution for its products. That is an important aspect of this tactic; the increasing number of steps between raw materials and consumer in the global economy makes it difficult to monitor human rights abuses. Reebok realized it needed to consolidate those steps in order to ensure that products were made without child labor.

This labeling tactic could be used to fulfill market demand for other "fair labor" goods: produce for which growers are paid a fair price; goods made in factories where laborers are paid a fair wage; and products made or grown in an environmentally friendly way.

Are there businesses that could be unexpected allies in your struggle?

New Tactics in Human Rights	**INTERVENTION**	Region	Initiating Sector	Target Sector	Focus	Human Rights Issue
	Incentive	Asia	Business	Business Society	International	Child labor

RESTORATIVE TACTICS

From 1980 to 2000 more than 70,000 people in Peru disappeared or were murdered. Most of the victims were from poor rural families who were largely excluded from economic and political life. The human rights community in Peru brought this issue to the attention of the media, the general public and international organizations, leading to the creation of the Truth and Reconciliation Commission on which I had the privilege to serve.

The Commission, which issued its final report in August 2003, made it impossible for the state to continue to ignore the cries for justice from the families of the disappeared. Its work, while a victory for human rights, was only a first step in a much larger process of restoring rights and justice for all people in Peru.

In this chapter you will read about other people and organizations, like the Truth and Reconciliation Commission, who were part of the process of restoring justice and rebuilding communities after horrific human rights abuses. Some recorded the abuses, making it impossible for the state or society to ignore them. Some helped heal communities and individuals damaged by abuse. Some sought justice for both victims and perpetrators.

In the Commission's work, justice meant punishing perpetrators, gaining reparations — both collective and individual — for victims and ensuring that the crimes that were committed will not happen again. Reparations are a crucial part of this mix in Peru, both because the Peruvian government owes a debt to the victims it failed to protect and because reparations will help restore rights to all members of Peruvian society.

Other groups have used other tactics to bring justice to their communities. I hope that you will find many of them useful to you in your work.

— Sofia Macher
Former Member, Truth and Reconciliation Commission
Former Executive Director, National Coordinator of Human Rights , Peru

Even when human rights violations end — when the war is over or the old regime has been toppled, when victims have been freed or have escaped, or time has simply passed — even then the need for creative human rights work does not end. The impact of human rights abuse extends beyond immediate suffering: it can destroy leadership in a community, lead to economic decline and erode civil society.

A silence can descend that prevents victims, families and communities from rebuilding leadership and social structures, prevents perpetrators from being brought to justice and prevents communities from reconciling and moving on. The tactics described in this chapter have all been used to seek healing, justice and reconciliation for victims and communities, to rebuild leadership and to advance a vision for a free and fair society.

Traditionally a distinction has been made between restorative and retributive justice, where restorative justice emphasizes healing the wounds of victims, offenders and communities and retributive justice emphasizes punishment for the offender and redress for the victim. Both approaches are useful and essential to the task of rebuilding and restoring a damaged community and both are included here.

These tactics also, while most often focused on the past, play an important role in preventing abuses in the future. They have been used to strengthen damaged communities; break down walls of impunity that protect abusers; punish abusers and make it known that abuse will not be tolerated in the future; create records of abuse that acknowledge and validate the pain felt by victims and victims' families; and record patterns of abuse that, if we are vigilant, could help us recognize and stop abuses in the future.

The tactics in this chapter are divided into three sections:

1   Remembering abuses — tactics that bring to light the nature and extent of abuses, or the identities of the perpetrators or victims.
2   Strengthening individuals and communities — tactics that employ mental health interventions, rehabilitation and other techniques to heal individuals and communities.
3   Seeking redress — tactics that seek justice through litigation, sanctions, reparations or other means.

REMEMBERING ABUSES

It would be easiest to forget the abuses we hear about, witness and experience, but we then leave wounds untended and a door open to future abuses. The tactics in this section create a permanent and public record of abuse and patterns of abuse. Without such a public record, memory will dissipate, because existing documents may be scattered or hidden within a deep layer of bureaucracy. Files regarding human rights abuses also have a tendency to "disappear" if not preserved. Where documentation does exists, special efforts may be needed to unearth it, preserve it and make it public. In situations where the best or only documentation lies with the bodies buried in unmarked or mass graves, other tactics put specialized forensic skills to use. In other cases the facts of abuse are already known to the public — perhaps it occurred a little further in the past — but people are in danger of forgetting what happened. These mechanisms not only keep the memory fresh, but also make it relevant. And in several situations below, where abuse has been widespread and pervasive, public commissions and tribunals give victims, victims' families and, in some cases, perpetrators, the chance to tell their stories.

Opening files and records that contain information about human rights violations — especially deaths, torture and disappearances — to the general public can serve several purposes. It can bring to victims' families a sense of "closure," helping them put the past to rest and move on or perform the rituals traditional in their culture. It also helps families gather information to build a solid record for litigation against abusers. Also, the public records can become a visible and tangible memorial, providing a focal point for public discussions and becoming, in some ways, a voice to the voiceless.

Answers for Victims' Families: Documenting records of abuse to promote healing and justice.

A group in Cambodia has documented abuses from the Khmer Rouge genocide and made the records of abuse accessible to the public, preserving the memory of both those affected by the genocide and those who committed the abuses.

The Documentation Center of Cambodia (DC-Cam) collects records of the victims and perpetrators of the genocide in Cambodia so that families and friends can learn the precise fate of the disappeared. At the same time, DC-Cam gathers possible legal evidence that can be used against former Khmer Rouge leaders in a court of law.

DC-Cam's Family Tracing File System helps families of both victims and perpetrators discover the fate of their loved ones by searching detailed records kept by the Khmer Rouge regime (1975–1979). DC-Cam has four databases that catalogue hundreds of thousands of pages of relevant documents, photographs and interviews. Its mapping project has used GPS technology to identify 19,466 mass graves, 168 prisons and 77 genocide memorials in 170 districts of Cambodia and nearly all of the country's provinces.

Although most often finding that relatives were executed by the Khmer Rouge, families can still find closure and relief in knowing exactly what happened, and the community can begin to heal from the trauma of the genocide. Records occasionally reveal the location of the missing's remains, allowing a family to perform the proper rites for the victim's spirit. An estimated 80 percent of families that come to the center inquiring about loved ones leave with answers as to what happened.

DC-Cam's ultimate goal is to keep the memory of the genocide alive, helping the people of Cambodia seek justice and build a strong future and preventing such atrocities from ever happening again.

DC-Cam's tactic has been very effective in Cambodia, where the population has suffered grave, long-term abuses. Other countries emerging from long periods of abuse could benefit from the group's experience. To create a central repository of information, a group must find how or whether the perpetrators left any documentation or evidence behind and may need to conduct exhumations and forensic work (see page 91). In Cambodia, the genocide targeted the educated class and destroyed the justice system, meaning that the information could only be put to use when the system was rebuilt.

How can you record the history of abuses in your community? How can you use this history to promote healing and justice?

Region	Initiating Sector	Target Sector	Focus	Human Rights Issue	**RESTORATIVE**	**New Tactics in Human Rights**
Asia	Civil Society	Government Society	National	Gross violations of human rights	Remembering Abuses	

www.newtactics.org   87

| **Opening the Archives of Terror:** Promoting justice by leveraging the legal rights to access victims' records.

In Paraguay, the Centro de Documentación y Archivo (the Center for Documentation and Archives or CDyA) is taking advantage of a law that gives former prisoners the right of habeas data — the right to control documents relating to their own cases — to create an "archive of terror."

The Centro de Documentación y Archivo (CDyA) opened police files to the public after the country's 35-year military dictatorship.

The constitution of Paraguay, like the constitutions of five other Latin American countries, includes the right of habeas data: the right of former prisoners to control data collected about them and their experiences. After filing a petition to obtain his own file, Martin Almada, a former political prisoner, accompanied by a local judge, found thousands of detention files in a police station in Lambare in 1992.

These files document prisoners' detention experiences in detail — including torture and other human rights violations — and have been used to corroborate individuals' stories of detention during several Latin American dictatorships, to confirm the disappearance of citizens and as evidence in the prosecution of former police and military personnel in several Latin American countries.

The Paraguayan courts, including the Supreme Court, eventually ordered that the files be made accessible to the public. The archive, now under the control of the CDyA, is open to researchers, investigators, human rights activists and the general public. CDyA has used the files as the basis for legal cases, to organize tribunals to prosecute the chief perpetrators of state-sponsored torture and illegal detention, and to inform the work of the Paraguayan truth commission. Twenty officials have been successfully prosecuted. The archive was also used to assemble the case for the extradition of General Augusto Pinochet from Great Britain to Spain in 1998 .

CDyA has transferred 90 percent of the material in the archives to microfilm and is digitizing it as well. The group is also seeking to have the archives included in UNESCO's World Heritage List.

The availability of detailed information about human rights abuses can have important effects on those who suffered abuses as well as on the administration of justice after the abuses have ended. Almada's efforts in Paraguay confirmed the experiences of many victims and made legal recourse an option.

While the files in Paraguay were discovered by accident, the tactic of purposefully opening files regarding human rights violations has been used by several governments. In Germany and several Eastern Europe countries, for example, governments have opened the files of victims of the secret police. In Germany, the files are maintained by an independent body called the Gauck Authority and open to victims but not to the general public. In Czechoslovakia and other countries, files were opened selectively and not made available to victims and some files slipped through cracks in the service of political purposes.

There have been numerous criticisms of and lessons learned from these tactical approaches. Tina Rosenberg at the Harvard Law School Human Rights program on truth commissions, for instance, states that "the fact that German files were opened helped to solve the problem of the files' unreliability. Victims could help confirm whether or not the person accused of informing could actually have done what he was accused of. It is a self-checking mechanism, which does not exist in the Czech version. Furthermore in Germany, the victim can choose whether or not he wants to publicize the information about who informed on him. That is not public information.

What laws exist in your country that might be useful in obtaining access to documents that confirm abuses and identify perpetrators?

	RESTORATIVE	Region	Initiating Sector	Target Sector	Focus	Human Rights Issue
	Remembering Abuses	Americas	Government Civil Society	Government Society	National International	Gross violations of human rights

Preserving Memories: Coordinating efforts to preserve archival information among several organizations and creating a system for accessing it.

"Never again" is a vow frequently heard after human rights abuses come to light, but that vow cannot be kept unless the memory of the abuses, the victims and those who fought against the abuse remains alive. Unfortunately, the powerful information stored in the files of numerous human rights organizations is often unknown to the outside world and inaccessible to those who may later be able to use it to make sure that such history is not repeated. Memoria Abierta is an alliance of eight human rights organizations in Argentina that have combined their efforts to create a publicly accessible database, one they hope will contribute to the articulation of a collective and lasting memory.

Memoria Abierta has created a system to make accessible all public archives of documents, photographs and interviews that testify to the horrors of state terrorism in Argentina, its victims and the people who stood against it. While anyone with Internet access can search the online catalogue of the files, the actual materials remain in the offices of each member organization or in Memoria Abierta's office. The database provides a single index of all materials, easily searchable by any user. It also tells the location of the original documents, photos and videos so that interested researchers can set contact organizations about them. The project has created special software developed in open-source format to help other organizations create similar databases.

The Patrimonio Documental (Documentary Heritage Program) archive includes five parts: 1) the Documentary Heritage Program itself, which includes about 22,000 documents on state terrorism; 2) the Topography of Memory Program, with maps, documents and oral testimony about historical sites related to state terrorism — over 340 torture centers that were hidden in ordinary places throughout the country; 3) the Photographic Archive Program, which includes digital images from human rights organizations, private collections and the media; 4) the Oral Archive Program, with summaries of more than 320 interviews with people whose lives have in some way been affected by the experience of state terrorism; and 5) Memoria Abierta's own documents.

Memoria Abierta is comprised of the Abuelas de Plaza de Mayo, Asamblea Permanente por los Derechos Humanos, Asociación Buena Memoria, Centro de Estudios Legales y Sociales, Familiares de Desaparecidos y Detenidos por Razones Políticas, Fundación Memoria Histórica y Social Argentina, Madres de Plaza de Mayo — Línea Fundadora, and Servicio Paz y Justicia. The alliance was formed to develop and support projects that encourage communities and individuals to remember events that occurred during the military dictatorship. Memoria Abierta also sponsors initiatives to promote debates on the creation of sites of memory and spaces for public reflection. The archives will one day form part of the main collection of a Museum of Memory.

The tactic of coordinating archives of multiple organizations could be used in any country where more than one group is collecting human rights-related data. It could be part of a "memory" project, but could also be used in countries where multiple human rights organizations are tracking ongoing abuses and need to maximize access to information.

Region	Initiating Sector	Target Sector	Focus	Human Rights Issue	**RESTORATIVE**	**New Tactics in Human Rights**
Americas	Civil Society	Civil Society	National	Gross violations of human rights	Remembering Abuses	

Forensic Anthropology: Using forensics to identify victims' remains and cause of death.

In cases where paper documents are insufficient or simply do not exist, forensic work can create a record for litigation and give victims' families the information they need for closure. Forensic work is an objective way to record abuses. Because the evidence is scientific, it can be even more powerful than testimony and written documentation in proving human rights violations. The exhumation of bodies can also allow families to perform traditional rituals, mourn and, though still hurting, move on with their lives.

Over the past two decades, Equipo Argentino de Antropologia Forense (the Argentine Forensic Anthropology Team, or EAAF) has identified the remains of victims of state violence. During Argentina's military dictatorship (1976–1983), 10,000 to 30,000 people were killed or "disappeared" by the state. The EAAF's goal is three-fold: to return victims' remains to their families and thus aid in the healing process; to provide evidence for legal cases against the perpetrators of state violence; and to train and support the formation of other forensic teams in countries that have suffered periods of violence and need to investigate the past.

The EAAF has a permanent investigative team that researches information on people who were disappeared. The group usually begins a case with a preliminary investigation to ascertain where the person might be buried, interviewing relatives, friends, other former prisoners, cellmates and former political activists about the victim's physical characteristics and the likely time and place of death. The EAAF also studies police and bureaucratic records, which contain physical descriptions, fingerprints and autopsy records, and must often obtain court orders to gain entrance to police archives. The process moves forward when the group has found ten written or oral documents.

Once the burial's likely location has been identified, the team approaches the family of the victim; the EAAF will not continue the investigation without the family's consent. Once the family agrees, and the group has received authorization from the prosecutor or legal authority, the team begins the exhumations. Families are welcome to participate in some of the steps. The group uses standard archaeological techniques to recover the person's remains, and work then proceeds to the laboratory, where the EAAF scientists attempt to match the remains with the gathered information and establish the cause and manner of death.

Through this process, the EAAF has identified hundreds of victims' remains, bringing closure to families and contributing evidence to national and international tribunals, truth commissions and local courts. The EAAF has also trained many other groups around the world in its techniques. EAAF team members say this has been an important process for increased cooperation among countries in the global South.

" " *It is a very difficult moment when we approach families with information about where their loved ones might be. This could end the search for loved ones, which families are not always prepared for. We build a relationship with the family and talk to them until they are prepared. We explain to them what they will see, what they can expect, and encourage them to ask any questions or participate in the process.*

— Luis Fondebrider, EAAF President, Argentina

New Tactics in Human Rights	RESTORATIVE	Region	Initiating Sector	Target Sector	Focus	Human Rights Issue
	Remembering Abuses	Americas	Civil Society	Government Society	National International	Gross violations of human rights

When the EAAF investigates deaths, it gives control of the process to the family and community. This is essential in communities that have not only been marginalized under abusive governments but have been excluded from the reconciliation process. The EAAF's approach requires a certain level of openness and political freedom, but the group's experience transferring the tactic to over 30 other countries demonstrates that total government support is not necessary.

Another group, in Guatemala, also works with the community during exhumations, but focuses on psychosocial services. The Equipo de Estudios Comunitarios y Acción Psycosocial (Community Research and Psychosocial Action Team, or ECAP) works with the the Fundación de Antropología Forense de Guatemala to provide support to families and communities before, during and after an exhumation.

ECAP organizes support groups in which families can safely share emotions related to their loss, where they can reflect, fearlessly tell their stories, learn to face the consequences of violence and understand the current situation so that they can plan for the future. Families also receive assistance in burying their relatives legally and according to their own traditions, helping to preserve the bond between the living and the deceased.

After providing counseling prior to an exhumation, counselors accompany families to the exhumation site to provide support as members confront the reality of their relative's death, and continue to work with families to help them accept this reality. In communities affected by widespread political violence, common in many rural areas of Guatemala, counselors identify the impact of the violence and create groups to foster discussions of how the community as a whole can heal. To contribute to the healing, ECAP also supports communities in the creation of memorials and other ways of recognizing the traumas of the past. These programs all promote a critical awareness of the community's shared history, present and future, along with the emotions and challenges involved in reclaiming their rights.

How might you use forensics or other technical expertise to document human rights violations?

Speaking Truth: Establishing a formal truth commission to investigate and acknowledge gross human rights violations.

In the past two decades, several countries emerging from long periods of abuse have created forums for victims, and sometimes perpetrators, to tell their stories. The truth-telling process can draw victims out of isolation; abusive regimes often maintain levels of secrecy that keep victims from knowing that their neighbors are suffering as well. Ideally, these truth-telling tactics engage the entire population, or at least large segments of it, so as to foster healing rather than be divisive.

Truth commissions are one kind of truth-telling tactic used by governments to start the process of reconciliation. Their mandates, which outline their purpose and authority, are typically established by country's legislative or executive bodies. In South Africa, a strategic decision was made at the end of apartheid to create a truth commission process rather than simply holding trials to prosecute perpetrators of gross human rights violations. The Truth and Reconciliation Commission was created by the country's parliament with a mandate to establish as complete a picture as possible of the nature, causes and extent of gross violations of human rights committed, by all sides of the conflict, between March 1, 1960, and May 10, 1994.

The South African Truth and Reconciliation Commission (TRC) was initiated by national legislation in 1995, after a period of public debate. Its mandate was to collect information about gross human rights violations committed by state bodies or the armed opposition during apartheid and its goal was to promote national unity and reconciliation. The Commission was expected to offer suggestions for policy reforms to prevent future abuses. In addition to amnesty and human rights hearings, special hearings focused on abuses suffered by women and children and others were held on the role of faith communities, the medical establishment, the legal sector, the business community and other institutions that had passively or actively contributed to rights violations. Hearings were held all around the country and the broadcast media carried clips and live coverage. All media covered the TRC extensively through the duration of the Commission.

Twenty thousand victims provided testimony. To make the process as comfortable for victims as possible, the TRC used briefers (also an interesting tactic), who were chosen from the caring professions — ministers, social workers, and nurses, among others — and offered support to the victims before, during and after the process. The briefers received extensive training on the process and the structure of the Commission.

One unique aspect of the Commission's mandate was a conditional amnesty for perpetrators of human rights violations willing to publicly admit the details of their actions. Criteria for amnesty included full disclosure of the crimes as well as a determination that the acts were politically motivated. This conditional amnesty was a policy not attempted in previous truth commissions of this magnitude and it resulted in public confessions detailing many of the most notorious crimes of the apartheid era, including the 1977 murder of activist Steven Biko. Amnesty was not guaranteed for those who provided testimony, though steps for prosecution of those who were not granted amnesty or did not come forward to testify have not been implemented.

The Truth and Reconciliation Commission Report was released in seven volumes between 1998 and 2002. Though its long-term impact remains to be seen, some of the report's immediate achievements include recommendations on how to prevent future violations, which have influenced the new government, and the collection of indisputable documentation of human rights abuses during the apartheid era. It is important to note that the TRC has not fulfilled all of its expectations. None of the abusers who refused to testify have yet been prosecuted, although the process allows for this, and the country continues to struggle with the issue of reparations.

ONLINE | Read more about the use of briefers within the Commission at www. newtactics.org, under Tools for Action.

New Tactics in Human Rights	RESTORATIVE	Region	Initiating Sector	Target Sector	Focus	Human Rights Issue
	Remembering Abuses	Africa	Government	Society	National	Gross violations of human rights

Truth commissions have been convened in dozens of countries and situations with a variety of mandates and results. Some are given subpoena powers, while others have no significant judicial tools at their disposal. Some hold open or even televised hearings, others work almost entirely behind closed doors. Some commissions recommend financial or other reparations for surviving victims and, in an effort to prevent future human rights violations, many have been asked to make substantial recommendations for changes in the political, military, police or judicial structures, or in the social or educational spheres.

Glenda Wildschut, a former commissioner on the South African Truth and Reconciliation Commission, notes that the commission operated under some limitations. Among them:

The TRC examined only gross violations of human rights. Victims of forced removals, land disposession, the mixed marriages act and a host of other legislation could not seek recourse from the TRC.

The TRC's reparations committee was mandated only to make policy recommendations to parliament, while the amnesty committee had the power to grant immediate amnesty.

The TRC had to cover a period of 34 years — from 1960 to 1994 — in just three years of work.

The TRC had very few resources to provide emotional and psychological support for victims.

The tactic is still controversial. Some believe that truth commissions add to people's suffering and feelings of powerlessness because abuses come to light without punishment for perpetrators, or that the commissions can be used as a substitute for legal action. Others argue that deeply divided societies cannot press legal prosecution without strengthening the resolves and power of perpetrators to resist democratic change. But truth commissions can be used as part of a larger strategy that includes both truth-telling and punishment for abusers, or, as in the case of Argentina, may help create the political climate needed to begin prosecution.

International Justice for War Crimes: Holding an international tribunal to raise awareness of and seek reparations for sexual war crimes.

A network in Asia organized an international tribunal to preserve the memory of abuses that occurred decades before, and to demand compensation.

The Violence Against Women in War Network, Japan (VAWW-NET) created a tribunal to acknowledge and seek justice for victims of sexual war crimes. In the first half of the twentieth century, the Japanese government created a system of sexual slavery through a network of "comfort stations," brothel facilities controlled by the military. An estimated 400,000 women and girls were forced into the system. For close to 50 years the atrocity remained behind a veil of silence.

In 1998, VAWW-NET proposed the establishment of the Women's International War Crimes Tribunal. An International Organizing Committee (the IOC) was formed, including representatives from nongovernmental organizations in victims' home countries, Japan and the international community. The IOC created a charter, set the procedures and rules for the tribunal and prepared for proceedings in Tokyo in December 2000. At the tribunal, prosecution teams from ten countries presented indictments, including a joint indictment from North and South Korea. A four-judge panel representing a balanced geographic and legal spectrum presided over the proceedings. The tribunal heard live and videotaped testimony from survivors — euphemistically called "comfort women" — as well as from two former soldiers. Experts also testified about Japanese military structure. The judges reviewed official documents, memoirs, diaries and legal briefs. The tribunal hall was packed throughout the proceedings with up to 1,000 observers and members of the international media. After three days, the tribunal issued preliminary findings of fact and law and recommended reparations.

The tribunal created a historical record and raised awareness in the international community about sexual war crimes. The government of Japan, with the citizens of Japan, set up the Asian Women's Fund (AWF) in 1995 to express its apologies and remorse and to provide compensation to victims. Although the fund has raised 483 million yen (approximately US$4 million) for victims, many survivors and supporters view the AWF as a means for the Japanese government to avoid paying direct compensation; some of the victims have declined compensation from this private fund.

This tribunal broke decades of silence surrounding a subject taboo in Japan and difficult for the international community to face. It brought worldwide attention to the suffering of the "comfort women," and even prompted private donations for the victims. It did not, however, succeed in holding the Japanese government to its responsibility to provide direct compensation.

A tribunal like this might be used on its own to break the silence around other issues — whether of this magnitude or on a much smaller scale — or to build momentum toward other international efforts, such as creating a fund for victims or building a powerful international movement.

Mock judicial procedures like these can also be used outside the country where the abuse occurred. In the United States, Minnesota Advocates for Human Rights organized a mock tribunal of the Khmer Rouge at which members of the local Cambodian community testified about the genocide in Cambodia. This gave Cambodians a chance to tell their stories, and local residents in the state of Minnesota a chance to learn about the new people arriving in their communities and what these people had survived. As part of the project a videotaped oral history was created that is now part of the permanent collection of the Minnesota History Center.

How might you organize allies in different countries to highlight your struggle?

New Tactics in Human Rights	RESTORATIVE	Region	Initiating Sector	Target Sector	Focus	Human Rights Issue
	Remembering Abuses	Asia	Civil Society	Government	International	War crimes
		Americas		Society	Local	Gross violations of human rights

94   www.newtactics.org

STRENGTHENING INDIVIDUALS
AND COMMUNITIES

Cycles of violence can be disrupted by traditional human rights approaches, but a peaceful environment can never be restored without first addressing the damage of repression on targeted individuals and the broader society. The tactics in this section aim to heal individuals and communities, beginning the complex task of creating cycles of positive events that pave the way for future progress.

Abuse that injures the individual also damages families and communities. It can destroy feelings of trust and security and can damage the institutions and relationships that allow us to rely on and support each other. Long-lasting and widespread patterns of abuse — whether under tyrannical regimes or during periods of civil conflict — can create large populations of displaced people and refugees and, even in communities that remain physically intact, can result in psychological devastation.

The tactics that follow include innovative ways of rebuilding communities and strengthening individuals whose lives have been affected by abuse. They include modern mental health interventions and techniques for rehabilitation (although the details of psychological treatment are outside the scope of this workbook), often combined with elements from traditional cultures. It is important to note that most, if not all, of these tactics draw support from within the community. A community devastated by conflict or tyranny may not seem to have many resources to draw upon. But recognizing and shoring up existing internal resources — whether they are cultural traditions or people with skills and potential they are eager to put to use — is essential to rebuilding that community.

The next three tactics focus on healing communities that have been torn apart by civil conflict, torture and displacement. Sometimes, especially following periods of civil war and tribal fighting, victims and perpetrators of abuse are forced to rebuild their lives side by side, in the same community. While it may seem most natural to focus on the needs of the victims while disregarding the abusers as evil, working with abusers can help fulfill important community needs.

**New Tactics
in Human Rights**

RESTORATIVE

Strengthening
Individuals and
Communities
www.newtactics.org

96

From Refugee to Mental Health Paraprofessional: Building local capacity for trauma-focused mental health services through an intensive training model.

The Center for Victims of Torture (which coordinates the New Tactics in Human Rights Project and published this book) is helping rebuild communities in which large portions of the population have suffered torture or war trauma and been forced to leave their homes.

The Center for Victims of Torture (CVT) trains refugees as peer counselors in Guinea and Sierra Leone. The refugees provide mental health services to others who have suffered torture and war trauma, increasing the number of people CVT can serve and creating a cadre of qualified mental health paraprofessionals in communities that had previously had no mental health services. Paraprofessionals perform many of the tasks of professionals, but within a system of supervision.

The wars and civil conflicts in West Africa have affected such a large proportion of the population, and driven so many people into refugee camps, that an international organization like CVT could not possibly bring in enough staff to meet the need for mental health services. Instead, CVT decided to draw on resources within the camps, eventually recruiting more than 120 refugees as peer counselors, or psychosocial agents (PSAs), in camps in Guinea and Sierra Leone.

The refugee camps provide a concentrated area of survivors needing assistance, as well as a good location for the prolonged close supervision and training needed to assist torture survivors. Many of the PSAs received up to four years of ongoing training and daily supervision before the program moved into the communities where the atrocities were committed.

The intensive hands-on training in CVT's model combines Western psychotherapy with local understandings of trauma and recovery. The program begins with a two-week training session, followed by day-long monthly and seven-day quarterly training sessions. These sessions focus on trauma theory, general psychology, counseling, and communication skills. CVT psychologists and social workers work daily in the camps, modeling behavior and helping PSAs practice their skills. On the job, the PSAs spend ten weeks observing mental health professionals facilitating therapy groups, ten weeks co-facilitating and ten weeks leading a group on their own with periodic supervision. By the end of their training, PSAs are well-versed in the effects of trauma and in trauma recovery facilitation and program evaluation. They are also skilled group facilitators and effective communicators.

Read more about this in a tactical notebook available at www.newtactics.org, under Tools for Action.

ONLINE

Essentially, CVT is using this tactic to help a community heal itself. The refugees who train as PSAs are empowered as they learn new skills and do something positive for their community. The people they serve see that someone from their own community, rather than an outsider, is in a position to help them. And at the same time, people in the camps receive the mental health care they need.

While this tactic has been applied here to help victims of torture and war trauma, it could also be used to serve other populations with large numbers of people deeply affected by violence.

Would the development of a cadre of paraprofessionals in the medicine, mental health or public health play a powerful role in your work? How might you develop this capacity?

Region	Initiating Sector	Target Sector	Focus	Human Rights Issue	**RESTORATIVE**	**New Tactics in Human Rights**
Africa	Civil Society	Society	International	Torture	Strengthening Individuals and Communities	

www.newtactics.org   97

| **Welcoming Child Soldiers Back Home:** Combining traditional and Western healing techniques to reintegrate child soldiers into their former communities.

Child soldiers are victims, but often abusers as well. Some have been forced to commit horrendous crimes, sometimes against their own communities and families. This not only causes terrible psychological damage, but can make it exceedingly difficult for their families and communities to accept them back. In Mozambique, a group has used a tactic that requires a great deal of collaboration and trust among the child soldiers, the community and the traditional leaders and healers, and that supports the overall healing process by helping communities reintegrate their children back into community life.

Reconstruindo a Esperança (Rebuilding Hope), in Mozambique, combined traditional healing and Western psychology to reintegrate former child soldiers. Thousands of children were used as soldiers by both sides in Mozambique's devastating civil war. Lucrecia Wamba, a psychologist with Rebuilding Hope, states that "child soldiers lived through unimaginable horrors and they processed these experiences through the lens of the culture and belief systems of their communities. Their healing necessarily had to be processed through the same lens, in order to achieve both individual rehabilitation and community reintegration." The organization recognized that neither traditional healing methods nor individualized Western psychology alone would be sufficient to address the needs of the children or the community.

Rebuilding Hope first conducted a survey to identify communities that were facing problems with returning child soldiers and to identify community resources. Recognizing that traditional healers are often the first people community members approach when they need help, Rebuilding Hope psychologists enlisted the support of community leaders to build relationships with the healers.

In the community, psychologists examined the role traditional healing processes were playing in promoting reconciliation and reintegration and approached families to see what the children needed. At first, families were reluctant to trust the outsiders, fearing that their children would be taken from them yet again. The psychologists also went to local leaders, describing the effects of trauma and asking if they were seeing particular problems among the returning child soldiers and were able to address these problems. When leaders acknowledged that these problems were continuing, the psychologists offered to work collaboratively with the traditional healers.

Local leaders accompanied the psychologists on visits to healers to encourage cooperation. Psychologists and healers realized that their approaches could complement each other. To build trust within the community, Rebuilding Hope also needed to work with the communities to identify material priorities and gain material assistance, connecting the community to resources such as housing, education and agricultural tools.

The result was an integrated approach to healing in which healers and psychologists built a collaborative relationship, referring children to one another to achieve the best results possible.

ONLINE | Read more about this in a tactical notebook available at www.newtactics.org, under Tools for Action.

Former child soldiers present communities with complex issues that are, sadly, not unique to Mozambique. This tactic may be applicable in other communities working to reintegrate survivors of war, communities in which leaders and traditional healers can play significant roles and in which the abused and the abuser need to live together. To heal, a community must overcome the assumption that perpetrators of abuse are evil and cannot be reintegrated into society in any positive or meaningful way. Scarce resources can make it difficult to implement this tactic, particularly if community members feel that such resources would be better used to help victims rather than those who have perpetrated abuses.

" " | *We went to each healer accompanied by the first lady of the community. She was our entry into the healers' homes. She would be the first to speak, describing our desire to help. "They are doctors," she said. "They are here to help. I just brought them to you because I think they have something to offer us." The healers would then tell us what they were doing for the children and we would describe the educational processes of our own discipline, focusing on the children and the community at large. We felt we could work together. If the healer can first wash away those evil spirits, then the children can come to us and we can help to build them up as men and women.*

— Lucrecia Wamba, Rebuilding Hope, Mozambique

	RESTORATIVE	Region	Initiating Sector	Target Sector	Focus	Human Rights Issue
	Strengthening Individuals and Communities www.newtactics.org	Africa	Civil Society	Society	National	Child soldiers

Peacemaking Circles: Involving the community in determining offenders' sentences and helping to rehabilitate them.

Rarely do victims and offenders have the chance to sit together and discuss a crime in a way that allows the community both to heal and to help prevent future offenses. In communities in the United States and Canada, a tradition that has existed for centuries is being adapted to deal with contemporary justice issues.

Peacemaking circles use traditional circle ritual and structure to create a respectful space in which all interested community members — victim, victim supporters, offender, offender supporters, judge, prosecutor, defense counsel, police and court workers — can speak openly in a shared attempt to understand a crime, to identify what is needed to heal all affected parties and to prevent future occurrences. These circles are built on the tradition of talking circles, common among indigenous people of North America, in which an object called a talking piece is passed from person to person around a circle, structuring the dialogue.

Peacemaking circles are community directed processes that work in partnership with the criminal justice system. They typically involve a multi-step procedure including application by the offender to the circle process, a healing circle for the victim, a healing circle for the offender, a sentencing circle to develop consensus on the elements of a sentencing agreement and follow-up circles to monitor the progress of the offender. The sentencing plan may incorporate commitments by the system, community and family members as well as by the offender.

During circle gatherings, participants sit in a circle without tables or other furniture. Circles are facilitated by "keepers," often trained community members, who are responsible for setting a tone of respect and hope that supports and honors every participant. Participants may only speak when holding the talking piece, which is passed clockwise around the circle to provide an opportunity for every participant to speak. Because it designates who will speak and who must listen, the talking piece reduces the role of the facilitator and eliminates interruptions. It also creates space for the ideas of participants who would find it difficult to insert themselves into the usual dialogue process. Each participant is encouraged to add to the understanding of the problem and to generate possible solutions.

The process may first involve separate circles for the victim and offender in which participants determine an action plan to address issues raised in the process. By consensus the circle may develop the offender's sentence and may also stipulate responsibilities of community members and justice officials. After the circle process, regular communication and check-ins are used to assess progress and adjust agreements as conditions change.

Peacemaking circles are a way in which people from many different perspectives can come together to have difficult conversations about conflict, pain and anger while creating the space to honor the presence and dignity of every participant. In addition to supporting victims and assisting offenders in making life changes, peacemaking circles are also being used to develop plans for families in crisis, resolve conflict in schools and in the workplace and bridge gaps between cultures and generations.

Circles are not appropriate for all offenders. The connection of the offender to the community, the sincerity and nature of the offender's efforts to be healed, the input of victims and the dedication of the offender's support group primarily determine whether the case is appropriate for the circle process. Because communities vary in their health and capacity to deal constructively with differences or conflict, the formal justice system participates in community sentencing circles to protect both victims and offenders from inappropriate community responses or power imbalances.

— Kay Pranis, Circle Trainer, United States

| **Telling Stories Online:** Creating a venue on the Internet for former child soldiers to share their stories and develop new skills.

New technologies provide an opportunity to build awareness about human rights violations.

Launched in 2000, the Child Soldier Project of the International Education and Resource Network in Sierra Leone (iEarn Sierra Leone) has created a web site on which former child soldiers can share their stories. The web site, www.childsoldiers.org, features the essays, poems, artwork and voices of former child soldiers and offers an on-line forum for discussion.

iEarn Sierra Leone visits schools, hospitals and camps, airs radio announcements and publishes newspaper articles to inform former child soldiers about the project. Participants are tutored in reading and writing, basic word processing and computer skills. They also receive trauma counseling from volunteer nurses and psychiatrists.

When participants become comfortable on a computer they use the web site to share their thoughts and experiences. Galleries of former child soldiers' accounts, drawings and voices have prompted support and solidarity from people around the world. An interactive forum allows participants to discuss and debate with fellow former child soldiers and others. Participants build confidence and learn skills that make it easier for them to create a place for themselves in society. To date, over 200 former child soldiers have participated in the project.

This tactic uses the Internet to help a scattered group of victims share their stories and connect with each other, and could be used in other cases where victims of abuse are dispersed or in which targeted minorities (e.g. people with disabilities or gays and lesbians) cannot talk about their experiences as easily in their own communities. The Internet can create a safe space for these people to connect with others who will understand. It is not always possible, however, to guarantee anonymity or security of personal information on the Internet.

This tactic clearly requires an adequate technological infrastructure, but by succeeding in Sierra Leone, a war-ravaged country ranked one of the poorest in the world, iEarn has proven that this obstacle can be overcome.

How can you enable people to tell their own stories?

" " | *The children, some of whom are talented in various art forms, are able to rediscover their talents, which makes them believe that their lives can be improved. Their songs, artwork and music, as well as the enormous responses they receive from peers, become a catalyst for social justice and positive change.*

— Andrew Benson Greene, childsoldiers.org,
Sierra Leone

RESTORATIVE	Region	Initiating Sector	Target Sector	Focus	Human Rights Issue
Strengthening Individuals and Communities	Africa	Civil Society	Society	National	Child soldiers
www.newtactics.org					

Bringing Hope to Children: Organizing summer camps to offer children a reprieve from violence.

In the West Bank a group is addressing the problem of trauma among children under occupation by providing them an opportunity to connect with other children in a peaceful environment.

The Treatment and Rehabilitation Center for Victims of Torture (TRC) in Ramallah, in the West Bank, organizes a free summer camp to rehabilitate traumatized children. The camp offers recreational, artistic and rehabilitative activities intended to help children support one another and deal with their personal traumas and fears.

The Israeli military has occupied the West Bank since 1967 and ongoing violence in the region has psychologically affected the entire Palestinian population, creating a culture dominated by violence. Born into oppressive and stressful living conditions, most of the children in the West Bank have witnessed atrocities.

TRC established its summer camp to alleviate some of the hardships these children face and to provide a setting for rehabilitative care. TRC promotes the camps in nearby villages, in refugee camps and among its clients. Most of the children selected (about 60–70) suffer symptoms of anxiety, depression or loneliness because of their exposure to trauma; many have witnessed the death or torture of family members.

The summer camp meets daily for four to five hours over a period of three to four weeks. Transportation is provided to and from the camp and most often the camp is located close to where the children live. The participating children are divided into groups based on the level or kind of trauma they have suffered. Each child has a mentor to assist, listen, counsel and integrate him or her into the group of other children. Each child also has access to a psychiatrist, psychologist and social worker. The first and last three days of the summer camp are usually dedicated to projects such as drawing, artwork and sports. The rest of the days are focused on group work, such as group dynamics and counseling, play and art therapy. Medical and behavioral reports are maintained in order to evaluate the camp's impact on each child.

Based on evaluation forms filled out by parents and counselors, many children leave the camp with fewer anxiety symptoms, fewer violent behaviors and more openness and are more integrated into their communities. During the drawing projects, children are asked to draw pictures representing their environments or hopes for the future. Most often, initial drawings portray dark images or colors. Final drawings, however, show a change in attitudes and hope about the future.

The camps give the children an opportunity to step out of the violence of their day-to-day lives and explore different ways of dealing with trauma without using violence themselves. The camps also offer a release for children, a place where they can come to express themselves through play and art, while at the same time receiving rehabilitative services.

Region	Initiating Sector	Target Sector	Focus	Human Rights Issue	**RESTORATIVE**	**New Tactics in Human Rights**
Asia	Civil Society	Society	Local	Children's rights	Strengthening Individuals and Communities	

Local Ownership of History: Documenting oral testimony to create a written history to help people in isolated communities understand the full extent of the war crimes suffered in their country.

History is traditionally written by those in power. Victims of abuse — whether they are poor communities or civilians caught in the middle of a civil war — rarely have their say, even after the abuse has ended. A group in Guatemala brings isolated communities ravaged by war into the process of writing that war's history. The concrete outcome of the work was a written report, but the report's creation began a process of reconciliation at the local level and gave a voice to people who would otherwise have remained silent.

As part of the ongoing REMHI (Recovery of Historical Memory) Project, several dioceses of the Catholic Church in Guatemala mobilized their members to collect testimonies from victims of state violence. These testimonies were compiled in a report used to return that history to the affected communities and individuals.

During Guatemala's 36-year civil war, nearly 200,000 people were killed, disappeared or suffered other human rights abuses, primarily by state security forces. The REMHI Project began in 1994, one year before the 1995 Peace Accords, as an initiative of the Human Rights Office of the Archbishop of Guatemala, under the leadership of Archbishop Juan Gerardi. While a truth commission had been outlined as part of an earlier Peace Accord, it had not been established, and the church felt that the commission would be unable to meet expectations due to extreme divisions and the degree of violence suffered by the society.

REMHI therefore decided to use the structure of the church and the enormous network of people associated with it to open a space for dialogue on the violence, and to facilitate the work of a future truth commission. The church publicized the project through posters, flyers and radio spots. Each participating parish nominated two parishioners as "facilitators of reconciliation." REMHI's approach differed from other reconciliation efforts in its grassroots mobilization of individuals, especially victims of the violence, who often served as facilitators. Across the country, close to 800 facilitators collected and analyzed testimonies from 5,000–7,000 people who had suffered violence, torture or the loss of a family member. Since the violence was ongoing, the collection of testimonials was carried out at great risk to the church and its members.

Analysis of the testimonies demonstrated that state security forces were responsible for most of the human rights abuses during the war. A final report, *Guatemala: Never Again,* was released in four volumes and presented to the public on April 24, 1998. Tragically, Archbishop Gerardi was assassinated two days after the report was released; military personnel were later convicted for his death.

Despite the Archbishop's death, many of the same facilitators have continued the project. They have presented participating communities with project results, helping place individual and community experiences into a historical and national context. When translations become available in local languages, participants are given copies of a popularized version of the report, meant to be read aloud in group discussions. From the report, they learn that what happened to them was not their fault and that it happened to many throughout the country. Facilitators have also assisted communities in their reconciliation efforts, contributing to the construction of a culture of peace by promoting nonviolent methods to resolve conflict. This process has occurred in conjunction with the ongoing exhumations and reburial of victims' remains, which form an important part of the healing process in Mayan culture. REMHI has also contributed to work of the Guatemalan truth commission (the Commission for Historical Clarification), supporting witnesses and the participation of community organizations and providing testimony.

New Tactics in Human Rights

RESTORATIVE
Strengthening Individuals and Communities
www.newtactics.org

102

Region	Initiating Sector	Target Sector	Focus	Human Rights Issue
Americas	Civil Society	Society	National	Gross violations of human rights

REMHI's tactic could be used to facilitate or contribute to the work of a truth commission in other countries, or could be used in situations where no truth commission exists, or where those most affected by human rights abuses cannot participate in processes like commissions and litigation.

In Guatemala this tactic was effective largely because of the extensive institutional structure and reach of the Catholic Church. Without a pre-existing, trusted network it would be difficult to gather personal stories on this scale. Funding is also necessary; in Guatemala, financial resources were limited and work was distributed among the individual dioceses.

This tactic can be risky. Many of the human rights violators remain in positions of authority in the army and government, and the army and paramilitaries have responded with threats and even assassinations of those associated with the project.

How might people in the local communities be actively engaged in your reconciliation process?

RESTORATIVE
Strengthening
Individuals and
Communities
www.newtactics.org

New Tactics
in Human Rights

103

SEEKING REDRESS

When great wrong has been done, is it ever possible to compensate victims fairly or adequately? Can punishing abusers help heal victims' wounds or prevent future abuse? Can the courts help right a wrong? Can enough money be given to compensate for the abuses? These are difficult questions and ones that the international community is constantly trying to answer. The tactics in this section all seek to bring some form of justice after human rights abuses have occurred, whether by seeking punishment for abusers or compensation for victims or by tearing down cultural and institutional structures that grant abusers impunity.

Legal cases against serious human rights abusers — those who have committed war crimes or crimes against humanity — can be arduous affairs. They require that a constellation of factors come into perfect alignment. The appropriate national or international legal structures must exist, as well as treaties or laws; there must be evidence; there must be a way to apprehend the accused and physically bring him or her to court; often there must be extradition treaties and mechanisms in place. When these cases do occur they are extraordinary, yet there is also much to be learned from them about the value of international conventions, treaties and legal structures, and about the role of the international community in preventing and redressing wrongs.

Often these court cases are less about punishing a particular human rights abuser than about sending the message that abuse will not be tolerated and that our society is one governed by laws and justice. Action against injustices can occur completely outside legal structures. People have found many creative ways to bring abuses to light and hold perpetrators accountable for their actions.

A First in International Justice: Applying international law to dictators traveling outside their home countries.

The arrest and extradition of former Chilean dictator Augusto Pinochet is among the most extraordinary of the legal cases. It set a precedent that may be used in the future to target current and former heads of state for international justice.

The Spanish and British governments used both international and national law to determine that Chilean dictator Augusto Pinochet could be tried for human rights violations committed during his rule.

In the early years of Pinochet's 1973–1990 dictatorship, human rights activists began documenting cases of illegal detention, forcible transfer, murder, torture and disappearances carried out by Pinochet's forces. After democracy was restored in Chile, an official truth commission compiled detailed information on approximately 3,000 cases of human rights violations. Pinochet could not, however, be brought to trial in Chile, because prior to leaving office he had given constitutional protection from prosecution to himself and most of his accomplices.

Lawyers acting on behalf of the people whose human rights were violated by Pinochet's government filed criminal complaints in Spain using a procedural device called *accion popular,* or people's action, in which Spanish citizens are permitted to file private criminal actions in certain circumstances. Spanish courts allowed the case to proceed based on the principle of universal jurisdiction, which allows cases that involve torture, genocide and other crimes against humanity to be tried in Spanish courts no matter where the crime was committed and regardless of the nationality of the perpetrators and their victims.

A Spanish warrant was then issued and Pinochet was arrested by British authorities in London, where he was visiting. Pinochet and his defenders challenged the warrant, arguing that as a former head of state he enjoyed immunity from arrest and extradition. The British House of Lords, however, twice rejected this argument, ruling first that, although a former head of state enjoys immunity for acts committed in his functions as head of state, torture and crimes against humanity were not "functions" of a head of state; and second that, once Britain and Chile had ratified the 1984 United Nations Convention against Torture and Other Cruel, Inhuman or Degrading Treatments or Punishments, Pinochet could not claim immunity from charges of torture.

Pinochet was ultimately sent back to Chile for medical reasons and so was not tried in Spain. The Chilean Supreme Court stripped him of the parliamentary immunity he had granted himself and determined that he should be tried; it later ruled, however, that he was too ill to stand trial.

The Lords' ruling set an important precedent, demonstrating to the world that a head of state enjoys no immunity from prosecution on charges of torture, that such crimes can be prosecuted anywhere in the world under the principle of universal jurisdiction and that national courts can be used to force states to fulfill their obligations under international law.

The international attention also changed the political equation in Chile, which could no longer cling to national laws that had protected human rights violators, including Pinochet, from being tried for their actions. Most importantly, Pinochet's prolonged detention in London diminished the fear he engendered in the Chilean population, which began to move ahead in new ways.

Region	Initiating Sector	Target Sector	Focus	Human Rights Issue	**RESTORATIVE**	**New Tactics in Human Rights**
Europe	Government Society	Government	International	Gross violations of human rights	Seeking Redress	

Accountability for Multinationals: Using national laws to bring to justice those who perpetrate crimes against humanity in other countries.

A group in the United States uses a longstanding federal statute to allow victims of human rights abuses in other countries to bring legal cases against corporations complicit in the abuse.

The International Labor Rights Fund (ILRF) uses the Alien Tort Claims Act (ATCA) to bring legal cases against multinational corporations complicit in human rights abuses. Dating to 1789 and created to address and prevent piracy, the ATCA is a United States federal statute allowing foreign nationals to bring civil actions against U.S. citizens and corporations for violations of international law. While legal tactics have long been used to provide redress for human rights, the use of national laws for abuses taking place outside of a country represents a new opportunity for victims of human rights violations. This approach is also unique in its focus on abuses committed by multinational corporations.

Many foreign nationals do not have the option to bring cases in their own countries. ILRF's first ATCA case, for example, was brought against the energy company Unocal on behalf of Burmese refugees for the use of forced labor on an oil pipeline in Burma. If the refugees had complained in Burma, they might have faced imprisonment, torture or death, since it is against the law to provide information to foreigners about the government. The ATCA, however, allowed the foreign nationals to bring the case to the United States. For a case to be considered, there must be evidence that the corporation knowingly participated in the violation; the ILRF is working to prove this.

In addition to the case against Unocal, the ILRF has brought cases against Coca-Cola, Exxon-Mobil, Drummond and Del Monte. None of these cases has yet been concluded. The ATCA is currently being reviewed by the United States Attorney General's office, which seeks to limit the reach of the statute.

Current mechanisms in international human rights laws are not particularly effective against transnational corporations. This tactic uses available national laws to broaden the opportunities for redress for victims of the most serious human rights abuses. It also sends a message to transnational corporations that they will be held responsible for human rights violations facilitated by their business ventures, while at the same time raising awareness among the general public.

The ATCA or similar laws could be used by victims in other countries where abuse is ongoing or where there is no opportunity for legal recourse. The ATCA itself, however, is interpreted narrowly to apply only to the most serious human rights abuses — genocide, war crimes, crimes against humanity, slavery, extrajudicial killing, torture and unlawful detention.

What universal jurisdiction laws exist in your country that could be used to hold entities accountable for violations?

New Tactics in Human Rights	**RESTORATIVE**	Region	Initiating Sector	Target Sector	Focus	Human Rights Issue
	Seeking Redress	Americas	Civil Society	Business	International	Gross violations of human rights

106   www.newtactics.org

Testing for Violations: Testing for discrimination.

When abuses are hidden, or accepted by members of society, it can be difficult for victims to prove that a human rights violation has taken place. A group in Hungary uses a testing method to provide evidence of discrimination and bring legal cases on behalf of victims.

Adapting a method used by United States organizations on housing discrimination, the Legal Defense Bureau for National and Ethnic Minorities (NEKI) uses a method of testing to collect evidence when there is an allegation of discrimination. The Hungarian court first recognized testing as a valid technique for documenting discrimination in a case in 2000.

The Roma form minority groups in several countries in Europe. They have been frequent targets of hate crimes and are often blamed for the increase of crime and unemployment in Hungary. Forms of discrimination faced by the Roma today include the inability to receive employment, housing and services in public accommodations. Since discrimination is often subtly carried out, direct evidence is rare.

NEKI uses testing to prove discrimination and obtain this direct evidence. The group identifies and trains people who are sent out as testers to replicate the actions of those who claim to have experienced discrimination. Each tester must be a reliable and objective observer and his or her profile must match that of the person who experienced discrimination as much as possible. In selecting testers, NEKI also evaluates whether each individual would make a credible witness during legal cases. Since litigation may last several years, testers must also be willing to stay in contact with the program for an extended period of time.

When NEKI receives a complaint, staff members assess the case and, if they decide to pursue it, send testers to the alleged place of discrimination. If the allegation concerns employment, for example, testing involves sending out a Roma and a non-Roma person with similar characteristics and qualifications, with ethnicity being their only major difference. They are sent out at closely spaced intervals on the same day to apply for a job and the testers take comparable actions in order to make the comparisons clear.

Testers record their experiences on assignment forms immediately after the test, detailing questions asked at the interview, treatment of the applicant and the manner in which the job was described, e.g. salaries and benefits. The test coordinator (the organization or the attorney) then evaluates whether or not differential treatment has taken place. This information is often used to support victims in legal cases.

As of 2002, NEKI had used the testing tactic fifteen times. In three cases, it was not possible to complete the test. Of the twelve completed tests, five did not produce evidence of systematic discrimination. The remaining seven tests, however, were convincing demonstrations of discrimination and sufficient to justify legal action.

Read more about this in a tactical notebook available at www.newtactics.org, under Tools for Action.

ONLINE

Adapted from work by U.S. organizations, the tactic is clearly a flexible one and other groups in the region have approached NEKI to learn about replicating their methods for human rights issues such as disability rights. Testing could also be used to look at the hiring practices of a range of institutions, including police departments or businesses.

Region	Initiating Sector	Target Sector	Focus	Human Rights Issue	RESTORATIVE	New Tactics in Human Rights
Europe	Civil Society	Government	National	Minority rights	Seeking Redress	

Demanding Compensation: Convincing the government to compensate victims of abuse by police, military and armed forces personnel.

In India, the National Human Rights Commission investigates complaints of human rights abuses and recommends that local governments provide compensation to victims.

The National Human Rights Commission in India responds to verified complaints of police abuse by requesting that the government provide financial compensation to victims and issue appropriate penalties to perpetrators.

Established as part of the Protection of Human Rights Act (1993), the Commission has the power to investigate and recommend responses to human rights violations by public servants — including abetting or neglecting to prevent violations. The majority of the complaints it receives are against the police, although the Commission has also recommended compensation for victims of abuse by military and armed forces personnel.

Complaints of abuse are received from activists and media sources as well as from victims or their relatives. Common complaints include physical abuse, harassment of individuals or families, failure to follow procedures concerning treatment of women, neglect while in detention, illegal detention and torture. The Commission also receives complaints related to child labor, bonded labor and violations of the rights of vulnerable members of society, such as children, women, the disabled, certain castes and tribes, refugees, minorities and others.

When a complaint is received, the Commission calls for an enquiry report or directs its investigative division to look into the case. If the case is verified, the Commission files a report with the government of the state in which the violation occurred. The report includes recommendations for financial compensation to victims and for disciplinary action against the perpetrators. The state involved is free to recover the amount of compensation from the public servant who committed the violations.

The Commission publishes details of important cases in its monthly newsletter, *Human Rights,* and in its annual reports. The media also covers big cases.

Compensation packages help victims and their families rebuild their lives only if the rewards are substantial; in addition, care must be taken to ensure that this tactic does not deflect attention from other reforms. Despite these difficulties, however, the work of these commissions does have the benefit of making officials aware of the consequences of their actions, and thereby possible deterring future abuse.

Creating a commission like this requires substantial support from governing officials and community outreach and or publicity campaigns are necessary to ensure that victims and their families know they can use this recourse without fear of retribution.

How can you begin to hold government agencies and infrastructures accountable and convince them to support your cause?

New Tactics in Human Rights	RESTORATIVE	Region	Initiating Sector	Target Sector	Focus	Human Rights Issue
	Seeking Redress	Asia	Government	Government	National	Police and military abuses

Mobilizing Against Impunity: Raising public awareness of impunity through a referendum or petition drive.

Sometimes legislative and government tools exist but the public is unaware of them or does not know how to put them to use. A group in Uruguay organized a remarkable public effort aimed at preventing abusers in the Uruguayan military from being granted immunity from prosecution.

Using a constitutional provision that had never been invoked, Comisión Nacional Pro-Referéndum (CNR) organized a referendum in Uruguay, so that the public could vote on the congressional decision to grant impunity to human rights abusers employed by the military. In order to petition the government to hold a popular referendum, CNR needed, within one year of the impunity law's passage, to collect the signatures of 25 percent of citizens who were qualified to vote.

Gathering one quarter of the population's signatures required tremendous organization as well as extensive volunteer involvement, most of which came from women's movements. Organizing the participants posed a significant challenge. For example, during a day-long national campaign to gather signatures, organizers coordinated the efforts of 9,000 *brigadistas*, or volunteer signature collectors. In this massive undertaking, they used computers and spreadsheets to tabulate the signatures.

After the signatures were collected and submitted to the government, CNR publicly defended their validity before the electoral review committee. Throughout the process of collecting and submitting the signatures, CNR used grassroots organizing to combat heavy governmental and media opposition. It distributed leaflets, hung banners and posters, and held rallies, music festivals and bike marathons.

Although the referendum was narrowly defeated, CNR's work created a new tool with which to shape Uruguayan democracy. One in three Uruguayans was visited personally by brigadistas during the campaign and eight more popular referendums have since been attempted. The brigadistas and leaders at CNR have continued to play a role in politics.

The CNR did not achieve its ultimate goal of overturning the law granting impunity, but it did mobilize civil society in Uruguay in an unprecedented way and made impunity a national issue. The brigadistas' visits made an extraordinary number of people aware of the law first-hand and many more became aware of the issue through media coverage.

Legal provisions like the little-used referendum power in Uruguay are not available in every country. Signatures can still be collected on petitions, however, as an avenue of public awareness and a declaration to the government that the public is dissatisfied with government policies.

Region	Initiating Sector	Target Sector	Focus	Human Rights Issue	**RESTORATIVE**	**New Tactics in Human Rights**
Americas	Civil Society	Government Society	National	Gross violations of human rights	Seeking Redress	

Taking Responsibility for the Past: Mobilizing public resources for a socially marginalized group.

Identifying and, when possible, punishing abusers is only part of the equation. In seeking to redress human rights abuses, some groups seek compensation for victims, often in the form of treatment, financial compensation or the return of confiscated property.

To be successful, groups must often force the current government to acknowledge its part in the abuse, and to take responsibility for compensating victims or helping them obtain treatment.

The ICAR Foundation in Romania pressured the government to help provide, first, the physical premises for torture treatment centers and, second, the rights to free medicine and to insurance coverage for the specialized care and services required by torture survivors.

ICAR's tactic is part of a strategy to convince the government to take responsibility for the nation's past in order to build a better future. Many of the torturers from communist-era Romania escaped with impunity and some now occupy influential positions in society. Victims face a society in which substantial forces would prefer to forget the past — and its victims — rather than learn from that past in order to build a deeper civil commitment to democracy and human rights.

ICAR first sought to gain the trust of victims, working with the Romanian Association of Former Political Prisoners, then identified the group's unmet needs, including access to appropriate medical care and financial and legislative support. To meet these needs, ICAR targeted, among others, civil servants, medical professionals and officials at city, municipal and state agencies, such as the Ministry of Health, to provide professional services. ICAR also created alliances with other small civil society organizations, the media and the International Rehabilitation Council for Torture Victims (IRCT) in Denmark.

It took ten years, but ICAR convinced Romania's government to acknowledge its responsibility to those who had suffered at the hands of the former regime.

ONLINE | Read more about this in a tactical notebook available at www.newtactics.org, under Tools for Action.

ICAR's success was hard-won, and depended in large part on the political transition Romania was undergoing at that time. ICAR recognized, and used its connections to take advantage of, this political opening. New laws and the newly open society also allowed victims to organize without fear of reprisals. ICAR's tactic served the dual purpose of compensating victims and ending government impunity.

How might you begin to engage government to invest resources in providing services to victims?

New Tactics in Human Rights

RESTORATIVE	Region	Initiating Sector	Target Sector	Focus	Human Rights Issue
Seeking Redress	Europe	Civil Society	Government	National	Torture

110   www.newtactics.org

Unmasking Abusers: Publicly exposing abusers through targeted demonstrations.

When perpetrators of abuse are granted impunity, whether by law or de facto, they may go on to lead relatively anonymous lives — sometimes in the same communities as their victims. A group in Argentina decided that, even if perpetrators cannot be prosecuted through the courts, they can be revealed — or "unmasked" — to the general public.

Hijos por la Identidad y la Justicia contra el Olvido y el Silencio (Children for Identity and Justice Against Forgetfulness and Silence, or H.I.J.O.S) organizes targeted demonstrations in front of the homes of people who have been identified as perpetrators of human rights abuses. These demonstrations, called *escraches* ("unmaskings"), publicly expose the abusers and allow communities to express their moral condemnation.

H.I.J.O.S., whose members are mostly children of the disappeared, starts by identifying an individual who carried out repression under the military government in Argentina (1976–1983). Then the *pre-escrache* begins. They talk to local unions, libraries and other social organizations that work in the neighborhood where the perpetrator lives. They hand out pamphlets and organize informal lectures in the neighborhood and in the schools. The purpose of the pre-escrache is to involve the community, whose participation is essential to the success of the tactic. On the day of the escrache, protestors gather at a square or other public place near the target's home, giving speeches condemning the individual and describing his or her crimes. They post pamphlets on walls with the person's photo, name, address, telephone number and biography. A variety of other actions may be taken when appropriate. A variant of the escrache is the *escrache-movil*, a mobile demonstration that targets more than one perpetrator, generally in a single neighborhood.

H.I.J.O.S. has legal representation to assist in solving any problems that might arise with the police or with counter-demonstrators, but the key to accomplishing its objective without conflict is to involve as many people as possible in the demonstrations.

After the escrache has finished, the effectiveness of the tactic remains in the hands of the target's neighbors. Sometimes the response is staggering. There are examples of shops closing or bars becoming empty when an abuser enters. Some abusers who have been targeted have had to move from their own homes because of the social rejection.

Even though amnesty laws have made it difficult to prosecute some perpetrators, H.I.J.O.S. bypasses political and legal systems to encourage a kind of social ostracism, while making use of humor, theater and other creative demonstrations.

This tactic has some serious risks. People adapting this tactic must be certain that they are targeting the right people and that the demonstrations are not used for other political purposes. Organizers of large demonstrations around emotional subjects must have mechanisms in place to prevent the events from degenerating into violence. In some situations, actions like this might turn people in the community against the protestors, as they may not want a disturbance like this in their neighborhood.

How might you use the power of an entire community to condemn an abuse or an abuser?

Region	Initiating Sector	Target Sector	Focus	Human Rights Issue	RESTORATIVE	New Tactics in Human Rights
Americas	Civil Society	Society	Local	Gross violations of human rights	Seeking Redress	

| **Rebuilding a Neighborhood:** Mapping personal histories and mobilizing memory to reclaim a place in history and recover lost land.

Oppressive regimes have often forced people from their homes, dislocated whole communities and confiscated land and property. Colonial powers as well as new societies have encroached on native land. Returning this property to its former owners can be a challenge and requires that property boundaries be positively identified and delimited. The District Six Museum in South Africa meets this challenge in an innovative way.

The District Six Museum in South Africa spearheaded a land claim in which people ultimately recovered both the property and dignity they had lost under apartheid. It continues to be a space where people can collect, disseminate and exchange memories of the neighborhood and is also actively involved in promoting civic dialogue about humane cities in South Africa.

In 1966, as a result of the Group Areas Act, the racially integrated neighborhood of District Six in Cape Town was razed to the ground to make way for a new "whites only" development, but construction never took place. The only buildings left were houses of worship.

As part of a campaign to defend the land and community integrity, a group of former residents built an exhibition with a map of the old area as the central installation. They covered the floor of a Methodist church with a detailed map of their destroyed neighborhood, and invited their neighbors to place their homes, streets, stores and community spaces on it.

This memory-mapping project became the foundation for land reclamation claims. The museum organized and hosted one of the Land Courts, where people could establish formal claims to land they or their families owned. Former residents sat in chairs directly on the map of their old neighborhood, as the court granted them, in the words of one, "our land back, our homes back, our dignity back." Since then, the museum has developed exhibitions on the histories of smaller neighboring communities destroyed under the Group Areas Act, including Kirstenboch and Two Rivers, to publicize and support their unresolved land claims.

The District Six Museum seeks to provide a sustained process of personal healing and reconciliation, as well as to promote a lasting democratic and human rights culture in the neighborhood. Its programs keep the memory of forced removals alive and pass it on to new generations. The public memory of the past in turn strengthens efforts to prevent segregation, displacement and other abuses of democracy in the future.

In coming years, former residents of District Six will begin returning to the neighborhood to reclaim their land and rebuild. The International Coalition of Historical Sites of Conscience, of which District Six Museum is a member, can suggest creative ways to use history and the sites where that history was lived to address present day human rights issues and challenges.

New Tactics in Human Rights

RESTORATIVE	Region	Initiating Sector	Target Sector	Focus	Human Rights Issue
Seeking Redress	Multiple	Civil Society	Government Society	Local	General human rights Displaced populations

112   www.newtactics.org

Ripples in the Pond

Redress is possible long after abuses have taken place. Native communities in the United States and other countries have worked for decades to regain control of their native land through the courts and legislative bodies. The White Earth Land Recovery Project in the U.S. state of Minnesota decided to restore the land and heritage of the Anishinaabe people in another way — by buying it. **Winona LaDuke** of the White Earth Land Recovery Project talks about strategic thinking, tactical flexibility and building alliances.

When we first started to try to get our land back, we struggled through every legal mechanism possible. We went to the courts but the courts ruled against us. We went to Congress, but we got a bad deal from Congress. I testified at the UN. We tried all those mechanisms and then we decided that we should try to figure out a better way to get back our land.

So we started a land trust. We buy land from willing sellers and people have started to donate land to us as well. We have about 1,700 acres now. We grow some old corn varieties, some raspberries and strawberries. We have a big maple syrup producing operation as well.

I think of my work as organizing by example. I've been an organizer for 25 years and I've learned that we not only have to fight what is wrong, we have to illustrate what is right. People have become accustomed to what is wrong. Even in our own Native American community we have become accustomed to being treated like second-class citizens. And we have become accustomed to thinking that we cannot get back our land, we cannot control our own economy.

So we've been changing this attitude piece by piece and getting our land back. Let's say you've got a Native American cemetery somewhere that somebody is running their cows over. So you go talk to the farmer and you figure out how to get that cemetery fenced off. It's a micro approach, not a macro approach. Think of it like tiny pebbles that make big ripples in the pond.

At the same time that you're dealing with the smaller issues, you have to have your eyes open to the larger issues. You have to be very attuned to what's happening politically. And, sometimes, to meet the needs of your community you may need to build alliances with people you never thought you'd be working with.

Those of us working in indigenous rights issues in the United States have been at this a long time. We have a lot of experience with national policy analysis and we've built strategic alliances not only with other native peoples but also with environmentalists and health care providers. Right now we're trying to build an alliance around organic food issues. We're fortunate to have the experience we do, but it doesn't mean we're winning. It just means that we are cognizant of our situation.

Region	Initiating Sector	Target Sector	Focus	Human Rights Issue	**RESTORATIVE**	**New Tactics in Human Rights**
Americas	Civil Society	Society	Local	Indigenous rights	Seeking Redress	

www.newtactics.org 113

BUILDING HUMAN RIGHTS CULTURES AND INSTITUTIONS

Every society defines human rights a little bit differently, shaped by its own traditions, culture and economic realities. But every society, no matter what its values, needs a common place where individuals, government agencies, civic institutions and people and groups of all sorts can come together to share responsibility for the collective well-being and to lay down the rules for acceptable behavior and conditions.

We can call this civil society, we can call it the public domain. This is the place where we have the opportunity to build cultures and institutions that respect human rights. In some countries — primarily in the West — this common space is strong, but even there it is not entirely safe from abuse. In other parts of the world, it exists but is not yet a permanent part of people's daily lives. In certain societies that public space is very weak; it is over-regulated by the state, squeezing out individuals who then retreat and hide in their own private lives, rather than getting involved. Without this civil society, without this public space, there is no civic activity and human rights become an arbitrary affair.

But as you will see in this chapter, more and more people are getting involved and working to advance and protect human rights locally, nationally and internationally. They are using new tactics to strengthen that public space and build strong human rights cultures. Some of them are starting small — in their own schools or village governments or focused on a single issue — but when people can successfully achieve modest aims they then have the spirit to dare to do something bigger, something better. And this is where new tactics can play a crucial role, giving people the tools they need to go that extra step.

— Murat Belge
President
Helsinki Citizens' Assembly
Istanbul, Turkey

Human rights advocates come in many forms. Whether they are working to alleviate hunger, to clean up the environment or to clean up politics; whether their focus is on children, women or minorities, the common thread is that all are working to build a world in which all human beings live in dignity and security.

The international agreements, conventions and treaties signed in the past few decades are a positive step, but they alone are not enough. Individuals and communities need to understand the rights codified in those agreements — the rights, for example, to equal protection before the law, freedom of movement or freedom from torture — and how to claim them.

Other tactics in this workbook focus on abuses that are imminent or ongoing, or on repairing the damage of past abuses. The tactics in this section are, for the most part, longer-term approaches, ones that strengthen the human rights culture and respect for human rights. They do this by getting new people and groups involved in human rights work, which not only increases what we are able to accomplish, but adds legitimacy to the movement. They do this by getting the right people and groups together, people who, as allies, can do more than the sum of their work as individuals. They do this by giving people the skills they need to do their work. And, finally, they do this by creating a broad awareness of the existence of these rights and their violations and persuading people to recognize abuse and define it as unacceptable in a civilized world.

Some of these tactics address a particular problem or focus on a particular right, but many have a broader goal: building the groundwork, institutions, alliances, awareness and attitudes that make possible the protection of all human rights.

The tactics in this chapter are divided into four sections:

1 Constituency-building tactics involve new groups in human rights advocacy.
2 Collaboration tactics are used to develop new and effective partnerships for change.
3 Capacity-building tactics create institutions and training systems to promote human rights.
4 Awareness and understanding tactics educate about human rights.

BUILDING CONSTITUENCIES

Human rights messages are often directed at people already familiar with the issues, people who have already expressed interest and support. Reaching out to new people and involving them in human rights work strengthens the potential for more effective action. It brings in fresh energy, fresh ideas, fresh resources and fresh contacts. The more diverse the group of people acting as advocates on a particular issue, the better able it will be to adapt to changes and the more difficult it becomes for abusers to defend their actions. A diverse and active constituency creates a far more resilient human rights movement.

The tactics in this section all build new constituencies for human rights issues. They reach out to individuals and groups who may never have had the chance to become involved in these issues — young people or local legislators, for example — or to those with particular authority in a community, such as religious leaders, who have great power to influence and engage others.

New Tactics
in Human Rights

**BUILDING HUMAN
RIGHTS CULTURES**
Building Constituencies

118   www.newtactics.org

Youth Against Fascism and Racism: Using popular culture to engage young people in human rights reporting.

TACTIC

Discussion groups, forums and workshops are all common tools for raising awareness of an issue and getting new people involved, but these tactics may not be dynamic enough to catch the attention of certain target groups — namely, young people. An organization in Poland has zeroed in on two effective ways to reach young people and hold their attention: music and sports.

Nigdy Wiecej (Never Again) is using pop culture to build an anti-racist youth network in Poland. At rock concerts and soccer matches the group reaches out to large numbers of young people and makes them aware of the problem. It then recruits some to join a network of correspondents who monitor and report on the activities of neo-fascist and racist groups in their hometowns.

As part of its rock campaign Music Against Racism, Nigdy Wiecej organizes concerts and publishes compilation CDs featuring well-known Polish and foreign rock bands. At the concerts and inside the cases of the CDs, Nigdy Wiecej educates the audience about the seriousness of the problem of racism in Poland and calls on audience members to become active agents of social change.

Poland's soccer stadiums had been almost completely dominated by a xenophobic subculture before Nigdy Wiecej started its Let's Kick Racism Out of the Stadiums campaign. As part of the campaign, the group publishes *Stadion,* an anti-racist magazine for soccer fans, has released a CD, organizes amateur soccer tournaments and provides banners and leaflets used during games to show their presence to other local anti-racist groups.

Through these youth-focused campaigns, Nigdy Wiecej has recruited a network of 150 voluntary correspondents who are required to report monthly on racist and xenophobic activity in their commuities. Nigdy Wiecej collects these reports, publishes them in its own monthly magazine and distributes them to the Polish and international press. The network and the publication help raise awareness of the problem of racism among a much larger cross-section of Polish society, well beyond young soccer and rock fans.

Read more about this in a tactical notebook available at www.newtactics.org, under Tools for Action.

ONLINE

Nigdy Wiecej uses pop culture to get young people — a sympathetic, but otherwise often uninvolved constituency — involved in human rights work, but it doesn't stop at concerts and sports. Once people have expressed interest and a commitment to volunteering, the organization ensures that they have the chance to get more involved. Adaptations of this tactic could be used to overcome widespread apathy in a variety of situations, but the issue itself is important: it must be something young people can feel connected to, something that could potentially touch their own lives.

> *The very existence of social problems such as racism and xenophobia is often denied by the authorities and the mainstream mass media in Poland, as it is in other Central and Eastern European countries.*
>
> — Rafal Pankowski, Nigdy Wiecej, Poland

" "

Region	Initiating Sector	Target Sector	Focus	Human Rights Issue	**BUILDING HUMAN RIGHTS CULTURES**	New Tactics in Human Rights
Europe	Civil Society	Society	National	Minority rights	Building Constituencies	

Making Human Rights a Local Issue: Passing international treaties at the local level to impact public policy and promote human rights standards.

Local legislators constitute a potentially powerful constituency that is rarely involved in human rights struggles. In some countries local officials are not accustomed to thinking of their work in terms of human rights; their day-to-day work centers around zoning decisions, permits and budgets. The Women's Institute for Leadership and Development (WILD for Human Rights) works with local government to help officials see the role they could play in shaping policies that protect human rights. They also engage local communities, the constituencies to which these legislators are accountable.

The Women's Institute for Leadership Development for Human Rights (WILD) has used the United Nations Convention to End Discrimination Against Women (CEDAW) to advocate for human rights at the local level.

In 1996, WILD for Human Rights began advocating for San Francisco to become the first U.S. city to pass a law promoting the principles of CEDAW. Discussing human rights standards in relation to discrimination and to setting up measurable community-based outcomes, WILD for Human Rights worked with government officials, public citizens and advocacy groups focused on domestic violence, poverty and health issues.

WILD for Human Rights held a public hearing at which community members were encouraged to record personal testimony relating to the rights of women and girls and to their pledges to uphold the principles of the Convention. Through this hearing, the group hoped to give community members and city officials a leadership role in the process, helping them feel personally committed to seeing the Convention's principles upheld throughout the city.

Testimony on the relevance of CEDAW in the lives of local women was presented to government officials at a public hearing in the fall of 1997. In April 1998 the city passed an ordinance requiring city departments to review budgets, employment policies and the delivery of services within the context of gender and human rights and allocating funds to help the departments put the ordinance into practice. The ordinance entered a new phase in 2003.

In response to the ordinance, the San Francisco city government has examined the Departments of Public Works, Juvenile and Adult Probation, and the Environment, as well as the Rent Board and the Arts Commission. And city departments have made a number of changes, creating, for example, nontraditional jobs for women in city government, and adding more streetlights in unsafe neighborhoods.

WILD for Human Rights is now extending its reach, and advising organizations in cities across the United States on how those cities might adopt the principles of CEDAW, as well as those of the Convention on the Elimination of All Forms of Racial Discrimination (CERD).

The people who testified at the public meetings may never have seen their experiences in terms of human rights, just as the local officials in San Francisco may never have considered their work in terms of fulfilling human rights obligations. But WILD for Human Rights helped them to put their work and their experience into that framework and drew them into the human rights movement.

This tactic could help change a national mindset, bit by bit, and eventually lead to the implementation and monitoring of human rights standards. Other groups working on a wide variety of issues may also decide that finding supporters and building constituencies on the local level can help them make more significant changes both locally and globally.

New Tactics in Human Rights	BUILDING HUMAN RIGHTS CULTURES	Region	Initiating Sector	Target Sector	Focus	Human Rights Issue
	Building Constituencies	Americas	Civil Society	Government	Local	Women's rights

120   www.newtactics.org

Fighting Social Stigmas: Involving religious leaders in modeling behavior toward stigmatized populations.

In many communities religious leaders hold positions of great respect and influence; people look to them for cues on how to behave and what moral standards to uphold. Here, Tibetan Buddhist monks and nuns fight the stigma of HIV/AIDS by modeling behavior toward sufferers who might otherwise be entirely ostracized.

The Sangha Metta project trains Buddhist monks, nuns and novices to provide practical and spiritual assistance to people with HIV/AIDS and to fight the myths, misconceptions and stigma surrounding the disease. The program now exists in Thailand, Cambodia, Laos, Burma, Bhutan, Vietnam, China and Mongolia and receives aid from the United Nations Children's Fund (UNICEF), AusAID, the Open Society Institute and the Burma Project.

While HIV/AIDS has become epidemic in the Asia Pacific region a lack of understanding about the disease's transmission persists, as does discrimination against those infected.

Centered on the moral and religious teachings of Buddhism, the Sangha Metta project was started in 1997 by monks in Thailand and has been a source of inspiration, training and technical assistance for Buddhist mobilization around AIDS. Sangha Metta arranges seminars, workshops and visits to AIDS hospices for Buddhist leaders, as well as leaders of other religions. In three- to five-day trainings, participants learn about prevention education, awareness-raising, social management skills and tools to encourage tolerance and compassion. Together they assess the problems in their communities and possible steps for combating them.

The Buddhist leaders then model behavior towards affected community members, eating, for example, food prepared and offered by people with HIV/AIDS. This simple, symbolic act has a powerful impact on community members by confronting their fears of transmission. The monks also guide meditation for people with HIV/AIDS, visit them in their homes, educate young people about the disease and care for children orphaned by it.

The monks and nuns working with Sangha Metta are helping to convince members of their communities to promote and respect human rights by modeling behavior — acceptance and tolerance for a group of people who had traditionally been outcasts. Temples in Asia are the spiritual heart of the villages and villagers see monks and nuns as respected teachers, confidants and examples of the purist way to live a Buddhist life. People are accustomed to seeing them as models for behavior. While it may not be as explicit in other religions or cultures, many people look to their religious leaders for guidance on how they should act. These leaders have the power to involve new people in promoting human rights.

Sangha Metta has now crossed religious barriers and is conducting workshops and trainings for leaders of the Christian, Hindu and Islamic faiths as well.

How can you mobilize respected leaders in your community?

I spoke to monks about what their role could be in regards to HIV/AIDS. I asked for their ideas and studied Buddhist scriptures with them. They came to the conclusion that HIV/AIDS was not simply a health issue but also a socioeconomic one. As traditional and religious leaders in their communities, the monks saw their role as strengthening their communities and playing an active role in combating HIV/AIDS.

" "

— **Laurie Maund, Sangha Metta, Thailand**

Region	Initiating Sector	Target Sector	Focus	Human Rights Issue	**BUILDING HUMAN RIGHTS CULTURES**	New Tactics in Human Rights
Asia	Civil Society	Civil Society	International	HIV/AIDS	Building Constituencies	

Going Door-to-Door to Find Allies: Using a nomination campaign to identify new potential allies for human rights.

Domestic violence is an issue that affects the lives of men, women and children, yet it is often seen solely as a woman's issue. A group in South Africa uses a unique tactic to get men involved in curbing domestic violence.

The Everyday Hero Campaign of the 5-in-6 Project in South Africa asks women to identify men with a positive attitude toward women and then invites these men to become new advocates for women's rights.

The rate of violence against women in South Africa is the highest in the world among all countries not at war. Research shows that one man in six here abuses the women in his life. The 5-in-6 Project targets the other five men, those who do not abuse women. The project has developed the Everyday Hero campaign to find these men and involve them in the struggle. Volunteers go house to house to ask women for information about the good, positive men who live there. With nominations also sent by mail, more than 50,000 responses have identified the "best" fathers, uncles, brothers, grandfathers and male friends in the country. The names and recommendation forms decorate local churches, spreading awareness of the campaign and increasing its popularity.

Volunteers from this list of names are invited to meetings discussing "community problems," and involving men of various ages, experiences, social classes and financial situations. Meetings focus on developing collaborative, nonviolent solutions to the problem of violence against women. Additional workshops help men understand the power relations between genders, build self-esteem and find positive ways to deal with difficult domestic situations. Many participants have noticed dramatic changes in their level of consciousness about domestic violence, and in their ability to engage other men on the issue. For many, it is the first time they have ever spoken out on these issues and the result has been powerful.

By recognizing and honoring local male role models, the 5-in-6 project is able to connect with a cross-section of positive male role models in the community, engaging them to discuss and identify solutions to domestic violence and to see that it is an underlying part of the other problems faced in their communities.

This nomination campaign helps identify "potential allies"—people who care about a particular issue but are not actively involved in it. They may be uninvolved because they don't see it affecting them or simply because they have never had the opportunity to do so or because society has traditionally distanced them from the issue.

Once the 5-in-6 Project identifies these passive allies, it helps some of them become active allies and the effect grows: these active allies, given the necessary tools and information, talk to other men, creating more allies for women's rights.

Who are your passive allies?
What tactics can you use to gain
their support and involvement?

New Tactics in Human Rights	BUILDING HUMAN RIGHTS CULTURES	Region	Initiating Sector	Target Sector	Focus	Human Rights Issue
	Building Constituencies	Africa	Civil Society	Society	Local	Women's rights

122   www.newtactics.org

Building Networks Through Text-Messaging: Using text-messaging to build constituencies for human rights action.

Modern technology can be used to create awareness about human rights and recruit large numbers of people, specifically youth, to be involved in human rights campaigns.

Amnesty International-the Netherlands uses text-messaging technology to attract new members — especially young people — to the organization, build awareness of its Campaign Against Torture and encourage people to respond quickly to urgent action appeals. More than 500 new members have joined as a direct result of the text-messaging recruitment and over 5,000 more have responded to urgent action appeals sent through text messaging.

The tactic was developed in 2001, within the framework of Amnesty International's Campaign Against Torture. When immediate action was required to protect someone from torture, the Dutch section of Amnesty International sent a text-message to the mobile phones of thousands of participants. These participants, who had signed up for a voluntary and free subscription to the SMS (text-messaging) campaign network, responded to the appeal, and within hours, Amnesty had collected thousands of protest "signatures" against a case or threat of torture. The organization then forwarded these protests by fax or e-mail to the authorities.

With a Tunisian man who had been both subject and beneficiary of an Urgent Action, AI-Netherlands introduced the technique on the most popular Saturday night television program, reaching 2.5 million people. Viewers learned that an Urgent Action is summarized in just 160 characters in the text-message. To respond, people need only respond with a 'JA' (Yes) to text-message number "4777." One minute later, participants receive another text-message to thank them and to tell them how many people have already sent a protest, and a later text-message informs them of the campaign's result, such as the release of the person from custody.

Although Amnesty International rarely claims direct responsibility for improvements in the situation of people featured in Urgent Action cases, about one-third of the cases have had successful outcomes: death sentences have been commuted, "disappeared" people have reappeared and the whereabouts of detained persons have been announced. The chances of torture have therefore been reduced, and the likelihood of seriously ill prisoners receiving medical attention has improved.

In addition, the campaign has convinced many — perhaps even thousands — of young people to join Amnesty's Urgent Action network.

All Amnesty campaigns direct a focused response to a place in the world where someone needs help, using simple actions in which large numbers of people can participate, and through which they feel they are making a difference. The campaigns also educate the public and build a global consciousness about human rights abuses such as torture. The text-messaging campaign generated a faster response to help the victim, while at the same time expanding Amnesty's educational impact into a new constituency.

The text-message campaign attracted new younger members into Amnesty in a way that other outreach and activities had not been able to do. Young people are the most frequent and numerous cell phone users, and it is the youth that Amnesty wants to reach. By using this popular tool of youth culture, Amnesty draws in new young activists who will add to its campaigning power for a long time to come.

Region	Initiating Sector	Target Sector	Focus	Human Rights Issue	BUILDING HUMAN RIGHTS CULTURES	New Tactics in Human Rights
Europe	Civil Society	Society	National	Civil and political rights	Building Constituencies	

Transforming the Police Force: Teaching police officers about their role in defending human rights.

A Brazilian group uses a comprehensive training approach to persuade police officers to transform their relationships with the communities in which they work.

The Centro de Assessoramento a Programas de Educação para a Cidadania (CAPEC, or the Center for Advising Citizenship Education Programs) provides training to police officers in Brazil to help them understand the vital role they can play as defenders of human rights. The training, which includes a wide variety of courses, emphasizes the human rights of all citizens, including the police officers themselves. The role of police is transformed through this process, leading to improved relationships with the community and greater civic engagement.

Police brutality and torture are widespread in Brazil. Compounding this problem, police officers are poorly paid and corruption is considered rampant. CAPEC's goal is to create "interactive security," in which public security efforts are planned and organized together with community members and in which responsibilities are shared, resulting in policing that effectively responds to the needs of citizens.

The training courses are carried out in three two-day modules over six months. So that its message reaches as many people as possible, CAPEC asks police departments to recommend officers who can share their training experience with others when they return to work. Community members participate in the courses with the officers.

CAPEC's trainings focus on showing law enforcement officers how important their role is in society and how their work affects the lives of individuals and communities. Officers explore what they believe and feel and how they relate with other human beings. They also learn about the many advantages of interactive security, including more effective policing and safer conditions for officers.

Trainers use many stories, metaphors and examples taken from the experiences of the students and focus on educating rather than judging behavior. In this dialogue, officers feel appreciated while learning how they can improve human rights in the community.

CAPEC's training has so far been used in 25 states in Brazil and with more than 30,000 participants, mainly from the civil police, military police, federal police, traffic police and municipal guards. CAPEC has worked with the federal government, state and city governments.

CAPEC's tactic is especially interesting because it involves a group that has been responsible for committing or allowing abuse and transforms them into advocates for human rights. This approach not only contributes to a stronger human rights culture in Brazil, it also directly reduces ongoing abuses by creating a favorable environment in which the police and community are looking for joint solutions to the problems they face.

" "

In interacting with their communities, officers can become educators, especially for those young people and children who have few heroes or good role models.

One episode in a neighborhood in the city of Macapá is particularly touching. This neighborhood was considered very dangerous because of the youth gangs that tormented the local population. When interactive policing was instituted in that neighborhood, a captain of the military police was assigned to the area. He found out who was the leader of the main gang and sent messages to invite him to come to speak with him. Finally the teen came and the officer began establishing a bond, as a caring adult and also as an educator and excellent role model.

It is possible that this boy had never had a similar role model before in his life. Today that teen is an ally to the police and through his leadership, many more also help the police. The neighborhood has become calmer and safer. This officer understood the importance of his job as educator and promoter of peace and by getting closer to the community where he worked he was able to have an impact.

— Rosa Almeida, CAPEC, Brazil

New Tactics in Human Rights	BUILDING HUMAN RIGHTS CULTURES	Region	Initiating Sector	Target Sector	Focus	Human Rights Issue
	Building Constituencies	Americas	Civil Society	Government Society	National International	Police and military abuses

**BUILDING HUMAN
RIGHTS CULTURES**
Building Constituencies

New Tactics
in Human Rights

www.newtactics.org   125

COLLABORATION

New alliances — especially with unexpected partners — can strengthen the efforts of human rights advocates in unexpected ways. Get a former adversary on your side and you have not only gained an ally, you've lost an opponent. Open channels of communication that had been closed and you lessen the possibility of conflict and abuse. Build relationships with groups outside your sector and you lend credibility to your cause and attract new audiences. Reach across international borders and you build an alliance that is stronger, more flexible and has more political clout.

Strategic collaboration can make advocates more prepared, more powerful and more representative of the communities they serve. It can give them legitimacy in the mainstream, in media and in government. When the human rights advocates have a powerful, diverse array of allies and are no longer working in isolation, their work is much more difficult to assail.

**New Tactics
in Human Rights**

**BUILDING HUMAN
RIGHTS CULTURES**
Collaboration

126   www.newtactics.org

Building a United Front: Building a coalition of a country's human rights organizations to speak with one voice against abuses.

When human rights groups work together they can often do much more to improve a country's human rights situation than individual groups could do on their own. The National Coordinator for Human Rights in Peru proves that this is possible even on a very large scale.

The National Coordinator for Human Rights (Coordinadora Nacional de Derechos Humanos) is a coalition of 63 of Peru's leading human rights groups. The Coordinadora, founded in 1985, has survived because of its ability to unite member organizations and adapt to a constantly changing political environment. Its mix of both urban and rural members has enhanced the group's legitimacy throughout the country and internationally, while constructive engagement of government officials has contributed to its power as a political player.

Following the military regime of General Francisco Morales Bermúdez and the launch of the Sendero Luminoso (Shining Path) armed revolution, human rights groups were overwhelmed by the increasing atrocities. During 1983 and 1984, nearly 6,000 Peruvians lost their lives as a result of political violence. It was vital to create a space for groups to collaborate that was independent of religion and politics.

The success and strength of the coalition is due to a number of factors, including:

1   **Clear principles of internal functioning:** The coalition decided from its first meeting that it would pledge to reject violence of all types, remain independent of political parties and the government, be committed to a democratic society and oppose the death penalty. Organizations that do not adhere to these principles are not allowed to be part of the coalition.

2   **Decision-making by consensus:** The decision-making process creates a sense of common agreement and solidarity. All groups must be in agreement. While groups in the coalition are all different sizes and come from various parts of the country, each has an equal voice when it comes to decision-making and to forming the National Board, elected by members at a General Assembly.

3   **Representing the collective:** The internal process of selection and agreement on a representative for the organization gives legitimacy, both internally and externally, to this person and to the organization. When someone is selected by the member organizations to participate in an international meeting, for example, the individual participates not as a representative of the specific organization that he/she represents, but rather as a representative of the Coordinadora.

4   **Agreement on priorities that will be carried out together:** Every two years, the member organizations come together in a national assembly and determine priority topics they will address as a coalition. Their work on these topics is then carried out collectively and nationally by the Executive Secretary, a permanent body that carries out the decisions of the National Board and General Assembly. The Executive secretary is elected for a two-year term and serves as the official spokesperson for the coalition, organizing and facilitating the meetings, and mobilizing the members. The Coordinadora only takes on activities that are distinct from those implemented by individual coalition organizations and related to the priority areas.

By coordinating its efforts, the Coordinadora efficiently and effectively mobilizes people on a national scale, having a much greater impact than individual organizations or a temporary coalition. For example, when former Peruvian President Alberto Fujimori threatened to withdraw participation in the Inter-American Court system, the Coordinadora mobilized people across the nation within one week. All of its member organizations signed a statement and carried out efforts against the president's proposal and more than 400 additional organizations were mobilized to act. Every organization then took steps in its own community to build support and engage people to speak out against the situation. If not for the Coordinadora's clear position, credibility and structure, this would not have been possible. The Coordinadora was created in an atmosphere of violence and extreme human rights abuses, demonstrating that it is possible to implement this coalition-building tactic in adverse situations. Yet the true success of this coalition is based on much more than a need to come together at a very difficult time. Clear objectives, a solid framework and principles for collaboration and a clear stance against violence have brought the organization greater legitimacy. These principles have also won the support of the international community and have served to ensure the coalition's long-term success.

Region	Initiating Sector	Target Sector	Focus	Human Rights Issue	**BUILDING HUMAN RIGHTS CULTURES**	New Tactics in Human Rights
Americas	Civil Society	Civil Society	National	General human rights	Collaboration	

| **Public Dialogue with the Police Force:** Creating a long-term public forum where the police and ordinary citizens can work together to resolve human rights grievances and other issues affecting police/community relations.

One friction point in many societies is the relationship between the police force and civilians. Poor communication can lead to abuses or compromise public safety. In Nigeria a group has found an innovative way to bridge that gap.

The CLEEN Foundation, formally the Centre for Law Enforcement Education in Nigeria, creates public forums where citizens and police can discuss concerns and grievances regarding crime and police conduct.

Communities and police forces can find themselves in an unproductive cycle of distrust. Community members are concerned about police misconduct, brutality and corruption. The police, in turn, can see the community as hostile and uncooperative in their investigations.

In Nigeria, the centralized structure of the police force has contributed to the problem: one set of agendas and policies is applied to the whole country, creating a gap between the law enforcement priorities of the police and the needs of the local communities.

CLEEN begins bridging this disconnect by sending letters to local governments, proposing the establishment of a public forum in their communities. The group follows up on this invitation only if local governments respond and the cooperation and commitment of the local police division can be secured. CLEEN then conducts a partnership workshop, where police and community members receive conflict-resolution training, discuss police responses to local complaints and discuss how CLEEN's program could be implemented in the area. These workshops allow each community to shape the program to its own needs. Two people from the community are then hired on a part-time basis to coordinate the forums for two years. After the two-year period is over, the community must find a way to sustain the program on its own.

CLEEN's tactic provides community members and police officers with a nonthreatening environment in which to share their concerns, overcoming the significant barriers created by bureaucracy. Both sides in a potentially contentious relationship have the opportunity to see the other as more human: someone to collaborate with, rather than to oppose. Over time, this process can interrupt the unproductive cycle of mistrust, laying a new foundation on which police embrace their role of service to citizens and citizens assist the police in their duties. This can reduce both police violence and civilian crime. The project has been implemented in fourteen local government areas drawn from the six geographical regions of Nigeria.

Because mistrust and misunderstanding cause friction among many groups, this tactic could be used to build stronger relationships between other groups in conflict, such as ethnic groups or business owners and farmers. One potential pitfall is the emotion and acrimony that can surround very difficult issues. Facilitators must be prepared to deal with this and to do so over a fairly long period of time. A one-time meeting is likely to be far less effective than CLEEN's long-term approach.

New Tactics in Human Rights	BUILDING HUMAN RIGHTS CULTURES	Region	Initiating Sector	Target Sector	Focus	Human Rights Issue
	Collaboration	Africa	Civil Society	Government Society	Local	Police and military abuses

128   www.newtactics.org

Getting to Know Your Allies: Identifying allies to hold constructive dialogue and maintain cooperative relationships.

Sometimes mistrust exists not only between human rights organizations and outside institutions, but among and within the human rights organizations themselves. In the Great Lakes Region of Africa, a group is working across international borders and entrenched lines of suspicion to overcome this problem in order to cooperatively monitor the region's human rights situation and quickly disseminate information.

The Ligue des Droits de la Personne dans la Region des Grands Lacs (Human Rights League of the Great Lakes Region, or LDGL) works as an umbrella group to maintain the alliance among 27 member organizations in Burundi, the Democratic Republic of Congo and Rwanda — a region rife with conflict. The Great Lakes region has long suffered from violence caused by ideological and ethnic mistrust or hatred. Some organizations in the region, including even some human rights groups, reflect these divisions, taking actions on behalf of narrow, ethnically-based constituencies.

The League's process of careful and systematic dialogue relies on the principles of *ubuntu* (humanness) as a basis for approaching its interactions with people from different backgrounds and cultures and for successfully building dialogue and sharing information.

When divisions within the LDGL emerge, leaders of the group try to understand the underlying problems creating the dispute. They then map out potential allies and identify the approach to dialogue that has the most potential for maintaining productive relationships. The LDGL selects individuals to participate in the dialogue based on their ability to build trust and cooperation. In everything it does, the LDGL chooses language and actions that build its credibility, thereby assuring alliance members that they are respected and that their concerns will be addressed.

Before approaching any issue to be addressed by member organizations, especially a contentious one, the League identifies the problem, the possible or real areas of contention, the desired goal and the alliances necessary to reach it. The league also identifies passive, potential and active allies to engage in dialogue.

Friction is natural among members of an alliance, especially one working in an area with a great deal of conflict. Rather than being the fault of "bad people," this friction signals the need for rigorous, sensitive systems of dialogue. A difficult part of the League's work is gaining mutual understanding for its actions within the region. If no consensus is reached at a meeting, the League sends reliable and trusted delegates from member organizations to the reluctant members in order to gain better understanding of the perspectives and build support.

Through this on-going process of building and maintaining relationships, the League has succeeded in creating a strong network of diverse organizations throughout the region and gaining their trust, in order to monitor human rights abuses and quickly disseminate information.

Creating mechanisms to carefully map out allies before convening members or groups for dialogues on contentious issues is critical for the successful implementation of tactics. This tactic could be applied in other situations where human rights groups are divided and competing with each other for scarce resources and attention. Coalitions are tenuous and always require constant dialogue and cultivation to continue to work effectively and stay together.

Region	Initiating Sector	Target Sector	Focus	Human Rights Issue	**BUILDING HUMAN RIGHTS CULTURES**	New Tactics in Human Rights
Africa	Civil Society	Civil Society	International	General human rights	Collaboration	

Coverco invites multinational corporations to improve human rights by comparing their corporate codes of conduct with on-the-ground reality in the overseas factories supplying their goods. Coverco gathers, examines and independently publishes information to remove any excuses the business may have for failing to respect human rights.

The Commission for the Verification of Corporate Codes of Conduct (Coverco) conducts long-term, intensive, independent monitoring of labor conditions in Guatemalan apparel factories and agricultural export industries, verifying compliance with internationally accepted labor standards. Based in Guatemala City, Coverco is an independent monitoring organization formed in 1997 by members of civil society groups; it does not work as a consultant to management nor as a worker advocate. The organization first establishes a relationship with a corporation (for example, Liz Claiborne Inc.) then negotiates an agreement permitting full, unannounced access to the production facility where the corporation commits to pay service fees. The organization independently publishes its findings on its web site.

Rather than conducting short-term visits and filing one-time reports, Coverco maintains a steady presence in the factories it monitors over a period of at least six months. It tries to "make movies" of the labor relationships in a production facility, instead of taking a snapshot. Trained monitors visit factories several times a month, unannounced. Monitors review factory records, have management explain official policy on issues as they arise, conduct "sensory inspections" of production facilities, meet with workers during and outside of normal business hours and maintain a telephone hotline to ensure that employees have full access to them. Interviews are conducted in Spanish and kept in strict confidence. Full access to the production facility, personnel files, management and workers is guaranteed by the multinational corporation.

Monitoring begins with a "social audit" whereby monitors characterize labor relations at the production facility — checking, for example, whether there is a grievance procedure and whether or not it works. Working conditions are thoroughly documented, including the presence and handling of industrial chemicals, the maintenance of and access to bathrooms, on-site health care and compliance with other health and safety criteria.

Monitors then undertake a thorough review of payroll records, payment of employee benefits and production bonuses and compliance with overtime regulations. They carefully investigate worker complaints and make certain to include management comments in all reports, noting situations where claims cannot be verified.

Coverco's monitoring and verification activities have led corporations to require suppliers to demonstrate systemic compliance with labor rights. For example, one minor working at a supplier to Liz Claiborne complained that her manager refused to allow her to leave work early to attend classes as required by both local law and the LCI Code of Conduct. When Coverco documented this violation, LCI intervened with local management to ensure that managers complied with this law. This led Coverco to review the files of all minors working at the factory; the supplier then acted to ensure that they had the required parental permission for all working minors and to comply with local law requiring that minors work no more than 35 hours per week.

Coverco has reported some problems with gaining access to supplier factories and reluctance by some suppliers to implement the remediation programs they have negotiated with the multinational corporations. Managers at one Gap supplier factory, for instance, refused for a time to let Coverco monitors walk unescorted through the production facility or speak unobserved with workers.

Although the record is hardly perfect, failure to implement remediation programs has led some supplier factories to reprimand or dismiss managers. Illegally dismissed workers have been reinstated, excessive overtime has been reduced and cases of incorrect benefit payments have been remedied.

New Tactics in Human Rights	**BUILDING HUMAN RIGHTS CULTURES**	Region	Initiating Sector	Target Sector	Focus	Human Rights Issue
	Collaboration	Americas	Civil Society	Business	International	Labor rights

130   www.newtactics.org

Different types of monitoring are being undertaken around the world, including confrontational approaches and those, like Coverco's, which involve working in cooperation with companies. Coverco uses a collaborative relationship with international businesses rather than an adversarial one. It negotiates with them to fund this external, independent monitoring program and then, in interesting ways, takes monitoring a step further than usual. It provides a safe venue where workers can complain without fear of reprisals, thereby encouraging them to take a hand in improving their own working conditions. It also employs local monitors who are more likely than foreigners to understand local conditions and make connections with workers. To make this tactic work, it is crucial to have the support of both workers and management. When it is successful, all stakeholders contribute to the creation of a culture of compliance.

BUILDING HUMAN   New Tactics
RIGHTS CULTURES   in Human Rights
Collaboration

www.newtactics.org   131

Self-Governance that Crosses Borders: Creating a transnational body to advocate for and promote the rights of indigenous people.

Sometimes potential allies are obvious, but ways of bringing them together are not. The indigenous Saami people, living in four different countries in the Arctic Circle, have built governing bodies that coordinate with each other across national borders to advocate for cross-national policies on rights of a minority — particularly for grazing rights that directly impact the their day-to-day life.

The Saami Council, established in 1956, emerged from the need to maintain strong connections across the political borders that divide the Saami people of northern Scandinavia, to promote cooperation and to preserve their rights as indigenous people. The Council advocates for rights in the area where the Saami have lived for more than 10,000 years, an area that currently spans four countries — Norway, Sweden, Finland and Russia's Kola Peninsula.

Saami Council members are typically involved with national Saami organizations in their home countries. The fifteen seats of the Council are divided proportionally based on the Saami population — totaling over 100,000 — in each of the four countries. The Council has given strong support to the creation of Saami Parliaments in the Scandinavian nations, established in Finland in 1973, and in Norway and Sweden in 1987 and 1993, respectively. Each parliament is an independent, democratically-elected political body that consults with its respective national parliament on matters of interest to the Saami. Though Saami Parliaments cannot pass their own legislation, they are able to promote initiatives before the national parliaments.

The success of the Saami Council can be attributed to its ability to organize its people simultaneously on local, national and international levels. In this way members are able to use their cross-border unity to build constituencies and leverage for a local policy changes, while at the same time drawing on smaller, local organizations to provide support for larger, transnational coordination of Saami issues. One effort currently underway is the drafting of the Nordic Saami Convention. In 2002, the governments and Saami Parliaments of Norway, Sweden and Finland agreed to establish an expert group made up of Saami and non-Saami members to produce a draft of the Convention by 2005. The Convention will deal with fundamental issues of self-determination and land rights, as well as the environment, cooperation between states and Saami parliaments and the preservation of cultural heritage. A critical area of consideration is cross-border land grazing rights for those who herd reindeer — a primary livelihood of the Saami people.

In addition, the Saami Council was instrumental in establishing the Permanent Forum on Indigenous Issues at the United Nations and played a significant role in creating the Special Rapporteur on Human Rights for Indigenous People under the UN High Commissioner for Human Rights.

As a minority in each of their home countries, separate Saami political bodies would have less power to shape the policies that affect them. But together they can be much stronger advocates for their own rights — a clear example of the value of collaboration. This also promotes human rights at the local level while simultaneously influencing the decisions of national, regional and international institutions. Similar collaborations could be effective in other situations where interest groups or human rights issues cross national borders, as is more and more often the case.

" "   *We try to have a good working relationship with the home governments, even though we do not compromise on our rights. We are in constant dialogue with the governments. We have always tried to be more informed and know more about the issues than the government people we are going to be negotiating with.*

— Mattias Åhrén, Head of the Human Rights Unit, Saami Council

New Tactics in Human Rights	BUILDING HUMAN RIGHTS CULTURES	Region	Initiating Sector	Target Sector	Focus	Human Rights Issue
	Collaboration	Europe	Civil Society	Government Society	International	Indigenous rights

Educating the Next Generation: Collaborating with government to incorporate human rights education into public schools.

Public schools can be important settings for building a human rights culture. In Albania, a group worked with the government to prepare citizens for democracy in a post-communist nation.

The Albanian Center for Human Rights (ACHR) collaborated with the Albanian Ministry of Education to bring human rights education into all public schools in the country. The group took advantage of the post-communist transition period, negotiating with officials in the new democratic government to launch a long-term and ambitious process in which they would prepare young Albanian citizens to participate fully in a democracy.

In 1991, after 45 years of an oppressive and isolationist communist dictatorship, Albania faced a new world of democratic possibilities, with mountains of inherited political, economic and social problems and an institutional infrastructure ill-prepared to face them. To make the most of their new democracy, Albanians needed an educational system that prepared its citizens for critical thinking and encouraged political participation.

ACHR developed an ambitious plan to integrate human rights education into the official curricula of all public schools in the country. The group took advantage of the unique political moment provided by the post-communist transition to secure a written commitment from the Albanian Ministry of Education and Science to implement human rights education projects in public schools.

ACHR then began establishing pilot projects, carrying out large training sessions for a core group of teachers, adapting international human rights education materials for Albanian classrooms and developing activity books for every grade level. They also created pilot schools, where teachers and administrators helped trained all of the other teachers in human rights and its history, international mechanisms and human rights methodologies and activities in and out of the classroom.

By the end of the decade, ACHR had developed special curricular material in many subjects for all age groups, trained thousands of teachers to use the materials, set up 42 pilot schools throughout the country and initiated a curriculum in the teachers colleges to integrate the teaching of human rights into their preparation.

ACHR had an ambitious vision for Albania and used a political opportunity to turn that vision into reality. The government was in transition and eager to show the international community its dedication to human rights. (Albania had ratified the Convention on the Rights of the Child in 1993.) ACHR offered the government a way to demostrate that commitment and help fulfill its obligations under the convention, and thereby secured its cooperation. It also sustained momentum by bringing in international support and educational experts.

Region	Initiating Sector	Target Sector	Focus	Human Rights Issue	BUILDING HUMAN RIGHTS CULTURES	New Tactics in Human Rights
Europe	Civil Society	Government Civil Society	National	General human rights	Collaboration	

BUILDING CAPACITY

BUILDING CAPACITY Resources for human rights practitioners are always limited. We are always trying to do more with less — with fewer people and less money and in less time than we feel we really need. But there is one important resource that is truly renewable: our skills. When we expand our own skills and those of our colleagues, and even take those skills out into the community to share them with new people, we can indeed do a little more with a little less in a little less time. The tactics in this section build capacity in two essential ways: they give human rights practitioners the skills they need to do their work better and faster, and they give people who are nominally outside of human rights work the skills they need to advance human rights.

New Tactics
in Human Rights

**BUILDING HUMAN
RIGHTS CULTURES**
Building Capacity

134   www.newtactics.org

Promoting Professionalism, Promoting Human Rights: Creating a professional organization that provides support and training to build professionalism among law enforcement personnel.

In Liberia, law enforcement officials saw the need to improve respect for human rights within their own ranks.

The Liberia National Law Enforcement Association (LINLEA) promotes professionalism among law enforcement personnel. LINLEA advances the perspective that law enforcement officers should be the leading human rights protectors and promoters, as prescribed by the law enforcement code of ethics and canons of police ethics. These codes challenge officers to respect the constitutional rights of all people to liberty, equality and justice. Unfortunately, due to lack of training, indiscipline, poor leadership or political manipulation, law enforcement personnel often engage in unprofessional conduct that leads to human rights abuses. LINLEA was established to meet police officers' needs for training, advocacy and assistance, and to do so in a context that makes them willing to join and participate.

To create LINLEA, respected law enforcement officers invited heads of public and private law enforcement departments and agencies to participate and establish an organizing committee. This committee developed the articles of incorporation and appointed a board of directors. The minister of justice attended the launch, adding legitimacy to the association. The association has since established a wide variety services for its members, including training in police and investigative procedures, human rights and leadership, as well as mechanisms to enhance enforcement of professional standards such as grievance procedures. In addition, the association reaches beyond the law enforcement network, working together with communities and organizations to improve the human rights conditions in Liberia.

Members make a personal investment in the organization by paying dues. LINLEA has now grown into a network of more than 500 law enforcement personnel, representing nearly 20 percent of the police force as well as many members of other law enforcement institutions. LINLEA's Center for Criminal Justice Research and Education has provided leadership and human rights training for 223 senior law enforcement officers. It has also conducted a training-of-trainers workshop for trainers and curriculum specialists of law enforcement agencies, as well as a workshop on policy formulation and development for law enforcement planners and administrators.

The association hosts annual social events which strengthen the bonds among members and their families and public forums to build relationships between law enforcement and communities. And it provides ongoing services that benefit law enforcement personnel, including certificates for participating in training workshops, which can help them receive promotions; support for their requests for advancement within the law enforcement structures; assistance with and some protection from professional problems such as dismissals and wrongful charges; and some assistance when facing personal problems such as financial distress due to a death in the family.

Many organizations have introduced training programs for law enforcement officials. LINLEA's approach, as a professional organization, requires an investment of time, money and effort from the police officers themselves. This adds an incentive for professional behavior — behavior that shows a respect for human rights — that comes from within rather than outside the profession. These incentives are critical to building the organizational strength needed to support law enforcement personnel who want to improve their own conduct, and to provide leverage for changing the behaviors of those who violate professional norms. Because they are law enforcement officials themselves, LINLEA's organizers have a particularly deep understanding of the challenges law enforcement personnel face and the kinds of support they need.

Region	Initiating Sector	Target Sector	Focus	Human Rights Issue	BUILDING HUMAN RIGHTS CULTURES	New Tactics in Human Rights
Africa	Government	Government	National	Police and military abuses	Building Capacity	

| **Making the Legal System Accessible in Rural Areas:** Training local leaders as mediators and resources on human rights.

In many rural or provincial areas, access to the legal system and to conflict resolution services is extremely limited. A group in Uganda is working to change this by training local people in mediation skills.

In Uganda, the Foundation for Human Rights Initiative (FHRI) trains local leaders to help community members with legal complaints in a way that avoids the problems and frustrations of using the formal judicial system. FHRI teaches these leaders how to educate their communities about their constitutional and human rights. It also gives them paralegal skills, enabling them to provide mediation, counseling and advice so that citizens can obtain redress for abuses and exercise their full human rights.

Many people in rural Uganda are unaware of their full constitutional rights and of what can be done when those rights are violated. They also perceive the legal system to be inaccessible, as it is located in the city: its costs are high and it uses unfamiliar language and behavior.

FHRI chooses participants who have demonstrated leadership skills and are important figures in their communities, such as teachers, business leaders, community elders or medical workers. The training is a week-long curriculum addressing legal processes, discussion methods and ways to create communication networks. It also provides participants with the skills they need to monitor, document and report human rights abuses. Some volunteers become responsible for specific groups in the community, such as women, children, the elderly or others.

When they have completed their training, these paralegal volunteers form meeting centers that address problems in ways tailored to their communities. This encourages alternative solutions — such as counseling, mediation, referrals to existing organizations and advice with paperwork — so people can avoid the challenges and costs of the formal judicial system.

FHRI has now trained more than 1,000 volunteer paralegals and has published the *Paralegal Reference Handbook* (available from FHRI).

This tactic increases access to justice. And, when too often the call for human rights comes from outside a community, it also creates local advocates for these rights. (The Thongbai Thongpao Foundation in Thailand also brings legal education to rural areas, but it focuses more on educating community members who may require legal services than on training local leaders to provide those services. See page 145.) FHRI's approach could be used in other situations where legal recourse is not an option for people and where community leaders are willing and able to take on this role.

The success of this tactic relies on the assurance that the leaders identified from the outside have genuine moral authority in their communities and will use it along with their new mediation skills. Also, the short-term training may need to be supplemented with long-term follow-up and support.

Is this type of tactic needed in your community? Who are the local leaders who might be trained to carry out such a tactic?

New Tactics in Human Rights

BUILDING HUMAN RIGHTS CULTURES

	Building Capacity	Region	Initiating Sector	Target Sector	Focus	Human Rights Issue
		Africa	Civil Society	Society	National	General human rights

136   www.newtactics.org

Helping Human Rights Advocates be More Effective: Utilizing an information specialist and systems to help human rights advocates work more effectively.

Human rights practitioners can often benefit from institutional strengthening tactics that provide new skills, technology or organizational systems.

The Human Rights Centre at the University of Sarajevo focuses on improving access to information for human rights advocates. Staff members have built a strong information system and a central role for an information specialist. Use of this system and of the specialist's skills has allowed other staff to better and more productively focus on their core programmatic missions.

Establishing a library or documentation unit within human rights organizations can help staff facilitate the flow of information, manage confidential documents, chronicle the organization's history and improve day-to-day operations. Key elements of this tactic include the involvement of a skilled librarian or information specialist, an organized physical space, a core collection of materials and appropriate software and other information technology.

Human rights librarians have particular skills to offer a human rights organization, including knowledge of technology and of human rights information and documentation. The role of the librarian is to acquire and evaluate materials in relation to the organization's core mission, arrange them for efficient use and disseminate them within the organization. This last role involves working closely with staff to sort and prioritize information.

It is important to have sufficient space to organize materials and provide for staff interaction. At a minimum, a documentation center includes space for the librarian's office needs, including a networked computer and shelving and file units. The core collection of books and other resources depends on the mission and scale of the organization. In general, an organization should try to include information essential to its present and future programs.

Finally, an efficient documentation center will have appropriate software (for cataloguing, classification, indexing, and so on) and an Internet connection to allow the librarian to freely access information.

Read more about this in a tactical notebook available at www.newtactics.org, under Tools for Action.

ONLINE

The work of the librarians at the Human Rights Centre in Sarajevo focuses on the information needs of human rights advocates themselves, allowing them to be more effective by freeing up their time and energy. The Centre is a fairly large and well-funded organization, but nearly all human rights work now relies on timely access to complete and accurate information. When an organization has the necessary resources — even if that involves only to a part-time employee or dedicated volunteer — an information center could help provide that access. The librarians and information specialists themselves, however, may need to employ persuasion tactics to convince the organization and its members of the importance of work that may at first seem peripheral to the core mission.

I brought back the Human Rights Centre's tactic and I already knew that it would be useful. I have spent several hours with the administrative staff person on this. The library was in chaos and she spent three months doing it in the right way — setting up library. That was a big job and the person worked all summer. It's helping me a lot.

" "

— Bea Bodrogi, NEKI, Hungary

Region	Initiating Sector	Target Sector	Focus	Human Rights Issue	**BUILDING HUMAN RIGHTS CULTURES**	New Tactics in Human Rights
Europe	Civil Society	Civil Society	Local	General human rights	Building Capacity	

Broadcasting Human Rights: Training victims of human rights abuses to use video technology to expose those abuses.

Human rights practitioners often need to get their message out to a broader public. In an age of advanced technology, this increasingly requires access to video and broadcast technology and the skills to use it.

Based in Hungary and Romania, the Black Box Foundation works to improve attitudes towards the Roma minority by training them in the production of television programs for local channels. The Foundation creates production teams, trains them in video production, secures airtime and sees that programs are exchanged between teams.

Since 1997, the Black Box Foundation has trained approximately 150 Roma at twelve locations within Hungary and Romania to inform local viewers about the issues affecting their communities. The Foundation solicits applications and creates ethnically-mixed teams of five people. Staff members first work to build trusting relationships with and among team members, discussing individual viewpoints and addressing the sensitive issues that will be brought up in the program. Teams then learn the fundamentals of television production and consult with experts on minority issues.

During the last three days of training, teams produce their first films. The Foundation provides cameras, lights, microphones and other necessary equipment. The teams go on to produce monthly programs at their local television stations, working independently and with their own resources, while the Foundation negotiates to secure regular airtime for the programs. The Foundation supervises and monitors teams for six months following training and teams exchange the videos they make with each other.

Outcomes among the production teams have varied. A number of teams continue to broadcast regularly on local television, while others now use their skills and equipment to record the activities of their organizations.

Due to the success of this approach, the Black Box Foundation has opened a successful one-year school for Roma students who are interested in becoming television professionals.

The Black Box Foundation program has helped to change the way minorities are viewed and treated in the region, reducing discrimination and prejudice. In Hungary and Romania the Roma are often segregated from the majority populations and their problems are hidden. They do not have access to the same educational and other resources used by the general population. The Black Box training program not only gives participants the skills they need to tell their own stories — as Roma — it also helps broadcast those stories on a medium members of the majority population are likely to see. This helps build a culture in which the minority and majority populations work together to promote human rights for all.

New Tactics in Human Rights

BUILDING HUMAN RIGHTS CULTURES	Region	Initiating Sector	Target Sector	Focus	Human Rights Issue
Building Capacity	Europe	Civil Society	Society	National	Minority rights

138   www.newtactics.org

Documenting Torture: Creating a network of professionals to document torture and support victims.

A Kenyan group is linking doctors and lawyers in order to expose human rights violations committed by law enforcement agencies, and to raise awareness about the use of torture.

The Independent Medico-Legal Unit (IMLU), a registered nongovernmental organization, is a network of doctors and lawyers who provide services to victims and their families. These services include independent postmortem examinations of suspicious deaths in the hands of law enforcement agencies, documentation of suspected cases of torture and medical and legal aid to prisoners and to torture survivors.

IMLU first organized its network by lobbying for the formation of professional committees, namely the Kenya Medical Association Standing Committee on Human Rights and a group of lawyers sympathetic to efforts to end torture. Once the committees were established, the IMLU developed ongoing workshops to strengthen the capacity of health workers and lawyers in dealing with torture. The workshops take place throughout the country, addressing topics such as defining human rights, building relationships with the Prison Department and educating professionals and government officials on human rights statutes and violations.

In order to reach victims of torture and their families, IMLU networks with various religious bodies, lawyers, doctors and NGOs throughout Kenya. Referred clients are able to request a postmortem on family members, the results of which are carefully documented according to medical and legal guidelines.

IMLU encourages clients to seek legal redress when evidence of torture is discovered. For clients who cannot afford legal aid, IMLU refers them to a network of lawyers and NGOs providing pro bono legal services. Its goal is to pursue public interest cases that will set a precedent against the use of torture and send to a message to the perpetrators of torture.

Because of IMLU's continued efforts to expose torture in Kenya, several cases have been taken to court, resulting in increased concern for the well-being and treatment of prisoners. Moreover, prison authorities are now demonstrating an interest in better prison conditions by reducing the use of physical punishment or torture and, since the new government took power in late 2002, more government officials have begun working with IMLU to improve their own human rights efforts.

By coordinating a professional network and training members in documenting torture, IMLU has raised awareness about torture in Kenya, resulting in increased pressure on authorities to prevent it. The network also draws on the desire of some doctors and lawyers to use their skills to promote human rights, strengthening support around the country for an end to torture.

This work, however, has not been without challenges. The demand for IMLU's services often exceeds its financial capacity to support victims and victims in rural Kenya often confront a slow response from network lawyers, most of whom reside in Nairobi. IMLU has also experienced police interference and intimidation in its attempt to document postmortem examinations. In such cases, the network has joined with other NGOs to publicize these issues by releasing press statements that condemn interference and to bring legal action against the police.

Region	Initiating Sector	Target Sector	Focus	Human Rights Issue	BUILDING HUMAN RIGHTS CULTURES	New Tactics in Human Rights
Africa	Civil Society	Civil Society	National	Torture	Building Capacity	

The Eyes and Ears of Human Rights: Empowering NGOs to use video in human rights advocacy.

WITNESS empowers human rights organizations around the world to incorporate video as an advocacy tool in their work. Rooted in the power of personal testimonies and in the principle that a picture is worth a thousand words, the videos of WITNESS and its partners have been used

as evidence in legal proceedings;

to corroborate allegations of human rights violations;

to complement written reports to international and regional organizations that provide a counterweight to official versions of a country's human rights performance;

to stimulate grassroots education and mobilization;

to provide information for news broadcasts;

to promote human rights via the internet; and

to produce documentaries for broadcast on television worldwide.

Founded in 1992 and based in New York City, WITNESS has created partnerships with more than 150 groups in 50 countries on a variety of issues, ranging from the "social cleansing" of street children in Central America and sexual abuse of women and girls during Sierra Leone's civil war to sweatshops in the United States and the plight of displaced people in Burma.

WITNESS chooses partners who seek to build a long-term capacity to use video effectively and also seeks specific campaign opportunities where video can tip the balance between success and failure. Once a partnership is established, WITNESS provides the group with video equipment and training, then follows up with workshops in camera techniques, intensive instruction in using video for human rights work, systemic evaluation of video footage, post-production assistance and constructive feedback to create powerful documentaries.

WITNESS and its partners then create video advocacy campaigns around the footage collected. These campaigns include many components, including broadcast and distribution platforms, collaboration with other organizations and networks, targeted screenings before key audiences and opportunities for individual viewers to take action. They may be as targeted as using video to influence a small group of key decision-makers or as broad as trying to mobilize youth around a particular issue. Footage is also kept in the WITNESS Archive, where it is available to the global community as a unique resource of human rights information.

WITNESS recognizes that, depending on the local context, a human rights advocate may be protected or endangered by using a camera. WITNESS uses the experience of its staff and partners to help others create safe and appropriate policies for their situations. It also stresses the importance of trust between the person filming and the person being filmed and clearly explains the risks and benefits of speaking to a camera.

	BUILDING HUMAN RIGHTS CULTURES	Region	Initiating Sector	Target Sector	Focus	Human Rights Issue
	Building Capacity	Multiple	Civil Society	Government	International	General human rights
				Business		
				Civil Society		
				Society		

Visual Evidence can Stop Violations

WITNESS partners have collected testimonies and produced powerful videos that have been used in many ways. One strategic and savvy use of video advocacy is WITNESS's work with Mental Disability Rights International (MDRI) to document the deplorable conditions in a Paraguayan psychiatric hospital.

Julio and Jorge are two adolescent boys being kept in the hospital along with 458 other people — naked, in bare cells without access to bathrooms. The cells reeked of urine and excrement and the walls were smeared with feces. The boys spent approximately four hours every other day in an outdoor pen, littered with garbage and broken glass.

In December 2003, MDRI filed an emergency petition before the Inter-American Commission on Human Rights (IACHR) at the Organization of American States (OAS), asking the IACHR to intervene on behalf of the boys, as well as the others in the hospital.

Along with a legal brief, MDRI submitted a video shot and edited with WITNESS and structured according to the articles set forth in several international human rights instruments to which Paraguay is bound. It was presented within this human rights framework to argue that the patients were legally entitled to protections of their rights to life and humane treatment. Using images that clearly demonstrated how Paraguay had failed to fulfill its obligations, the video put a human face on the issue.

This led the IACHR, for the first time, to approve urgent measures to protect the lives and physical integrity of those in psychiatric institutions, a precedent that can now be used in other countries in the region. MDRI and WITNESS subsequently brought the issue to the general public by streaming the video over their web sites and by collaborating with CNN en Español on a follow-up story. The president of Paraguay and the minister of health visited the hospital, after which the hospital director was fired and a commission was formed to investigate the issue.

By exposing the situation to a broader public, MDRI and WITNESS called attention to the appalling conditions of the state-run mental health facility and garnered further support for change. The press also played a pivotal role in the unfolding of events, helping to bring about significant changes.

Although Julio and Jorge's ward is still being renovated as this book goes to press, they are no longer locked in tiny cells and now have access to showers and clothes, as well as to 24-hour nurses. The Paraguayan Health Ministry is working with the Pan-American Health Organization (PAHO) to promote community integration for people with mental disabilities.

The collaboration between WITNESS and MDRI has produced system-changing results, but the challenge lies ahead, in ensuring that human rights advocates pick up the momentum created by the video and follow up on the case to ensure that people with mental disabilities have the support and services necessary for their successful integration into the community.

While this case has relied upon strong visual evidence of a violation, it is important to note that WITNESS partners have successfully used video without relying upon such graphic images. Many, for instance, have created powerful videos by collecting testimonies and telling the stories of those most directly affected, which can have an equally powerful impact within a human rights campaign.

Region	Initiating Sector	Target Sector	Focus	Human Rights Issue	BUILDING HUMAN RIGHTS CULTURES	New Tactics in Human Rights
Multiple	Civil Society	Government	National	Mental disability rights	Building Capacity	

Does the Government Keep its Promises? Creating a network of volunteer monitors to persuade local and national governments to abide by international human rights commitments.

In Slovakia, a group is monitoring government adherence to its international human rights commitments and using what it finds to persuade the government to keep those promises.

The League of Human Rights Advocates (LHRA) in Slovakia has developed a network of volunteer human rights monitors within the minority Roma population to ensure that international human rights treaties are implemented at the local level. As part of its work to become a member of the European Union, Slovakia ratified a number of treaties relating to human rights and was vulnerable to criticism of their human rights record. In addition, the constitution of the Slovak Republic gives priority, over domestic laws, to international human rights treaties ratified and passed into law by its parliament.

LHRA's monitoring approach helps to bridge the gap between the locus of abuse and the policies, laws and treaties created to prevent or stop a violation. Often the only discussion of these abuses and the laws or policies to prevent them occurs in high-level political and diplomatic forums. The LHRA recruits people from the disenfranchised population to serve as human rights monitors. The monitors learn, often for the first time, about their own rights under national and international law and then work with the LHRA to enforce those rights — which were signed into existence in far-off capitals — in their own town halls, police stations, schools and communities. The information from local monitors is used to present the true, on-the-ground impact of national and international laws in the country.

The Roma monitors are recruited through word of mouth. LHRA educates them about the relevant human rights instruments and the government authorities responsible for their implementation, then arranges introductory meetings with the police, mayors, community leaders and others, adding legitimacy and authority to the monitors' work. The network is divided into eight regions; regional coordinators work with LHRA headquarters to recruit and train monitors (roughly 48 in all).

When the monitors are prepared for their work, they are issued an LHRA identity card and provided with letters of introduction to present to local authorities. When an alleged abuse occurs, they go to the community to compile information from victims and from the involved authorities. The monitoring focuses on a number of issues, including employment, living conditions, education, health care, political participation, racially motivated violence and access to public facilities and services.

LHRA's national office synthesizes all the monitors' work into regular national reports and publishes its own periodical. As a result of this monitoring tactic, a range of human rights abuses occurring at the local level have been exposed and more victims of abuse have started to come forward with more complaints. The government, over time, has implemented policies to address discrimination in education, housing and employment.

ONLINE Read more about this in a tactical notebook available at www.newtactics.org, under Tools for Action.

LHRA's tactic is a unique combination of pressure and promotion. The Roma monitors learn about their rights, empowering them to take action. And the government's desire to join the European Union has made it more sensitive to reports of abuse, thus providing an opportunity to heighten the impact of the monitors' work. The tactic is also a unique application of international law to people's day-to-day reality. It has increased power to affect human rights abuses in countries that have signed international human rights treaties and that have an interest in how their human rights record is perceived by the international community.

" " *Our tactics make the Slovak government uncomfortable, and sometimes we have experienced persecution by state agents. But our aim — ensuring respect for the fundamental rights of citizens — has gradually been met. And the state has turned out to be our friend and sometimes our partner in this.*

— Columbus Igboanusi, League of Human Rights Advocates, Slovakia

New Tactics
in Human Rights

**BUILDING HUMAN
RIGHTS CULTURES**

	Region	Initiating Sector	Target Sector	Focus	Human Rights Issue
Building Capacity	Europe	Civil Society	Government Society	National	General human rights

142   www.newtactics.org

Children as Advocates for their Own Rights: Empowering children with information, skills and support to advocate for their own rights.

When equipped with skills and with access to appropriate information, children can defend and advocate for their own rights.

In India, the group Concerned for Working Children (CWC) enables children to create formal structures such as unions and governance bodies to advocate for their own rights. Through this work, CWC strengthens the participation of children, especially those who are working or otherwise marginalized, in decision-making and governance on all matters that concern them. CWC has been actively involved in this cause since 1980 and is currently working in five Karnataka districts.

CWC's efforts to empower working children led initially to the formation of Bhima Sangha — a union of, by and for working children. Bhima Sangha has a membership of 13,000 children in Karnataka and is an important partner in CWC's work to enable children to play a proactive role in decision-making and governance. Since its inception in 1990, Bhima Sangha has been a powerful advocate for the rights of working children and is equally concerned about improving the quality of life of their parents and communities. At the national and regional level, Bhima Sangha is assisting other working children with the formation of their own unions; it was also instrumental in forming the National and International Movements of Working Children.

So that they could influence the programs and policies that affect them, the children also demanded a formal role in governance. This led to the creation of what was later called the Makkala Panchayat, or Children's Government, elected by children in the community. The children designed its structure and determined its purpose and leadership style. Because the children wanted it to have a formal status with the local government, or Panchayat, CWC devised a mechanism to formally integrate the Makkala Panchayat with the village government through a task force, which is chaired by the district minister. The task force is comprised of both adults and children. Elections to the Makkala Panchayat are held by the formal government administration and the secretary of the adult Panchayat acts as the secretary of the children's Panchayat.

CWC teaches the children skills such as research, documentation, communication, negotiation and advocacy. The children use theater, puppetry, songs, publications, wall magazines and audio and video tools to support their stands and principles. They spell out their priorities, substantiate their claims and advocate for change. To maintain good relations with the local government, the children avoid political or other affiliations, but are actively involved in political debates.

Through their organized participation in politica l structures and local governance the children become more self-aware and they make the state accountable. Their participation in political space also enables other marginalized groups such as women and ethnic groups to change their immediate situation and strengthen democracy.

Thousands of children now participate in the governance of their villages and adults who were traditionally feudal and patriarchal have become advocates for children's rights. They see a value in the active and equal participation of children, as they have seen it translated into overall benefits for the whole community[1].

The children's organizations have been powerful in addressing a wide range of issues at the local level, including water and fuel problems, housing, pensions for the elderly and disabled, exploitative child labor, substance abuse and child marriage. They have also contributed substantially to the policies on children at the state, national and international levels.

The foundation of CWC's work is the empowerment of working children so that they may be their own first line of defense and participate in an informed manner in all decisions concerning themselves. CWC has shown that the troubling living conditions and challenges facing children can be mitigated through education, empowerment and partnerships with adults. CWC works in concert with local governments, communities and working children themselves to implement viable, comprehensive, sustainable and appropriate solutions. The outcome is an enhanced quality of life for all community members, made possible by the input of children themselves.

---

[1] Journey in Children's Participation, Nandana Reddy and Kavita Ratna, The Concerned for Working Children, India, 2002

Region	Initiating Sector	Target Sector	Focus	Human Rights Issue	BUILDING HUMAN RIGHTS CULTURES	New Tactics in Human Rights
Asia	Civil Society	Government Business Society	Local	Children's rights	Building Capacity	

BUILDING AWARENESS

Making people — all people — in a community aware of human rights is the first step toward building a community that cherishes those rights. When people don't know their rights, abusive actions by the government, ruling class or other power may be accepted, tolerated or simply overlooked. The tactics in this section build awareness both of the larger concept of human rights and of the more specific issues of how those rights apply to individuals and communities.

The challenge faced in most of the situations described lies in making people see the relevance of human rights in their own lives. People in isolated communities may not feel that they have rights. They may not know about international conventions or national laws, or may not feel that such acts apply to them. Conversely, people in developed nations may believe that the very words "human rights," and the concepts they convey, belong only to faraway, impoverished nations.

New Tactics
in Human Rights

**BUILDING HUMAN
RIGHTS CULTURES**

Building Awareness

144   www.newtactics.org

Legal Education in Rural Areas: Teaching people in rural areas about their rights and connecting them to lawyers to defend those rights.

In communities isolated geographically, by culture or by custom, lack of knowledge may be the biggest obstacle keeping people from taking full advantage of their rights. A group in Thailand combines community education — through skits and seminars — with access to the legal system, ensuring that people are not only aware of their rights, but can actively claim them.

The Thongbai Thongpao Foundation (TTF) in Thailand brings free legal assistance to rural residents, along with training on basic human rights and laws affecting their daily lives. While Thailand enjoyed rapid economic growth in the 1990s, much of the improved standard of living was concentrated in metropolitan areas. Rural populations lag behind economically and have little awareness of the rights guaranteed by modern Thai law. This leaves them vulnerable to exploitation by corrupt officials and moneylenders.

TTF's Law to the Villages course targets teachers, students, community leaders, poor farmers and women. TTF staff and a team of volunteer lawyers hold weekend training workshops in the villages, usually at the request of villagers who are facing problems with state officials. Over two full days of training, participants learn about constitutional law, human rights, marriage, loans and mortgages, labor law and other legal issues that concern them. Dramatizations of court cases complement the lectures and discussion.

Participants receive photo identity cards with the name and signature of their personal lawyer after completing the course. The back of each card lists the rights of suspects: the right to silence, to legal assistance, to know the charges against them and to post bail. After the program, a local paralegal committee of five to seven people is set up in the village to ensure that human rights standards are followed and to help organize courses.

Rather than distant, abstract concepts, TTF teaches practical information and skills that villagers can use to assert their rights. The power of the business card given to each person should not be underestimated: knowing that you have someone to call in case of abuse is not only a psychological boost, it could also dissuade someone from violating your rights in the first place.

This tactic could be valuable in rural and isolated areas around the world where people are unaware of their rights or do not feel empowered to access the justice system. It also offers legal action as a possible recourse for victims in case of abuse. A similar tactic in Uganda educates people in outlying areas about their rights, and creates avenues for mediation (see page 136).

What other "tokens of power" (like the business cards in this example) might help people who are otherwise prevented from exercising their rights?

Region	Initiating Sector	Target Sector	Focus	Human Rights Issue	BUILDING HUMAN RIGHTS CULTURES	New Tactics in Human Rights
Asia	Civil Society	Society	National	General human rights	Building Awareness	

Theater Breaks the Silence: Using theater to break the silence around sensitive human rights issues and provide legal rights education.

In Senegal, a group provides information on legal rights to a sector of society that isolated not by geography, but by cultural norms.

The African Resource for Integrated Development (Réseau Africain pour le Dévelopement Integré, or RADI) educates women about domestic violence through theatrical sketches and informal, paralegal-led discussions about the protective legal resources available to them. Through the use of theater, RADI aims to break the silence around domestic violence in Senegal.

Domestic violence, especially of a sexual nature, is a taboo subject in Senegal, and is rarely reported to authorities. In a country where ninety-five percent of the Senegalese population are practicing Muslims and many believe that religious law permits some forms of domestic violence, RADI needed to find an effective way to raise awareness regarding newly passed legislation. Because illiteracy is rampant, and because theater has experienced a remarkable resurgence, RADI chose theatre as the means to enhance its ability to reach its audience, raise awareness on domestic violence issues and make people aware of available resources.

RADI brings in well-known actors who select women from the audience to join them in 10-minute improvised sketches portraying scenes of domestic abuse. The spontaneous actions of the women and the audience members reveal their familiarity with these situations. The sketches are left unresolved in order to allow the paralegals to facilitate discussions on possible remedies and options that can be taken to address the domestic violence situation. The paralegal also makes sure to present the legal resources available and the penal and civil penalties for violence.

RADI draws on two important cultural resources in its tactic. First, theater is already a widely accepted and well-understood method of teaching in Senegal. Second, the programs are organized around *mbottayes,* traditional informal gatherings of women that generally guarantee very good attendance at the group discussions. RADI reports that most participants in the theater and discussion sessions not only learned more about their own rights but also passed this information along to family members and friends.

Many groups have used theater and performance to promote human rights, but RADI combines law and theater in a unique way. Part of the reason RADI succeeds in reaching its audience is that it uses the existing social structures of the mbottayes. The theatrical aspect offers further incentive to participate — it's entertaining — and offers the participants a layer of protection that facilitates conversation without asking them to discuss personal situations.

What are the cultural traditions in your community that create barriers against speaking out on certain human rights issues? What cultural traditions could be engaged to overcome the barriers and break the silence?

" " *The number of women presenting themselves to denounce cases of violence has increased and on the same note in some cases women have been leaving [marriages] and seeking annulment.*

— **Deputy Public Prosecutor of the Republic, Senegal**

New Tactics
in Human Rights

BUILDING HUMAN RIGHTS CULTURES	Region	Initiating Sector	Target Sector	Focus	Human Rights Issue
Building Awareness	Africa	Civil Society	Society	Local	Women's rights

146   www.newtactics.org

Reclaiming Tradition: Using the arts to connect human rights to local culture and tradition.

Human rights may seem like something imposed from outside or above. A regional human rights institution at work in the Arab world is strengthening human rights by demonstrating that they are already a part of the region's cultures.

The Cairo Institute of Human Rights Studies (CIHRS) in Egypt uses arts and literature to demonstrate that human rights are, and have long been, celebrated in Arab cultures. Although many Arab states supported the Universal Declaration of Human Rights (UDHR), several have since portrayed the UDHR, and human rights protection more generally, as a Western concept.

CIHRS uses a variety of approaches to illustrate the roots of human rights in Arab Islamic societies — in their folklore, literature and film. Artists are invited, for example, to monthly film screenings at which guest speakers discuss the films within the context of human rights. The film director or critics are often present at the screenings. This Cinema Club for Human Rights is one of the first experiences of its kind in the Arab world.

In addition, CIHRS publishes a series of booklets entitled *Human Rights in Art and Literature* that highlights the role of art and literature in disseminating the concepts of human rights; they have so far published ten books. Artists are always encouraged to present, in an engaging manner, their own experiences related to positive human rights values.

Through the Cinema Club and booklets, CIHRS has built a network of artists with an interest in promoting human rights, encouraging them to create projects that promote human rights in contemporary society. At times CIHRS also chooses a specific theme or issue, identifying how artistic approaches could play a role and then approaching network members who could successfully address that theme through a variety of artistic media.

Through all of these approaches, CIHRS has contributed to a greater awareness of the cultural relevance of human rights in Egypt and the Arab world.

CIHRS is using film, art and literature to help people throughout the region claim ownership of the principles of human rights, refuting claims that human rights is foreign and making it possible to build a base of widespread support for a human rights movement.

This approach is long-term and unlikely to cause any rapid changes in a community, and it is most likely to appeal to people already drawn to the arts. But if deeply-rooted cultural examples are chosen — ones to which most of the population feels directly connected, such as national epics and children's stories — it could reach a larger segment of the population.

Local cultural traditions, myths and text can also be used as educational tools, as readily understood examples of the principles of human rights. The Sisterhood is Global Institute (SIGI), currently based in Canada, uses an informal education model that helps Muslim women easily identify universal human rights concepts in local cultural terms. SIGI developed a series of manuals that can be used anywhere women gather, both in public and in private. The manuals encourage discussion of human rights concepts in terms that have relevance in the women's daily lives.

Every culture celebrates the values of justice, dignity, freedom, equality. Arts and literature help create a human rights culture. We approach the heart of the people, not just the minds, to make them aware of human rights.

" "

— **Bahey El Din Hassan, Cairo Institute of Human Rights Studies, Egypt**

Region	Initiating Sector	Target Sector	Focus	Human Rights Issue	**BUILDING HUMAN RIGHTS CULTURES**	**New Tactics in Human Rights**
Africa Multiple	Civil Society	Society	International	General human rights Women's rights	Building Awareness	

A New Way to Understand Social Justice: Training organizations to place their social justice work into the context of human rights, thereby providing advocates with a new set of tools and access to new alliances.

Because many people in developed countries see the term "human rights" only in relation to the developing world, human rights concepts and ideals can seem far-removed and foreign. This attitude can lead to a damaging complacency, something a group in the United States is working to combat.

The National Center for Human Rights Education (NCHRE) trains organizations in the United States to frame social justice issues as human rights issues. While many organizations in the United States work on social issues, few think of their work in terms of human rights.

In a 1997 poll conducted by NCHRE, over 90 percent of Americans did not know of the existence of the Universal Declaration of Human Rights. To respond to this lack of understanding of human rights in the United States, NCHRE has created a human rights education curriculum for grassroots social justice organizations.

NCHRE also holds conferences, meetings and community events and has distributed nearly half a million copies of the Universal Declaration of Human Rights.

In its training sessions, NCHRE emphasizes the universal nature of human rights by demonstrating that anyone can be either a perpetrator of abuse or a victim. NCHRE also teaches ways to protect human rights, particularly through education on the legal and technical aspects of human rights. Trainers then work with participants to develop human rights action plans to be used in their own communities.

Participants in the training sessions bring back to their organizations the ideas and skills learned in the workshops, increasing exponentially the reach of NCHRE's work. Since its creation, NCHRE has trained over 16,000 social justice advocates in human rights. A number of the groups trained by NCHRE have used a human rights framework to make positive changes in their communities. The Georgia Citizens Coalition on Hunger, for example, used human rights-based arguments to persuade the state legislature to pass the first minimum wage increase in more than 30 years.

NCHRE is countering a pervasive attitude in both the government and the general public that human rights principles are not relevant in the United States and that human rights problems, as such, do not exist there. To groups already fighting problems like hunger, poverty and homelessness NCHRE provides a new tactic. When these groups start framing their work in a new way, they may recognize new allies and may be able to attract new people to their cause.

" "   *There are intractable problems [the United States], such as lack of*
health care, welfare reform, racism. The Constitution doesn't offer
sufficient protection to the citizens in these areas. Our only option
is to turn to the global framework of human rights that raises these
issues to the proper level, that changes the nature of discourse and
politics in this country.

— Loretta Ross,
National Center for Human Rights Education, USA

New Tactics in Human Rights	BUILDING HUMAN RIGHTS CULTURES	Region	Initiating Sector	Target Sector	Focus	Human Rights Issue
	Building Awareness	Americas	Civil Society	Civil Society	National	General human rights

148   www.newtactics.org

Making Your Point With Mapping: Visual mapping to create public awareness and pressure for policy change.

No matter what audience you are trying to reach, visual representations of the problem you are addressing can be a very strong asset. Greenpeace Lebanon effectively used mapping to illustrate environmental hazards along Lebanon's coast.

The Greenpeace Lebanon office mapped environmental violations along the country's coast in order to educate the general public about the problem of toxic industrial waste and to pressure the government to institute policies to remedy the problem.

The group generated huge public interest in the environmental condition of the Lebanon coastline by traveling to a new site each week in an inflatable boat, focusing its efforts on the coastline's most heavily populated and used areas. It highlighted the most egregious environmental problems at each site by using Geographical Information System (GIS) software to produce a map of testing results. The public followed the progress of the Greenpeace boat on TV, in newspapers, on the group's web site or even along the beach front, where maps were posted during testing. The boat's weekly progress generated a great deal of interest and even suspense: What would they find, people wondered, at the next site? By the end of the campaign, the map itself was a graphic illustration of the toxic sites and of the extent of environmental problems all along the coast.

Greenpeace used several other tactics in combination with the mapping project. Members lobbied politicians, government agencies, residents and business owners along the coast. One staff member was assigned to keep the media informed and interested and ensure that coverage was timed to maintain public interest. The group also attracted attention with radio spots, fact sheets, huge mobile posters and an animated television spot that illustrated the long-term effects of pollutants.

The public awareness generated by the campaign helped pass Law #444, an environmental code that included the right to access information.

Greenpeace Lebanon turned dry, technical information into a compelling picture — making facts understandable to members of the public while attracting and holding their interest in its work, and at the same time moving them to take action to remedy the problem. The problem of environmental violations had been largely hidden, so that the people affected weren't even aware of the abuse. By revealing it, Greenpeace created a new constituency to work against it. The key to this success — the raised awareness and the passage of the new law — was strong outreach and media coverage to highlight the mapping effort as the group also lobbied for specific policy changes.

GIS mapping is being used to illustrate and combat other human rights problems, such as sex trafficking. It could also be used to show reported incidents of torture at police precincts, illustrate widespread poverty by describing average household incomes in an area, or portray access (or lack of access) to vital services by showing the locations of wells, hospitals or schools to illustrate access. When we can see the extent of a problem, we are better equipped to respond to it.

"A picture is worth a thousand words."
How can you use images to promote your cause?

Region	Initiating Sector	Target Sector	Focus	Human Rights Issue	**BUILDING HUMAN RIGHTS CULTURES**	**New Tactics in Human Rights**
Asia	Civil Society	Society	National	Environment	Building Awareness	

Understanding How We Got Here and Where We're Going: Using the emotional power of a historic site and personal stories to raise awareness of current human rights questions.

Stories can help bring seemingly dry or distant human rights issues to life. The Tenement Museum in New York City uses stories from the past to generate discussion and awareness of current labor rights issues.

Recreating an 1897 apartment and dressmaking shop, the Lower East Side Tenement Museum brings together representatives from conflicting sectors of the garment industry to discuss what needs to be done — and by whom — to address the problem of sweatshops today.

The Tenement Museum restores the apartments at 97 Orchard Street, where more than 7,000 immigrants from 20 different nations lived between 1863 and 1935, and tells the stories of their struggles in America. In 1897, Harris and Jennie Levine, immigrants from Plonsk (now in Poland) operated a garment shop from their apartment, representing the very space the word "sweatshop" was first coined to describe. Today, there are more than 400 garment shops in the U.S. employing nearly 15,000 immigrant workers. The U.S. Department of Labor classifies nearly three-quarters of them as "sweatshops," but the debate still rages over what a sweatshop is, what should be done to address labor abuses and who is responsible.

The museum has transformed the Levine home into a center where people in the garment industry can exchange ideas about how to solve problems. For its first meeting, in 2002, it invited an unusual mix of participants that included representatives from Human Rights Watch, UNITE! (the garment workers' union), Levi's and Eileen Fisher (clothing brands), the King's County Manufacturers Association and more. Packed in an intimate circle, these leaders of what are often considered opposing sectors of the garment industry listened to the story of how this immigrant family slept, ate, raised a family and turned out hundreds of dresses in a tiny 325-square-foot space.

In conjunction with this meeting, the group held a day-long summit about the new perspective to be gained by looking at the garment industry's past and the new ideas it suggested for preventing sweatshop conditions in the future. Since the first meeting in 2002, the museum has hosted similar dialogues with dozens of garment industry groups.

ONLINE

Read more about this in a tactical notebook available at www.newtactics.org, under Tools for Action.

It is crucial to have a strong facilitator and to carefully construct the dialogue so that people move from personal reactions to larger civic issues, appreciate and listen to opposing views and have the opportunity to exchange views in small group settings as well as large forums.

" "
These were people who refused to come together in other settings, but agreed to meet and talk at the museum. We had to emphasize that our interpretation of the past would be from multiple perspectives, raising questions for debate, rather than telling a single story.

In general, participants told us they felt comfortable coming together at a history museum while they would not feel comfortable in other settings. As one participant put it, "The environment here puts everyone a little off-balance, in a way that really opens discussion. It provides a wonderful opportunity to look at all these issues together."

— Liz Sevcenko,
Lower East Side Tenement Museum, USA

BUILDING HUMAN
RIGHTS CULTURES
Building Awareness

New Tactics
in Human Rights

www.newtactics.org   151

TOOLS AND RESOURCES

The individuals and organizations described in this book have chosen tactics based on their own unique situations, knowing their own strengths and risks, and have used these tactics as part of larger strategies to achieve well-defined goals. While some tactics — or some aspects of them — may be useful to you, it is crucial that you first assess your own situation: your context, goals, resources and allies.

This section of the workbook includes tools that we hope will help you in this task.

Developing Creative Strategies and Tactics

Use this section to identify your goals and targets and to brainstorm possible strategies and tactics. Use it to structure a conversation with people in your organization or to organize your own thoughts.

Sharing Your Tactic: A Sample Tactic Presentation

Use this sample presentation to train others to use tactics that have worked well for you. A vital part of the New Tactics in Human Rights Project is the creation of networks of practitioners who share their tactics with each other. We hope that this book will inspire you to do so.

Adapting Tactics

Use the questions in this section to decide whether a particular tactic, or aspect of a tactic, will advance your goals. Remember that not all tactics are right for every situation.

Self-Care: Caring for Your Most Valuable Resource

While you are examining your assets and liabilities, it is important to keep in mind your most valuable resources: yourself and your colleagues. Use this worksheet on your own or with your colleagues to think about ways you can take care of yourselves and each other.

DEVELOPING CREATIVE STRATEGIES AND TACTICS

Strategy without tactics is the slowest route to victory. Tactics without strategy is the noise before defeat.
— Sun Tzu

Sun Tzu's statement, written more than 2,000 years ago, tells us that planning without action is futile and action without planning is fatal. Today, we can learn a great deal from the three areas of analysis Sun Tzu identified so long ago to lay the foundations for success.

Know yourself

Don't believe your own propaganda. You must have a realistic view of your own strengths, weaknesses, resources, capacities and supports. It is equally important to have a clear understanding of the capacities and limits of your allies.

Know your opponent

Don't believe your opponent's propaganda either. It is just as important to understand your opponent's strengths, weaknesses, resources and capacities. in order to seize the momentum and the initiatives that can be opportune or even pivotal for advancing your human rights issue. Sun Tzu counsels particular attention to understanding — and disrupting — your adversary's strategy.

Know the terrain

Terrain can be the literal ground upon which you will meet your opponent. Terrain also includes the time or space, the legal, social and cultural conditions, or the environment in which you operate.

When you have gathered the information you need to analyze these areas you are ready to develop your strategy. Strategy is the gathering, toward a goal, of many decisions, which may include:

key objectives and appropriate targets

constituencies and resources

which tactics to use and when

A tactic is a specific or concrete action taken to affect a given situation. It is important that your tactics are part of and serve a larger strategy.

GETTING STARTED

These are some important things to keep in mind as you begin:

Work with others

Whenever possible, try to bring together a group that includes people with different perspectives, backgrounds and life experiences. Not only will this enrich the pool of ideas generated in your group, it will also allow more people and groups to share their ideas and learn from others.

Agree to some basic ground rules for discussion before you begin. These might include:

Everyone is respected.

Only one person speaks at a time.

If two people want to speak, the person who has not yet spoken should be given the opportunity first.

All ideas are welcome.

Disrespectful comments are not acceptable and should be redirected in a respectful but firm manner.

When you evaluate ideas, do so in a positive and constructive way.

You should also agree to an acceptable way for the group to intervene if a member begins to dominate the discussion.

Brainstorm freely

Get as many ideas out in the open as possible. Encourage everyone to contribute their ideas and don't dismiss any as too hard to implement, too simple or too strange. Without exception, however, all ideas should be nonviolent. Nonviolence is the cornerstone of legitimacy and credibility.

List all ideas as they arise. Some will be chosen for further discussion, some will not, but don't discard any of them. An idea that seems strange or outrageous at first may on second look have just the needed element of surprise. You will later need to conduct more in-depth analysis, but at first the goal is to generate as many ideas as possible.

Document the process

Write ideas on large sheets of paper or a blackboard so that the whole group can follow the process as it unfolds. Documenting the process creates a collective memory of the experience and provides an opportunity to return to these ideas at another time or share them with others. Do, however, evaluate the risks of keeping written records of your process.

Step One: Identify the Problem

What is the problem that needs to be addressed?

To help you examine it in smaller pieces, list some of the key elements of the problem. You will probably want to take on these smaller pieces individually, working to solve the larger problem step by step.

Is the problem related to a particular behavior, institution, policy, law or individual?

State the problem in a single concise sentence.

Step Two: Identify your Target(s)

Your target is the person, place or thing you intend to affect.

Who or what has responsibility for the problem you have identified?

Who are the key actors involved in creating or prolonging the problem?

Are there policies, laws or practices that prolong the problem?

Are there institutions responsible for addressing the problem? If so, why are they unable to do so?

Identify one or two key actors or targets that your group would like to affect.

Step Three: Identify your Goal

What impact do you want to have on the problem?

Briefly describe the desired outcome of your effort. Consider this: If you had the power to make all things come true, what would that be? Don't worry about being too grandiose — that's the benefit of group process. There are usually optimists, pessimists and realists to balance each other out.

How could the key actors or targets help you work toward achieving your stated goal?

Note: This goal is likely to be different from your organization's mission, but it is helpful to keep that mission in mind to ensure that the strategies and tactics you choose are consistent with it.

Step Four: Identify your Allies and Opponents

Keep in mind your goal and targets.

Who are your allies and potential allies — individuals, organizations, institutions — in your own country or internationally? Why do they or would they have an interest in supporting your effort?

Who are your opponents and potential opponents? Why do they oppose your efforts or why might they perceive your efforts as contrary to their interests?

Who are your current passive allies and opponents? Most people will fall into these categories.

Finding ways to influence these groups of people will be an important consideration when choosing your tactics.

Step Five: Identify your Resources

A resource is anything that is available that helps you to reach your goal.

What concrete resources do you have already in place? Think about people, other organizations, networks, finances and social, political or legal conditions.

What connections do you or your allies have to the key actors responsible for addressing the problem, as you identified earlier? These are resources, too.

Consider how you do or intend to take care of yourselves (See: Caring for Your Most Valuable Resource, page 164.).

Step Six: Identify Your Strategy

Defining your strategy entails making a great number of decisions. In completing the steps above, you have provided valuable information for making your strategic decisions.

Considering the previous steps, in what areas does your group have the greatest potential for making an impact?

Make a brief list of these areas, keeping your goal in mind.

What steps are needed to maximize your impact on your target?

Is there a specific order in which these steps should be implemented? Do they need to take place simultaneously or in coordination with other efforts? Do you have the necessary resources?

Discuss your course of action and how this action will help you move closer to your goal. Keep in mind that your strategy will most likely bring you to another level of action rather than immediately to the goal itself. Be sure that this course of action is consistent with your overall goal rather than taking you in a different direction entirely.

Step Seven: Identify your Tactics

Now it's time to decide what tactics you will use to implement the strategy you have identified. When choosing tactics consider both what is within your capacity and what your priorities are. Take time to review the key actors, constituencies, allies and opponents, as well as your and your opponent's strengths, weaknesses and resources.

Inventory the tactics you know about or have access to.

What tactics might encourage passive allies to become active allies?

What tactics might help ensure that your passive opponents remain passive, or even encourage them to become allies?

What tactics might stop or soften opposition?

Can your group do this alone or do you need to collaborate with other groups?

Choose one tactic at a time for further discussion that fits your strategy and goal.
Each tactic will very likely require a more in-depth discussion and a number of steps or even additional tactics for implementation.

Step Eight: Evaluate One Tactic

Discuss why you chose this tactic. How does it have the greatest potential to move you toward your goal given your current situation?

How might this tactic be adapted to have the most impact for your situation?

Does this tactic make the best use of your resources?

How can you generate additional resources? Who else can you work with? What tactics would you need to use to convince others to work with you or contribute resources?

What other tactics would you need to use to help you implement the tactic you chose? Is there an initial target you must address before you can reach the ultimate target (e.g., gaining allies within an institution before the director can be approached on a policy change)?

Do you need to gain the support of other organizations before you begin to carry out the tactic?

Outline as many steps as you can toward implementing the tactic effectively. Continue to evaluate your available resources.

Step Nine: Adapting Tactics from the Workbook

Refer to Adapting Tactics for more tips on adapting tactics.

Choose some tactic examples that you would like to explore.

What are the similarities between the tactic example and your situation? What are the differences? What lessons can you learn from the other organization's experience?

What additional resources do you have that the example in the workbook did not have? How can you use these resources to make the tactic even more effective?

What additional obstacles do you face?

How might you need to adapt the tactic to fit your situation?

What additional information is needed and who will obtain it?

This process can serve as a means to generate new ideas for reaching your goals and as a good training ground for your organization, allowing you to develop sharper analytical skills that will help you realistically plan and assess your strategy and tactics.

ADAPTING TACTICS

The tactics described in this workbook are meant to inspire you to think about new ways of doing your work. We also hope that you will find tactics that are transferable to your situation.

When we say that tactics are transferable, we mean that they can be adapted for use in contexts and countries other than the ones in which they originated. This does not usually mean that you could or should try to use a tactic — from this book or elsewhere — in exactly the same way it was originally used. You need to evaluate your own situation and resources and assess the risks involved. You may need to combine one tactic with another or you may find that some component or aspect of a tactic is applicable in your situation while the tactic as a whole is not.

The questions below will help you evaluate and adapt new tactics to your own situation.

Is this tactic right for my issue and situation?

Who else can I discuss this with?

What other groups should I tell about this?

Have I ever seen or used a tactic like this?

Was it successful?

Why or why not?

How would it help me achieve my goals?

Would it have the intended effect on my target?

Has this tactic already been used on my target?

What resources would I need?

What resources do I already have?

How can I get those resources that I don't have?

Who can I to talk to in order to get more information about this tactic?

What alliances would I need to make to use this tactic?

How can I make those alliances?

How might those who oppose my issue react to this tactic?

How risky would this tactic be for me or my organization?

Am I prepared to accept the level of risk involved in this tactic?

How can I reduce the risks that may be involved in using this tactic?

Can I use some part of this tactic?

Can I combine this tactic with other tactics?

What is my back-up plan?

What would I do if this tactic doesn't work the way I expect it to?

SHARING YOUR TACTIC:
A SAMPLE TACTIC PRESENTATION

The New Tactics project is about both learning and teaching new tactics. We want you not only to think about your own work in terms of tactics and to learn from the tactics in this book, but also to share your tactics with others. Sharing tactical innovations benefits those who developed the tactics (by building their leadership and presentation skills) as well as those whom they teach.

A basic outline for a 40-minute presentation on your tactic follows. Use this outline to help you choose the information that will best help your audience understand and implement your tactic.

1 minute
State your tactic.

Begin your training with a brief description of your tactic. Remember to focus first on your tactic rather than on the problem or the context (there will be time to explain that). Review the definition of tactic on p. 21 and read "The Need for New Tactics" (p. 12) to be sure that you are clear on this.

Also, think about an interesting way to tell your audience why this tactic is unique, important or successful. Tell a quick story. Ask a question that will grab your audience's attention.

5 minutes
Describe the context.

You want your audience to understand why this particular tactic was used in this situation. Help them do that in the following ways:

Describe current or past social issues that demanded response, particularly those that will help others understand your tactic.

Describe the process by which this response was organized.

Outline the desired outcome for using the tactic, i.e. your goals and objectives.

Briefly explain the strategy employed and how the tactic fit into it.

You don't need to spend a great deal of time on each of these question areas, but be sure to touch on each area briefly.

20 minutes

Explain how the tactic works.

This is the core of your presentation. You are providing your audience with the key information they would need to implement your tactic in their own situations.

Provide a step-by-step description of how you carried out the tactic. We recommend you use a single, specific case as an example. Imagine a colleague in another country who is going to try to use your tactic. What do they need to know? Where do they start? How many people are involved? What support do they need? What resources do they need?

Remember to take it step by step!

7 minutes

Review the development of the tactic.

Talk about the targets: What behavior, institution, policy or individuals was the tactic intended to influence? Keep in mind that there may be initial targets as well as long-range or ultimate targets.

Explain the actual outcomes: How do the people involved describe the outcome and impact? Use quotes or comments from people involved.

7 minutes

Discuss what you learned and how this tactic could be used in another context.

Explain what you learned from implementing this tactic: What worked? What would you do differently? What recommendations do you have for others?

From your experience, what factors need to be considered before implementing this tactic? What are its limitations?

If you are aware of other applications of the tactic, briefly tell people about how it was implemented differently and why.

SELF-CARE: CARING FOR YOUR MOST VALUABLE RESOURCE

In doing the difficult work of advancing and protecting human rights you may work long hours in dangerous situations. You may be exposed to sights and sounds and stories that are very hard to bear. What you are doing could be traumatizing or stressful for you, whether you are experiencing it firsthand or through others.

People cope with stress in many ways. Some people try to work harder at the expense of their family and friends, or decide they've had enough and frequently change jobs or volunteer positions. Others may smoke more cigarettes or drink more often or more heavily. Still others may lose sight of positive experiences and think that people shouldn't be having fun when others are suffering.

To maintain your strength, your commitment and your joy in doing this work you need to manage unhealthy stress. (Not all stress is unhealthy! Some stress actually pushes us to do better work.)

The ABCs of Self-Care

The ABCs of self-care are Awareness, Balance and Connection (Saakvitne & Pearlman, 1996).

Awareness

You must first be able to identify the signs and symptoms of unhealthy stress and the effects of trauma (whether experienced first- or second-hand). This requires awareness.

Be aware of your own body: Are you getting sick more often, feeling tense, becoming angry or frustrated more quickly?

Be aware of your relationships: Do you take time for the people you love and let those people take time for you?

Be aware of how you've changed: Do you no longer enjoy hobbies or activities that helped you to relax or were ways that you connected and spent time with family and friends? Have your beliefs changed, about your faith or about other people? Do you look at the world differently?

Balance

Seek balance among a number of different types of activities, including work, personal and family life, rest and leisure.

You will be more productive when you've had opportunities to rest and relax. What helps you and relax may be very different from your family members and colleagues do. It's important that the ways you relax aren't damaging to your health and well-being or to the relationships that are important to you. Becoming aware of when you are losing balance in your life gives you an opportunity to change.

Connection

Build connections and supportive relationships with your coworkers, friends, family and community.

All the work you do to create a better society will have little meaning if you don't experience positive and healthy connections along the way to this better place. Once again, becoming aware of when you are losing connection with people important to you provides you with an opportunity to think and take action that will bring more balance back into your life.

Discussing Self-Care

It can be very helpful for your organization to take time to discuss the ways in which you are all coping — individually and collectively — with the stress of doing human rights work.

Use any of the following questions to open discussion in pairs, in small groups or with your organization as a whole.

Share what you like about doing human rights work. Why do you continue to put your valuable time, energy and resources into the work?

Share something you enjoy that has nothing to do with your work. Do you take the time to do this?

Share an experience that made you change the way you view yourself, your family, your community, your country or something else.

Share what you notice about yourself when you get overwhelmed, tired, frustrated or angry. How do you try to cope with these feelings and situations? Does it involve others? Does what you do help the situation? Does it make the situation worse?

Share what you notice about the group when stress levels rise. What do you do as a group to cope?

Share a time when you felt supported or not supported by your family in doing the work you're doing. What did they do to help you or make it more difficult for you?

Share a time when you felt supported or not supported by one of your colleagues in doing the work you're doing. What did they do to help you or make it more difficult for you?

Share ways in which you as colleagues or as an organization can help each other bear the burdens of working with people who have experienced rights violations or of witnessing violations yourselves.

Finally, share one thing you'll do differently now that you've explored the ABCs of handling stress.

Now you're ready to take a step in maintaining your own awareness and activities in self-care. You are aware of what your colleagues are doing to help themselves. Take time to reinforce these positive steps and activities. Check in on a regular basis to continue discussing the importance of maintaining our most valuable resource — ourselves!

FURTHER RESOURCES

The best source of practical information and know-how is usually other people — people who have faced challenges and found ways to overcome them. The resources in this section were all created by people who wanted to share the benefit of their experiences.

The section "Tactic-focused Resources" includes books, articles, web sites and CD-ROMs relating to particular tactics in this book. Most of these were produced by the organizations that originated the tactics in question, although there are a few exceptions. Keep in mind that not all tactics will work in all situations; the resources below are starting points as you adapt tactics for use in your own struggle, not how-to guides or recipe books.

In the section "Tactical and Strategic Thinking," we have included historical and theoretical works as well as practical guides to building strategies and implementing tactics. Most of these resources were created by practitioners who have spent years, if not decades, doing human rights work; together these people speak from a deep well of experience about the value of thinking tactically and strategically.

A great deal of material exists on most of these topics, so this list is far from exhaustive. If you would like to suggest a resource for inclusion on our web site (www.newtactics.org), which we update regularly, please e-mail us at newtactics@cvt.org (please write "resource suggestion" in the subject line) or use the form at www.newtactics.org.

The New Tactics in Human Rights Project — www.newtactics.org
Tactical Notebook Series [online]. Minneapolis: Center for Victims of Torture [Updated March 2004: cited March 2004]. Available from World Wide Web:
(http://www.newtactics.org/main.php/ToolsforAction/TacticalNotebooks)
A series of 20+ page guides detailing how particular tactics were implemented, what factors influenced their use and the challenges that surfaced along the way.

Tactic Database [online]. Minneapolis: Center for Victims of Torture [Updated March 2004: cited March 2004]. Available from World Wide Web: (http://database.newtactics.org/NewTactics/Default.aspx)
A searchable (and growing!) database of more than 100 innovative tactics from around the world.

TACTIC-FOCUSED RESOURCES
PREVENTION TACTICS

Physical Protection Tactics
Mahony, Liam and Luis Enrique Eguren. *Unarmed Bodyguards: International Accompaniment for the Protection of Human Rights*. Bloomfield, Conn.: Kumarian Press, 1997.
Draws lessons from a decade of practice with a new tool in human rights protection, where unarmed international volunteers physically accompany those who are threatened with violence.

Peace Brigades International Publications [online]. London: Peace Brigades International [updated November 2001: cited March 2004]. Available from World Wide Web: (http://www.peacebrigades.org/publications.html)
Books, videos and studies about protective accompaniment and nonviolence. Available in English, French and Spanish.

Sharing Critical Information
Community Relations Council [online]. Belfast: Tibus [updated 2003: cited March 2004]. Available from World Wide Web: (http://www.community-relations.org.uk/about_the_council/CRC_publications/)
A list of publications available to download or to request, including *Action Against Intimidation — Information and Advice Manual, Anti-Sectarianism in Voluntary and Community Sectors, Approaches to Community Relations Work*.

Hall, Michael, ed. *It's Good to Talk; The experiences of the Springfield Mobile Phone Network.* Pamphlet. Newtownabbey: Island Publications, 2003.
Describes a mobile phone network enabling community activists to assist one another in reducing incidents of violence at the interface.

Removing Opportunities for Abuse

Nevitte, Neil and Santiago A. Canton. "The Rise of Election Monitoring: The Role of Domestic Observers." *Journal of Democracy.* (1997): 47–61.
Profiles of a number of domestic election monitoring organizations and campaigns (in 12 countries from South Asia and South America to the West Bank and Eastern Europe).

Stoddard, Michael. *NDI Handbook: How Domestic Organizations Monitor Elections: An A to Z Guide.* Washington, DC: National Democratic Institute for International Affairs, 1995.
A detailed guide to initiating and carrying out a domestic election monitoring program.

*Traditional Ecological Knowledge * Prior Art Database* [online]. Washington, DC: Science & Human Rights Program, American Association for the Advancement of Science [Updated October 2003: cited March 2004]. Available from World Wide Web: (http://ip.aaas.org/tekindex.nsf)
A searchable index of Internet-based public documentation concerning indigenous knowledge and plant use.

INTERVENTION TACTICS

Resistance Tactics

O'Rourke, Dara and Gregg P. Macey. "Community Environmental Policing: Assessing New Strategies of Public Participation in Environmental Regulation" [online]. *Journal of Policy Analysis and Management.* (2003): 383–414. Available from World Wide Web: (http://www.bucketbrigade.net/downloads/community_environmental_policing.pdf)
Report evaluating public participation in environmental monitoring and regulation through local "bucket brigades," including steps for implementation, impact and lessons learned.

Selected Writings on MKSS and Right to Information Campaign in India. [CD-ROM] Rajasthan: Mazdoor Kisaan Shakti Sangathan, 2003.
Uses modes of struggle and constructive action for changing the lives of the rural poor.

"Tips and Tools for Organizing Resolutions in Defense of the Bill of Rights." *Bill of Rights Defense Committee* [online]. Northampton, Mass.: BORDC. ca. 2002 [updated 2004: cited March 2004]. Available from World Wide Web: (http://www.bordc.org/Tools.htm)
Tools used by hundreds of U.S. communities in protesting the erosion of human rights.

Disruption Tactics

Treatment Action Campaign [online]. Muizenberg: TAC [updated March 16 2004: cited March 2004]. Available from World Wide Web: (http://www.tac.org.za/)
Extensive online library of documents related to HIV/AIDS, pharmaceutical companies and copyright law.

Persuasian Tactics

Coetzee, Erika and Shirley Robinson. *Measuring the Impact of Public Spending.* Cape Town: Idasa, 2000.
Provides a framework for thinking about ways to measure the impact of public spending, including tools for developing a monitoring strategy. Order online at **www.idasa.org.za.**

Fölscher, Alta. *Budget Transparency and Participation: Five African Case Studies.* Cape Town: Idasa, 2002.
Investigates budget transparency and participation in Ghana, Kenya, Nigeria, Zambia and South Africa, asking what information is necessary to assess the link between policy priorities, government spending and the delivery of services. Order online at **www.idasa.org.za.**

The International Budget Project [online]. Washington, DC: The Center on Budget and Policy Priorities [cited March 2004]. Available from World Wide Web: (http://www.internationalbudget.org/resources/howto/index.htm)
Collection of recommended online resources for applied budget analysis, including how-to tips.

Incentive Tactics

Liubicic, Robert. "Corporate Codes of Conduct and Product Labeling Schemes: The Limits and Possibilities of Promoting International Labor Rights Through Private Initiatives." *Law and Policy in International Business 30* (1998): 111–158.

Surveys private initiatives by the business community aimed at promoting labor rights (particularly codes of conduct and labeling schemes). The article recommends standardization and effective monitoring regimes to make codes of conduct and labeling schemes more effective.

The Proxy Resolutions Book. New York: Interfaith Center on Corporate Responsibility, 2004.

The complete texts of socially responsible shareholder resolutions submitted for 2004 annual company meetings. Covers: healthcare, finance, pay disparity, global warming, food and water, militarism, human rights and vendor standards. Available from www.iccr.org.

RESTORATIVE TACTICS

Remembering Abuses

Bloomfield, David, Teresa Barnes and Luc Huyse, eds. *Reconciliation After Violent Conflict: A Handbook* [online]. Stockholm, Sweden: International Institute for Democracy and Electoral Assistance (International IDEA), 2003 [cited April 2004]. Available from World Wide Web: (http://www.idea.int/conflict/reconciliation/reconciliation_full.pdf)

Designed to inform, assist and equip citizens and leaders in post-violence contexts, this practical handbook documents reconciliation processes, relationship-building strategies and structures for coexistence.

Hayner, Priscilla B. "The Contribution of Truth Commissions." *An End to Torture: Strategies for its Eradication.* London and New York: Zed Books, 1995.

A survey of truth commissions and their impacts and limitations with regard to reporting past, and preventing future, human rights abuses (particularly torture).

Hayner, Priscilla B. *Unspeakable Truths: Confronting State Terror and Atrocities.* New York: Routledge, 2002.

Examines the twenty major truth commissions established around the world, paying special attention to South Africa, El Salvador, Argentina, Chile and Guatemala.

International Center for Transitional Justice [online]. New York: International Center for Transitional Justice [cited March 2004]. Available from World Wide Web: (http://www.ictj.org/)

Assists countries pursuing accountability for mass atrocity or human rights abuse. Its strategies comprise five key elements: prosecuting perpetrators, documenting violations through nonjudicial means such as truth commissions, reforming abusive institutions, providing reparations to victims and advancing reconciliation.

Kritz, Neil J., ed. *Transitional Justice: How Emerging Democracies Reckon with Former Regimes.* Washington, DC: United States Institute of Peace, 1995.

Expansive and thorough three-volume work. The first covers general considerations, the second examines country studies and the third looks at laws, rulings and reports.

Otras Voces de la Historia. [CD-ROM] Buenos Aires: Memoria Abierta, 2002.

Documents state terrorism in Argentina between the years 1976 and 1983.

The Truth Commission Project [online]. Cambridge, MA: The Truth Commission Project [cited March 2004]. Available from World Wide Web: (http://www.truthcommission.org/)

Extensive research on five of the most successful truth commissions of the last 25 years: in Argentina, Chile, El Salvador, South Africa and Guatemala.

Strengthening Individuals and Communities

Pranis, Kay, Barry Stuart and Mark Wedge. *Peacemaking Circles.* St. Paul: Living Justice Press, 2003.

Offers experiences to support the work that many pioneering community members and criminal justice professionals are doing around the world to explore a more healing, constructive response to crime.

Jaranson, James M and Michael K. Popkin, eds. Caring for Victims of Torture. Washington, DC: American Psychiatric Press, Inc, 1998.

Collective wisdom of international experts in the treatment of victims of government torture — all distinguished physicians and pioneers in the field of traumatic stress.

Seeking Redress

International Labor Rights Fund. International Labor Rights Fund [online]. Mar. 2003. Available from World Wide Web: (http://www.laborrights.org/)
Reports, papers and books on labor rights for sale and download, including *The Alien Tort Claims Act — A Vital Tool for Preventing Corporations from Violating Fundamental Human Rights*, by Terry Collingsworth.

Violence Against Women in War Bibliography. VAwwNET. Violence Against Women in War [online]. March 2003. Available from World Wide Web: (http://www1.jca.apc.org/vaww-net-japan/english/resources/bibliography.html)
Bibliography of reports on women's rights, sexual slavery and international law relating to these topics.

BUILDING HUMAN RIGHTS CULTURES AND INSTITUTIONS

Constituency-Building

Levi, Robin. "Local Implementation of the UN Convention on the Elimination of All Forms of Discrimination Against Women (CEDAW)." WILD, 1999. Available from World Wide Web:
(http://www.wildforhumanrights.org/local_implement%20_paper.html)
A guide for people considering passing legislation implementing CEDAW in their own cities.

Collaboration Tactics

Stern, Katherine. *Techniques of Independent Monitoring in Guatemala and El Salvador.* New York: Lawyers Committee for Human Rights, 2002 [cited March 2004]. Available from World Wide Web:
(http://www.coverco.org/eng/media/Approved-Public-Report.pdf)
A practical, step-by-step report on how COVERCO and GMIES carry out their work, with a focus on how monitors are trained in everyday, practical details of their job.

Youngers, Coletta A. and Susan C. Peacock. *Peru's Coordinadora Nacional de Derechos Humanos: A Case Study of Coalition Building.* Washington Office on Latin America, October 2002. Available from World Wide Web:
(http://www.wola.org/publications/peru_Coordinadora_eng.pdf)
Examines Peru's history of abuses and the Coordinadora's success in advocacy campaigns and coalition building, highlighting the organization's work and accomplishments over the past 15 years.

Capacity-Building Tactics

Human Rights Institution-Building: A Handbook on Establishing and Sustaining Human Rights Organizations.
New York: Forefront Publications, 1994.
A guide to establishing organizational procedures and structures to prevent and combat institutional problems.

Video for Change [online]. New York: WITNESS [cited March 2004]. Available from World Wide Web:
(http://www.witness.org)
Training video for human rights advocates, illustrating how they can use video and communications technology to further their causes. Accompanied by a manual. Both are available to order or download.

Awareness and Understanding Tactics

Cairo Institute for Human Rights [online] [cited March 2004]. Available from World Wide Web:
(http://www.cihrs.org/BOOKS/booksHome.htm)
Publishes educational materials on human rights and the arts for Arab human rights organizations.

TACTICAL AND STRATEGIC THINKING

History and Theory

Ackerman, Peter and Christopher Kruegler. *Strategic Nonviolent Conflict: The Dynamics of People Power in the Twentieth Century.*
Westport: Praeger Publishers, 1994.
A theoretical and historical assessment of the importance of strategy in successful nonviolent resistance movements.

Ackerman, Peter and Jack Duvall. *A Force More Powerful: A Century of Nonviolent Conflict.*
New York: St. Martin's Press, 2000.
Examines how popular movements have used nonviolent weapons to overthrow dictators, obstruct military invaders and secure human rights. Jack Duval directed a companion film of the same name.

Johnson, Douglas A. and Kate Kelsch. "Tactical Innovations for Human Rights." *Effective Strategies for Protecting Human Rights*, David R. Barnhizer, ed. Dartmouth Pub Co., 2002.

Explores the importance of tactical thinking in human rights work and includes eight brief case studies of effective tactic.

Keck, Margaret E. and Kathryn Sikkink. *Activists Beyond Borders.* New York: Cornell University Press, 1998.

Examines the networks of activists that coalesce and operate across national frontiers to target international organizations or the policies of particular states.

Risse, Thomas, Stephen C. Ropp and Kathryn Sikkink. *The Power of Human Rights: International Norms and Domestic Change.* New York: Cambridge University Press, 1999.

Evaluates the impact of these norms on the behavior of national governments in many regions of the world.

Sharp, Gene. *From Dictatorship to Democracy: A Conceptual Framework for Liberation.* Boston: Albert Einstein Institution, 1993.

Focuses on the generic problem of how to destroy a dictatorship and to prevent the rise of a new one.

Sharp, Gene. *There are Realistic Alternatives* [online]. Boston, MA: The Albert Einstein Institution, 2003 [cited March 2004]. Available from World Wide Web: (http://65.109.42.80/organizations/org/TARA.pdf)

Brief introduction to nonviolent struggle and strategic thinking.

Practical Guides

Alexander, Sylvia. *Generating Local Resources: Case Histories and Methods for Supporting Human Rights Organizations In-Country.* New York: Forefront Publications, 1996.

A guide to strategies that allow human rights organizations to identify and cultivate domestic sources of funding.

Alexander, Sylvia. *A Handbook of Practical Strategies for Local Human Rights Groups.* New York: Forefront Publications, 1999.

A discussion of strategies used to overcome a variety of challenges, from coping with threats and violence, to building alliances and establishing ties with the international community, illustrated by examples from around the world.

Bobo, Kim, Jackie Kendall and Steve Max. *Organizing for Social Change: A Manual for Activists in the 1990s.* Santa Ana: Seven Locks Press, 1991.

A handbook on fundamental organizing techniques and methods of building a successful direct action organization.

Circle of Rights. *Economic Social & Cultural Rights Activism: A Training Resource* [online]. Minneapolis: Human Rights Resource Center, 2000 [cited March 2004]. Available from World Wide Web: (http://www1.umn.edu/humanrts/edumat/IHRIP/circle/toc.htm)

A detailed account of economic, social and cultural rights, as well as a guide, for trainers and activists, to useful strategies and tactics aimed at promoting and protecting rights through national and international organizations.

Johnson, Douglas A. "Confronting Corporate Power: Strategies and Phases of the Nestlé Boycott." *Research in Corporate Social Performance and Policy 8* (1986): 323–344.

A detailed account of the strategies and tactics employed during the Nestlé Boycott in the late 1970s.

Kehler, Randall, Andrea Ayvazian and Ben Senturia. *Thinking Strategically: A Primer on Long-Range Strategic Planning for Grassroots Peace and Justice Organizations.* Amherst: Peace Development Fund.

A guide to strategic planning that outlines steps in the planning process (setting goals, defining a mission and developing strategy) as well as measures for establishing accountability, designating responsibilities, identifying tactics and timing action. Also available to download free at www.newvisionsproject.org/ThiStrat.pdf.

McChesney, Allan. *Promoting and Defending Economic, Social, and Cultural Rights: A Handbook* [online]. Washington, DC: Association for the Advancement of Science, 2000 [cited March 2004]. Available from World Wide Web: (http://shr.aaas.org/escr/handbook/)

A resource for NGOs and others active in civil society who want to prevent or stop violations of economic, social and cultural rights and promote fulfillment of these rights at the national and international levels.

Milne, Paul and Glen Schneider. *The Effective Action Concept: A Value-Based Tool for Social Good and Personal Power.* San Diego: Institute for Effective Action, 1992.

A planning and management tool for deliberately creating change, whether at the personal or social level.

Sharp, Gene. *198 Methods of Nonviolent Action.* Boston: 1973. Available from World Wide Web: (http://www.peacemagazine.org/198.htm)

A simple, straightforward and powerful list of ways to reach your audience, make your point and begin to make change.

"Using the Internet Strategically." The Association for Progressive Communications [Cited March 2004]. Available from World Wide Web: (http://www.apc.org/english/capacity/strategy/index.shtml)

Profiles of civil society organizations that use technology and the Internet to promote human rights.

Human Rights for the Business Community

Business for Social Responsibility [online]. San Francisco: Business for Social Responsibility. [Cited March 2004]. Available from World Wide Web: (http://www.bsc.org)

A collection of tools and practical guidelines for responsible business practices, including descriptions of business-related tactics for promoting human rights.

By the Sweat & Toil of Children: Efforts to Eliminate Child Labor (volume V) [online]. U.S. Department of Labor Bureau of International Labor Affairs, 1998 [cited March 2004]. Available from World Wide Web: (http://www.dol.gov/ILAB/media/reports/iclp/sweat5/overview.htm)

A congressionally-mandated series of annual reports that reviews the child labor situation in 16 developing countries and analyzes the level and types of action being undertaken to reduce child exploitation.

An Economic Consideration of Child Labor [online]. U.S. Department of Labor Bureau of International Labor Affairs, 2000 [cited March 2004]. Available from World Wide Web: (http://www.dol.gov/ILAB/media/reports/iclp/sweat6/overview.htm)

This sixth report in the By the Sweat and Toil of Children series examines the economic benefits of the elimination of child labor and the increased enrollment of children in school.

Frankental, Peter and Frances House. *Human Rights: Is It Any of Your Business?* London: Amnesty International and The Prince of Wales Business Leaders Forum, 2001.

Information on human rights issues encountered by the business community and a discussion of ways companies can prevent abuses, e.g. through shareholder activism, improved transparency or government regulation.

The Human Rights and Business Project [online]. Copenhagen: Danish Institute for Human Rights [cited March 2004]. Available from World Wide Web: (http://www.humanrightsbusiness.org/)

A clearinghouse of news and resources regarding human rights issues and the business community, including the unique Human Rights Compliance Assessment. The HRCA is a diagnostic test made up of more than 1,000 indicators.

Unleashing Entrepreneurship: Making Business Work for the Poor. Report to the Secretary-General of the United Nations, Commission on the Private Sector and Development.

Recommendations for enabling businesses to advance development.

Region	Initiating Sector	Target Sector	Focus	Human Rights Issue
Multiple	Civil Society	Civil Society	International	Civil and political rights
Asia	Civil Society	Civil Society	National	Civil and political rights
Asia	Civil Society	Civil Society	National	Civil and political rights
Americas	Civil Society	Civil Society	National	Civil and political rights
Asia	Civil Society	Civil Society	National	Civil and political rights
Americas	Civil Society	Civil Society	National	Civil and political rights
Americas	Civil Society	Civil Society	National	Civil and political rights
Americas	Civil Society	Society	National	HIV/AIDS
Europe	Civil Society	Government Society	National	Torture
Asia	Civil Society	Government	Local	Freedom of movement
Europe	Civil Society	Society	Local	Peace
Africa	Civil Society	Government	National	Democracy

"Civil Society" here refers to nongovernmental organizations and the like, while "Society" refers to the general public.

Page	Organization	Contact Information		Tactic
37	Maiti Nepal	PO Box 9599, Gaushala Kathmandu Nepal	Tel. +977 1 449 4816 Fax +977 1 448 9978 info@maitinepal.org www.maitinepal.org	Involving survivors of human rights abuse in identifying and rescuing potential victims.
38	Kenya Domestic Observer Programme			Transmitting vote tallies by mobile phone to prevent tampering.
38	Transparencia			
38	Centre for Equality Rights in Accomodation	340 College Street Suite 101A, Box 23 Toronto, ON M5T 3A49 Canada	Tel. +1 416 944 0087 +1 800 263 1139 Fax +1 416 944 1803 cera@equalityrights.org www.equalityrights.org/cera	Informing potential victims of their rights when there is a time limit on protecting those rights.
39	Gobi Women's Project	Mongolia	Tel. +976 11 326410 Fax +976 11 326410 u-nies@magicnet.mn	Giving an at-risk population the skills they need to thrive in a changing economy through nonformal education techniques.
40	Soldiers' Mothers of St. Petersburg	Razjezhaja Street 9 St. Petersburg 91002 Russian Federation	info@soldiersmothers.spb.org www.soldiersmothers.spb.org	Empowering people to use the legal system to exert their rights.
41	Online Procedures Enhancement	Division for Public Administration and Development Management Department of Economic and Social Affairs United Nations Two UN Plaza, Room DC2-1712 New York, NY 10017 United States	Tel. +212 963 3393 Fax +212 963 9681 gianh@un.org www.unpan.org	Tracking the work of government officials online to fight corruption.

Removing Opportunities for Abuse

Page	Organization	Contact Information		Tactic
43	Movimiento Nacional de Fabricas Recuperadas por los Trabajadores			Using an expropriation law to ensure economic rights are protected.
44	Center for Victims of Torture	71 Reyukai Marg, Kathmandu Metropolitan City Ward No. 3, Bansbari PO Box 5839 Kathmandu Nepal	Tel. +977 1 43 73 900 Fax +977 1 43 73 020 cvict@cvict.org.np www.cvict.org.np	Creating alternative dispute resolution mechanisms to prevent the involvement of the police, who are potential abusers.
45	American Library Association	50 E. Huron Chicago, IL 60611 United States	Tel. +1 800 545 2433 library@ala.org www.ala.org	Protecting the freedom of thought and right to privacy by destroying records that could be demanded by the government.
46	American Association for the Advancement of Science	1200 New York Avenue NW Washington, D.C. 20005 United States	Tel. +1 202 326 6400 webmaster@aaas.org www.aaas.org	Protecting cultural and economic rights of indigenous people by recording traditional ecological knowledge.

Region	Initiating Sector	Target Sector	Focus	Human Rights Issue
Asia	Civil Society	Government Society	National	Trafficking
Africa	Civil Society	Government	National	Democracy
Americas	Civil Society	Government	National	Democracy
Americas	Civil Society	Society	Local	Right to housing
Asia	Government	Society	National	Development
Europe	Civil Society	Society	National	Police and military abuses
Asia	Government	Society	Local	Corruption
Americas	Society	Business	Local	Economic rights
Asia	Civil Society	Society	Local	Torture
Americas	Civil Society	Government	National	Freedom of thought
Multiple	Civil Society	Society	International	Indigenous rights

"Civil Society" here refers to nongovernmental organizations and the like, while "Society" refers to the general public.

Page	Organization	Contact Information		Tactic
	INTERVENTION TACTICS			
	Resistence Tactics			
53	Campaign of Darkness for Light			Creating a single mass expression of protest based on a simple activity that citizens can carry out safely in their own homes.
54	Estonian Heritage Society			Asserting cultural identity in masse to express opposition to an oppressive regime.
55	Mazdoor Kisan Shakti Sangathan	Devdungri Post Barar District Rajsamand Rajasthan 313341 India	Fax +91 1 463 88206 Tel. +91 2 951 43254 mkssrajasthan@yahoo.com	Using people's platforms (public hearings) where citizens can publicly challenge officials on the difference between promises and reality.
56	Bill of Rights Defense Committee	241 King Street, Suite 216 Northampton, MA 01060 United States	Tel. +1 413 582 0110 info@bordc.org www.bordc.org	Encouraging local governments, organizations and individuals to oppose federal legislation that endangers human rights through education and resources.
57	Poder Ciudadano	Piedras 547 (C1070AAK) Ciudad de Buenoa Aires Argentina	Tel. +541 1 43314925 Fax +541 1 43314925 fundacion@poderciudadano.org	Organizing a large-scale petition drive to pressure the government to change.
58	Bucket Brigades	1036 Napoleon Avenue New Orleans, LA 70115 United States	Tel. +1 504 269 5070 Fax +1 504 324 0251 info@labucketbrigade.org www.labucketbrigade.org	Collecting air-quality data independently in one's own community in order to pressure for change.
	Refinery Reform Campaign (A project of GCM/Tides) *These are two of several independent organizations engaged in this work*	222 Richland Ave. San Francisco, CA 94110 United States	Tel. +1 415 643 1870 www.refineryreform.org	
59	Chiapas Community Defenders Network Red de Defensores Comunitarios por los Derechos Humanos	Calle Ejército Nacional No. 108-A Barrio de Guadalupe San Cristóbal de Las Casas Chiapas 29230 Mexico	Tel. +52 967 6740343 comunitarios@prodigy.net.mx defensorescomunitarios.org	Training victims of human rights abuses to monitor and defend their rights.
60	Operation SalAMI	C.P. 55031 Succ. Fairmount Montreal, Quebec H2T 2M8 Canada	Tel. +1 514 524 8088 Fax +1 514 524 8096 salami@operationsalami.org	Using what it called a "Citizen Search and Seizure Operation" to pressure the Canadian government to release a secret draft treaty that they believed could undermine human rights.
	Disruption Tactics			
63	Brazilian Landless Workers Movement Movimento Dos Trabalhadores Rurais Sem Terra	Alameda Barão de Limeira 1232 Campos Elíseos São Paulo, SP 01202-002 Brazil	Tel. +55 11 3361 3866 semterra@mst.org.br www.mstbrazil.org www.mst.org.br	Settling landless people on unfarmed land to pressure the government to carry out land reforms.

Region	Initiating Sector	Target Sector	Focus	Human Rights Issue
Asia	Civil Society	Government Society	National	Corruption
Europe	Society	Government	National	Cultural rights
Asia	Civil Society	Government	Local	Corruption
Americas	Civil Society	Government	National	Civil and political rights
Americas	Civil Society	Government	National	Right to food
Americas	Civil Society	Business	Local	Environment
Americas	Civil Society	Society	Local	Indigenous rights
Americas	Civil Society	Government	National	Right to information
	Civil Society	Government Society	National	Economic rights

"Civil Society" here refers to nongovernmental organizations and the like, while "Society" refers to the general public.

Page	Organization	Contact Information		Tactic
64	Treatment Action Campaign	34 Main Road Muizenberg 7945 South Africa	Tel. +27 21 788 3507 Fax +27 21 788 3726 info@tac.org.za www.tac.org.za	Defying patent laws in order to pressure for change in those laws.
65	Ekota Sex Workers Association			Involving people with direct experience and knowledge in surveillance teams to rescue victims of abuse.
66	South Asian Coalition on Child Servitude	SACCS Global March L-6, Kalkaji New Delhi 110019 India	Tel. +91 11 626 898 55 Fax +91 11 623 6818 childhood@globalmarch.org www.globalmarch.org	Rescuing child laborers through factory raids.
67	Free Burma Coalition		info@freeburmacoalition.org www.freeburmacoalition.org	

Persuasion Tactics

Page	Organization	Contact Information		Tactic
69	African Public Radio			Using the power of the media to send targeted messages to people in a position to end abuses.
70	Commission on Human Rights and Administrative Justice	Old Parliament House High Street Accra Ghana	Tel. +233 21 664785 Fax +233 21 660020 chraj@ighmail.com	Engaging local leaders to use their influence to help end abuse.
71	Institute for Democracy in South Africa	Cape Town Democracy Centre PO Box 1739 Cape Town 8000 South Africa	Tel. +27 21 467 5600 Fax +27 21 461 2589 info@idasa.org.za www.idasa.org.za	Examining budgets to reveal social and economic inequities and persuade the government to rectify them.
72	Citizens' Watch	87 Ligovsky Prospect, Office 300 St. Petersburg 191040 Russian Federation	Tel. +7 812 380 6030 Fax +7 812 380 6030 citwatch@mail.wplus.net wwwwin.wplus.net/pp/citwatch	Building collaborative relationships with government officials to promote change from within the system.
73	The Interfaith Center on Corporate Responsibility	475 Riverside Drive, Room 550 New York, NY 10115 United States	Fax +1 212 870 2023 Tel. +1 212 870 2295 info@iccr.org www.iccr.org	Presenting shareholder resolutions to press companies to use more socially responsible business practices, including the adoption of comprehensive human rights policies and practices.
74	BAOBAB for Women's Human Rights and Civil Resource Development and Documentation Centre	232A Muri Okunola Street Victoria Island, Lagos Nigeria	Tel. +234 1 2626267 Fax +234 1 2626267 baobab@baobabwomen.org www.baobabwomen.org	Organizing mock tribunals to raise awareness of human rights abuses and influence public policy.

Incentive Tactics

Page	Organization	Contact Information		Tactic
77	Bolsa Escola	Brazil	prefeitobolsaescola@mec.gov.br www.mec.gov.br/secrie/ default.asp	Providing parents with funds that allow them to send their children to school rather than to work.
78	Bangladesh Rural Advancement Committee	75 Mohakhali Dhaka 1212 Bangladesh	Tel. +880 2 882 4180 Fax +880 2 882 3542 public-affairs@brac.net www.brac.net	Offering loans with favorable terms to small-business owners with the condition that they not use child labor.

Region	Initiating Sector	Target Sector	Focus	Human Rights Issue
Africa	Civil Society	Government Business	National International	HIV/AIDS
Asia	Society	Society	Local	Trafficking
Asia	Civil Society	Business Society	National	Child labor
Asia	Civil Society	Government	International	Gross violations of human rights
Africa	Civil Society	Government	National	Civil and political rights
Africa	Government	Society	Local	Slavery
Africa	Civil Society	Government	National	Children's rights
Europe	Civil Society	Government	National	Corruption
Multiple	Civil Society	Business	International	General human rights
Africa	Civil Society	Government Society	National	Women's rights
Americas	Government	Society	National	Child labor
Asia	Civil Society	Society	National	Child labor

"Civil Society" here refers to nongovernmental organizations and the like, while "Society" refers to the general public.

Page	Organization	Contact Information		Tactic
79	Rugmark	733 15th Street, NW, Suite 912 Washington, D.C. 20005 United States	Tel. +1 202 347 4205 Fax +1 202 347 4885 info@rugmark.org www.rugmark.org	Creating a market to support fairly produced products.
80	Reebok International Ltd	Reebok Human Rights Foundation, Reebok Int'l LTD 1895 J.W. Foster Blvd Canton, MA 02021 United States	rhrfoundation@reebok.com www.reebok.com	Concentrating all steps in the production process in facilities to make it easier to monitor and eliminate the use of child labor.

RESTORATIVE TACTICS
Remembering Abuses

Page	Organization	Contact Information		Tactic
87	Documentation Center of Cambodia	PO Box 1110 Phnom Penh Cambodia	Tel. +855 23 211 875 Fax +855 23 210 358 dccam@online.com.kh www.dccam.org	Documenting records of abuse to promote healing and justice.
88	Centro de Documentación y Archivo	Palacio de Justicia Testanova y Mariano Roque Alonso 8th Floor, Office 13 Asuncion Paraguay	Tel. +595 21 424212 Int. 2269 cdya@pj.gov.py www.unesco.org/webworld/ paraguay	Leveraging legal rights to access victims' records to promote justice.
88	The Gauck Authority			
89	Memoria Abierta	Av. Corrientes 2560 2nd floor C1046AAQ Buenos Aires Argentina	Tel. +54 11 4951 4870 memoriaabierta@memoriaabierta.org.ar www.memoriaabierta.org.ar	Coordinating efforts to preserve archival information among several organizations and creating an integrating system for accessing it.
90	Argentine Forensic Anthropology Team Equipo Argentino de Antropologia Forense	Rivadavia 2443, dpto 3 y 4, 2ndo piso Buenos Aires, C1034ACD Argentina	Tel. +54 11 4951 8547 Fax +54 11 4954 6646 eaaf@velocom.com.ar www.eaaf.org	Using forensics to identify victims' remains and cause of death.
90	Community Research and Psychosocial Action / Team Equipo de Estudios Comunitarios y Acción Psicosocial	4 Calle 21-61 Interior "C", Zona 14 Guatemala City Guatemala	Tel. +502 363 5270 Fax +502 363 5403 ecap@itelgua.com	
90	Fundación de Antropología Forense de Guatemala	3a Calle 3-18, Apto.B, Edificio Packard, Zona 1 Ciudad de Guatemala, CP01001 Guatemala	Tel. +502 254 0882 eafg@eafg.org.gt	
92	South African Truth and Reconciliation Commission	9th Floor, Old Mutual Building 106 Adderly Street Cape Town, 8001 South Africa	Tel. +27 21 44 5161 Fax +27 21 424 5225 nlouw@justice.gov.za www.doj.gov.za/trc	Establishing a formal truth commission to investigate and acknowledge gross human rights violations.
94	Violence Against Women in War Network, Japan		vaww-net-japan@jca.apc.org www1.jca.apc.org/vaww-net-japan/english	Holding an international tribunal to raise awareness of and seek reparations for sexual war crimes.
94	Minnesota Advocates for Human Rights	650 3rd Ave S, #550 Minneapolis, MN 55402 United States	Tel. +1 612 341 3302 Fax +1 612 341 2971 hrights@mnadvocates.org www.mnadvocates.org	

Region	Initiating Sector	Target Sector	Focus	Human Rights Issue
Asia	Civil Society	Business	International	Child labor
Asia	Business	Business Society	International	Child labor
Asia	Civil Society	Government Society	National	Gross violations of human rights
Americas	Civil Society	Government Society	International	Gross violations of human rights
Europe	Government	Society	National	General human rights
Americas	Civil Society	Civil Society	National	Gross violations of human rights
Americas	Civil Society	Government Society	National International	Gross violations of human rights
Americas	Civil Society	Society	National	Gross violations of human rights
Americas	Civil Society	Society	National	Gross violations of human rights
Africa	Government	Society	National	Gross violations of human rights
Asia	Civil Society	Government	International	War crimes
Americas	Civil Society	Society	Local	Gross violations of human rights

"Civil Society" here refers to nongovernmental organizations and the like, while "Society" refers to the general public.

Intervention Tactics / Restorative Tactics

Region	Initiating Sector	Target Sector	Focus	Human Rights Issue
Africa	Civil Society	Society	International	Torture
Africa	Civil Society	Society	National	Child soldiers
Africa Americas	Government Civil Society	Society	Local	Peace
Africa	Civil Society	Society	National	Child soldiers
Asia	Civil Society	Society	Local	Children's rights
Americas	Civil Society	Society	National	Gross violations of human rights
Europe	Government Society	Government	International	Gross violations of human rights
Americas	Civil Society	Business	International	Gross violations of human rights
Europe	Civil Society	Government	National	Minority rights
Asia	Government	Government	National	Police and military abuses
Americas	Civil Society	Government Society	National	Gross violations of human rights
Europe	Civil Society	Government	National	Torture

"Civil Society" here refers to nongovernmental organizations and the like, while "Society" refers to the general public.

Page	Organization	Contact Information		Tactic
111	Children for Identity and Justice Against Forgetfulness and Silence Hijos por la Identidad y la Justicia contra el Olvido y el Silencio	Calle Laprida 520 CP 5000 Córdoba Argentina	Tel. +54 351 428 3655 Fax +54 351 428 3655 hijoscordoba@ famdesapcba.org.ar www.famdesapcba.org.ar/ Hijos.htm	Publicly exposing abusers through targeted demonstrations.
112	District Six Museum	PO Box 10178 Caledon Square, 7905 Cape Town, 8001 South Africa	Tel. +27 0 21 461 8745 Fax +27 0 21 461 8745 info@districtsix.co.za www.districtsix.co.za	Mapping personal histories and mobilizing memory to reclaim a place in history and recover lost land.
112	International Coalition of Historical Sites of Conscience	91 Orchard Street New York, NY 10002 United States	Tel. +1 212 431 0233 Fax +1 212 431 0402 lestm@tenement.org www.sitesofconscience.org/fre/ lestm.htm	
113	White Earth Land Recovery	32033 East Round Lake Road Ponsford, MN 56575 United States	Tel. +1 218 573 3448 Fax +1 218 573 3444 info@welr.org www.welrp.org	

BUILDING HUMAN RIGHTS CULTURES AND INSTITUTIONS
Building Constituencies

Page	Organization	Contact Information		Tactic
119	Never Again Nigdy Wiecej	PO Box 6 03-700 Warszawa 4 Poland	rafalpan@zigzag.pl free.ngo.pl/nw	Using popular culture to engage young people in human rights reporting.
120	Women's Institute for Leadership Development	3543 18th St. #11 San Francisco, CA 94110 United States	Tel. +1 415 355 4744 Fax +1 415 355 4745 wild@wildforhumanrights.org www.wildforhumanrights.org	Passing international treaties at the local level to impact public policy and promote human rights standards.
121	Sangha Metta	Wat Sri Suphan 100 Wualai Road Tambon Haiya Muang District Chiang Mai 50100 Thailand	Tel. +66 53 201 284 Fax +66 53 201 284 laurie@cm.ksc.co.th www.buddhanet.net/ sangha-metta/project.html	Involving religious leaders to model behavior toward stigmatized populations.
122	5-in-6 Project 3	P.O. Box 8348 Roggebaai 8012 South Africa	Tel. +27 21 425 2095 Fax +27 21 425 4295 fivein6@mweb.co.za	Using a nomination campaign to identify new potential allies for human rights.
123	Amnesty International The Netherlands	Postbus 1968 1000 BZ Amsterdam The Netherlands	Tel. +31 20 6264436 Fax + 31 20 6240889 amnesty@amnesty.nl www.amnesty.nl	Using text-messaging to build constituencies for human rights action.
124	Center for Advising Citizenship Education Programs Centro de Assessoramento a Programas de Educação para a Cidadania	Av. Venâncio Aires, 1203 conj. 24 Bairro Bonfim CEP. 90040193 Brazil	Tel. +55 51 3335 3713 Fax +55 51 3335 3713 capec@terra.com.br	Teaching police officers about their role in defending human rights.

Region	Initiating Sector	Target Sector	Focus	Human Rights Issue
Americas	Civil Society	Society	Local	Gross violations of human rights
Africa	Civil Society	Government Society	Local	Displaced populations
Multiple	Civil Society	Society	International	General human rights
Americas	Civil Society	Society	Local	Indigenous rights
Europe	Civil Society	Society	National	Minority rights
Americas	Civil Society	Government	Local	Women's rights
Asia	Civil Society	Civil Society	International	HIV/AIDS
Africa	Civil Society	Society	Local	Women's rights
Europe	Civil Society	Society	National	Civil and political rights
Americas	Civil Society	Government Society	National International	Police and military abuses

"Civil Society" here refers to nongovernmental organizations and the like, while "Society" refers to the general public.   Restorative Tactics / Building Human Rights Cultures

Page	Organization	Contact Information		Tactic
	Collaboration			
127	National Coordinator for Human Rights La Coordinadora Nacional de Derechos Humanos	Jr. Tupac Amaru 2467 Lince Lima 14 Peru	Tel. +51 1 441 1533 Fax +51 1 422 4827 webmaster@dhperu.org www.dhperu.org	Building a coalition of human rights organizations in a country to speak with one voice against abuses.
128	Center for Law Enforcement Education in Nigeria	1 Afolabi Aina Street Ikeja 100281 Lagos Nigeria	Tel. +234 1 493 3195 Fax +234 1 493 5338 cleen@cleen.org www.cleen.org	Creating a public forum where the police and ordinary citizens can work together to resolve human rights grievances.
129	Human Rights League of the Great Lakes Region Ligue des Droits de la Personne dans la Region des Grands Lacs	LDGL B.P. 3042 Kigali Rwanda	Tel. +250 57 3307 Fax +250 57 6762 ldgl@rwandatel1.rwanda1.com www.ib.be/grip/afri/ldgl.html	Identifying allies to hold constructive dialogue and maintain cooperative relationships.
130	Commission for the Verification of Corporate Codes of Conduct	1a Calle 7-68, Zona 1 Edificio Pena, Segundo Nivel, Oficina B Guatemala City Guatemala	Tel. +502 232 0195 Fax +502 253 5025 coverco@coverco.org	Contracting with multinational corporations to monitor labor conditions in their factories.
132	Saami Council	Sveavagen 99 S-113 50 Stockholm Sweden	Tel. +358 16 677 351 Fax +358 16 677 353 saamicouncil@saamicouncil.net www.saamicouncil.net	Creating a transnational body to advocate and promote indigenous people's rights.
133	Albanian Center for Human Rights	Rruga Kont Urani 10 Tirana Albania	Tel. +355 42 391 21 Fax +355 42 391 21 qshdnj@albaniaonline.net www.achr.org	Collaborating with government to incorporate human rights education into public schools.
	Building Capacity			
135	Liberia National Law Enforcement Association	Corner of Carey & Gurley Streets Monrovia Liberia	Tel. +231 6 552280 cbgriffiths@yahoo.com	Creating a professional organization that provides support and training to build professionalism among law enforcement personnel.
136	Foundation for Human Rights Initiative	Human Rights House Plot 1853, Lulume Road Nsambya P.O. Box 1102 Kampala Uganda	Tel. +256 41 510262 Fax +256 41 510498 fhri@fhri.or.ug www.fhri.or.ug	Training local leaders as mediators and resources on human rights.
137	Human Rights Centre at the University of Sarajevo	Zmaja od Bosne 8 71000 Sarajevo Bosnia and Herzegovina	Tel. +387 33 66 82 51 Fax +387 33 66 82 51 irld@see-hrc.net www.sarajevo.see-hrc.net	Creating a strong information storage and retrieval system to support human rights advocates to work more effectively.
138	Black Box Foundation		Tel. + 330 746 2186 peter@artscouncil.com	Training victims of human rights abuses to use video technology to expose those abuses.
139	Independent Medico-Legal Unit	1271 Sarit Center Nairobi 0606 Kenya	Tel. +254 20 4456048/9 Fax +254 20 4450598 medico@imlu.org www.imlu.org	Creating a network of professionals to document torture and support victims.

Region	Initiating Sector	Target Sector	Focus	Human Rights Issue
Americas	Civil Society	Civil Society	National	General human rights
Africa	Civil Society	Government Society	Local	Police and military abuses
Africa	Civil Society	Civil Society	International	General human rights
Americas	Civil Society	Business	International	Labor rights
Europe	Civil Society	Government Society	International	Indigenous rights
Europe	Civil Society	Government Civil Society	National	General human rights
Africa	Government	Government	National	Police and military abuses
Africa	Civil Society	Society	National	General human rights
Europe	Civil Society	Civil Society	Local	General human rights
Europe	Civil Society	Society	National	Minority rights
Africa	Civil Society	Civil Society	National	Torture

"Civil Society" here refers to nongovernmental organizations and the like, while "Society" refers to the general public.

Page	Organization	Contact Information		Tactic
140	WITNESS	353 Broadway New York, NY 10013 United States	Tel. +1 212 274 1664 Fax +1 212 274 1262 witness@witness.org www.witness.org	Empowering NGOs to use video in human rights advocacy.
141	Mental Disability Rights International	1156 15th Street NW, Suite 1001 Washington, D.C. 20005 United States	Tel. +1 202 296 0800 Fax +1 202 728 3053 mdri@mdri.org www.mdri.org	Empowering NGOs to use video in human rights advocacy.
142	League of Human Rights Advocates		Tel. +2 524 94 720 Fax +2 524 94 720 www.lhra-icpr.org admin@lhra-icpr.org	Creating a network of volunteer monitors to persuade local and national governments to abide by international human rights commitments.
143	Concerned for Working Children	303/2 L.B. Shastrinagar Vimanapura Post Vimanapura, Bangalore 560017 India	Tel. +91 80 5234270 Fax +91 80 5234272 cwc@pobox.com www.workingchild.org	Creating children's parliaments that can work with local governments to create better social policy.

Building Awareness

Page	Organization	Contact Information		Tactic
145	Thongbai Thongpao Foundation	15/138-139 Soi Sueyaiuthid Ratchadapisek Road Chatuchak, Bangkok 10900 Thailand	Tel. +662 5416468 Fax +662 5416416	Teaching people in rural areas about their rights and connecting them to lawyers to defend those rights.
146	African Resource for Integrated Development Reseau Africain pour le Developpement Integre	Immeuble Arame Faha NDIAYE Parc a Mazout Colobane Senegal	Tel. +221 864 23 45 Fax +221 825 75 36	Using theater to break the silence around sensitive human rights issues and provide legal rights education.
147	Cairo Institute of Human Rights Studies	PO Box 117 (Maglis el- Shaab), Cairo Egypt	Tel. +202 7951112 Fax +202 7921913 webmaster@cihrs.com www.cihrs.com	Using the arts to connect human rights to local culture and tradition.
147	Sisterhood is Global Institute	1200 Atwater, Suite 2 Quebec City, Montreal H3Z 1X4 Canada	Tel. +1 514 846 9366 Fax +1 514 846 9066 sigi@qc.aibn.com www.sigi.org	
148	National Center for Human Rights Education	PO Box 311020 Atlanta, GA 31131 United States	Tel. +1 404 344 9629 Fax +1 404 346 7517 nchre@nchre.org www.nchre.org	Training organizations to put social justice work in the context of human rights in order to wpro-vide advocates a new set of tools and access to new alliances.
149	Greenpeace Lebanon	PO Box 13-6590 Beirut 1102 2140 Lebanon	Tel. +961 1 785 665 Fax +961 1 785 667 gp.mediterranean.lebanon@ diala.greenpeace.org www.greenpeacemed.org.mt	Visual mapping to create public awareness and pressure for policy change.
150	Lower East Side Tenement Museum	91 Orchard Street New York, NY 10002 United States	Tel. +1 212 431 0233 Fax +1 212 431 0402 lestm@tenement.org www.tenement.org	Using the emotional power of a historic site and personal stories to raise awareness of current human rights questions.

Region	Initiating Sector	Target Sector	Focus	Human Rights Issue
Multiple	Civil Society	Government Business Civil Society Society	International	General human rights
Multiple	Civil Society	Government	National	Mental disability rights
Europe	Civil Society	Government Society	National	General human rights
Africa Asia	Civil Society	Government Business Society	Local	Children's rights
Africa Asia	Civil Society	Society	National	General human rights
Africa	Civil Society	Society	Local	Women's rights
Africa	Civil Society	Society	International	General human rights
Multiple	Civil Society	Society	International	Women's rights
Americas	Civil Society	Civil Society	National	General human rights
Asia	Civil Society	Society	National	Environment
Americas	Civil Society	Business Civil Society Society	Local	Labor rights

"Civil Society" here refers to nongovernmental organizations and the like, while "Society" refers to the general public.

SHARE A TACTIC

The New Tactics project collects and disseminates innovative approaches to advance human rights and end persistent challenges around the world. Many innovations have demonstrated great value in advancing human rights, yet are not well known outside their countries or regions. The New Tactics in Human Rights Project promotes the use and sharing of the widest possible range of tactics.

If you know about an innovative tactic being used — in the public, private or voluntary sector, anywhere in the world — please let us know! Appropriate tactics will be added to our online searchable database of tactics at www.newtactics.org, or included in future editions of this workbook.

Please complete and mail this form to:
The New Tactics in Human Rights Project
The Center for Victims of Torture
717 East River Road
Minneapolis, MN 55455 USA

Or fax it to:
+1 612 436 2606
ATTN: New Tactics

Or e-mail this information to:
newtactics@cvt.org

You can also fill out an online form at:
www.newtactics.org

Your name:

Your contact information:

Organization or name of the people who use this tactic:

If you were not directly involved in using this tactic, whom might we contact to learn more about it?

What is the tactic that you would like to share?
A tactic is a specific action used to affect a given situation.

What is the human rights situation the tactic is addressing?

What are the steps for carrying out this tactic?

What is unique about the tactic?

What was the impact of the tactic? Please provide an example.